DISTANCE AND DUTIES:

DETERMINANTS OF MANUFACTURING IN AUSTRALIA AND CANADA

By
R.M. CONLON

Carleton University Press
Ottawa, Canada

© Carleton University Press Inc., 1985
ISBN 0-88629-029-5 (paperback)

Printed and bound in Canada

Canadian Cataloguing in Publication Data

Conlon, R.M. (Robert Maxwell) 1946-
   Distance and duites : determinants of
manufacturing in Australia and Canada

(The Carleton Library ; 135)
Bibliography: p.
ISBN 0-88629-029-5

1. Canada — Manufactures. 2. Australia —
Manufactures. 3. Tariff. 4. Transportation —
Economic aspects. I. Title. II. Series.

HD9738.A82C65 1985   338.4'0971   C85-090180-4

Distributed by:
  Oxford University Press
  70 Wynford Drive
  DON MILLS, Ontario, Canada, M3C 1J9
  (416) 441-2941

ACKNOWLEDGEMENTS

Carleton University Press gratefully acknowledges the support extended to
its publishing programme by the Canada Council and the Ontario Arts
Council.

This book has been published with the help of a grant from the Social
Science Federation of Canada, using funds provided by the Social Sciences
and Humanities Research Council of Canada.

DISTANCE
AND
DUTIES:

TABLE OF CONTENTS

Page

CHAPTER
1.   *INTRODUCTION: THE SCOPE OF THE STUDY*   1
    1.1 PROTECTION IN AUSTRALIA AND CANADA   2
    1.2 COMPARISONS OF AUSTRALIAN AND CANA-
    DIAN MANUFACTURING INDUSTRIES   4
    1.3 SCOPE OF THE STUDY   7
CHAPTER
2.   *AUSTRALIAN AND CANADIAN COMMER-*
    CIAL POLICY   10
    2.1 THE DEVELOPMENT OF COMMERCIAL POL-
    ICY IN AUSTRALIA   10
    Australian Commercial Policy to 1900   10
    Commercial Policy from Federation to War's End,
    1901-1920   11
    The Tariff Board and Tariff Policy, 1921-1939   12
    The Post-War Period, 1945-1971   14
    Australian Commercial Policy, 1971-1974   15
    The Tariff and Industrial Development: A Summary   16
    2.2 THE DEVELOPMENT OF COMMERCIAL POL-
    ICY IN CANADA   19
    Canadian Commercial Policy to 1879   19
    The "National Policy", 1879-1913   21
    The Economic Consequences of the National Policy   22
    The Inter-War Period, 1919-1939   23
    World War II and Post-War Commercial Policy   25
    The Tariff and Canadian National Development   26
    2.3 AUSTRALIAN AND CANADIAN COMMER-
    CIAL POLICIES: A SUMMARY   27
CHAPTER
3.   *TRADE BARRIERS AND INDUSTRIAL STRUC-*
    TURE AND PERFORMANCE: SOME THEORETI-
    CAL CONSIDERATIONS   29
    3.1 SOME ASPECTS OF THE THEORY OF TARIFF
    PROTECTION   29
    Nominal Tariffs and Efficiency   29
    Effective Protection and Resource Allocation   30
    3.2 TRANSPORT COSTS, TARIFFS AND THE
    RANGE OF COMMODITIES PRODUCED   32
    Transport Costs and Non-Traded Goods   33
    An Analysis of Transport Costs and Tariffs with a
    Continuum of Goods   35
    The real model   36

        Extensions of the model   37
         (i) Transport costs   37
         (ii) Tariffs   38
   3.3 *SOME IMPLICATIONS FOR INDUSTRIAL*
      STRUCTURE AND PERFORMANCE   39

CHAPTER
 4.   *TRADE BARRIERS AND THE STRUCTURES*
      AND PERFORMANCES OF AUSTRALIAN AND
      CANADIAN MANUFACTURING INDUSTRIES   42
   4.1 *TRADE BARRIERS AND ECONOMIES OF SCALE*   42
      Size of the Market   43
      Firm-Specific Economies   44
      Plant-Specific Economies   45
      Product-Specific Economies   46
   4.2 *TRADE BARRIERS AND THE STRUCTURE*
      AND PERFORMANCE OF INDUSTRIES: A
      SUMMARY OF EVIDENCE   48
      Market Size   48
      Output Diversity   49
      Foreign Participation   50
   4.3 *THE COSTS OF PROTECTION*   51

CHAPTER
 5.   *A REVIEW OF THE EMPIRICAL EVIDENCE*
      CONCERNING DISTANCE, INTERNATIONAL
      TRANSPORT COSTS, AND TARIFFS AS
      BARRIERS TO TRADE   54
   5.1 *DISTANCE AND TRANSPORT COSTS AS*
      DETERMINANTS OF INTERNATIONAL TRADE
      FLOWS   54
      Distance and Trade Flows   54
      Distance, Transport Costs and Trade Flows   57
   5.2 *THE RELATIVE HEIGHTS OF TARIFFS AND*
      INTERNATIONAL TRANSPORT COSTS: THE
      UNITED STATES' CASE   58

CHAPTER
 6.   *TRADE BARRIERS TO AUSTRALIAN AND*
      CANADIAN EXPORTS   62
   6.1 *THE CONTRIBUTION OF DISTANCE TO*
      TRANSPORT COSTS FOR AUSTRALIAN
      EXPORTS   63
      The "Cost" of Distance as a Barrier to Total Exports   63
      The "Cost" of Distance and Barriers to Exports of
      Individual Commodities   67
      The Case of Australian Exports to the United States   68
      Transport Costs of Australian Exports of Manufactures   72
   6.2 *TRADE BARRIERS TO CANADIAN EXPORTS*   73
   6.3 *SUMMARY AND CONCLUSIONS*   79

CHAPTER
7.   *TRADE BARRIERS TO AUSTRALIAN AND
         CANADIAN IMPORTS*   81
    7.1 *DESCRIPTION OF TARIFF AND TRANSPORT
         COST DATA IN THIS STUDY*   81
         Australia   81
         Canada   83
    7.2 *CHARACTERISTICS OF TRANSPORT COST
         AND TARIFF PROTECTION OF AUSTRALIAN
         MANUFACTURING*   84
    7.3 *CHARACTERISTICS OF TRANSPORT COST
         AND TARIFF PROTECTION OF CANADIAN
         MANUFACTURING*   93
    7.4 *COMPARISONS OF THE PROTECTIVE STRUC-
         TURES OF AUSTRALIA AND CANADA*   95
CHAPTER
8.   *A COMPARISON OF AUSTRALIAN AND
         CANADIAN MANUFACTURING INDUSTRIES:
         A BIVARIATE APPROACH*   101
    8.1 *BIVARIATE COMPARISONS OF MEANS AND
         DISTRIBUTIONS OF CHARACTERISTICS OF
         AUSTRALIAN AND CANADIAN MANUFAC-
         TURING INDUSTRIES*   102
         Industry structures   103
         Labour forces   105
         Foreign trade   108
         Use of resources   109
         Other industry characteristics   111
    8.2 *BIVARIATE CORRELATION ANALYSIS OF
         CHARACTERISTICS OF AUSTRALIAN AND
         CANADIAN MANUFACTURING INDUSTRIES*   111
         Protection and Industry Characteristics   113
         Industry structures   113
         Foreign participation   113
         Labour forces   118
         Research and development   118
         Production techniques and resource use   118
         Foreign trade   118
         Size of markets   120
         *Other Characteristics of Australian and Canadian
         Manufacturing Industries*   121
         Size of markets   121
         Foreign participation   123
         Industry structures   123
         Comparison of industry characteristics   126

8.3 *BIVARIATE COMPARISONS OF AUSTRALIAN AND CANADIAN MANUFACTURING SECTORS: A SUMMARY*   128
Comparisons of Means and Distributions   128
Simple Correlation Analysis   129

CHAPTER
9. *AN ANALYSIS OF AUSTRALIAN AND CANADIAN MANUFACTURING INDUSTRIES: A MULTIVARIATE APPROACH*   131
9.1 *MULTIVARIATE DISCRIMINANT ANALYSIS*   132
Discriminant Analysis of Four Aspects of Australian and Canadian Manufacturing Industries   132
     Industry structures   133
     Labour forces   135
     Foreign trade and the use of resources   137
Discriminant Analysis of Selected Attributes of Australian and Canadian Manufacturing Industries   137
     Selected industry characteristics   138
     Selected industry characteristics and Protection   139
Summary of Discriminant Analysis Results   141
9.2 *REGRESSION ANALYSIS*   143
Tariffs, Transport Costs and Characteristics of Australian and Canadian Manufacturing Industries   144
     Aspects of diversification   144
     Foreign trade performance   145
     Foreign control   150
Summary of Regression Analysis Results   153

CHAPTER
10. *SUMMARY AND CONCLUSIONS*   157
10.1 *PROTECTION OF AUSTRALIAN AND CANADIAN MANUFACTURING: A REVIEW OF THE LITERATURE*   157
10.2 *BARRIERS TO AUSTRALIAN AND CANADIAN TRADE: THE EMPIRICAL EVIDENCE*   159
Barriers to Exports   159
Barriers to Imports   160
10.3 *TRADE BARRIERS AND THEIR EFFECTS ON AUSTRALIAN AND CANADIAN MANUFACTURING*   161
Similarities Between Australian and Canadian Industries   162
Differences Between Australian and Canadian Industries   163
The Likely Role of Trade Barriers   164
The "Costs" of Protection   165

    10.4 *POLICY PRESCRIPTIONS?*   166
        Tariffs   167
        Transport Costs   170
APPENDIX
    8.1 *The Concordance of Australian and Canadian Manu-*
        facturing Activities   173
APPENDIX
    8.2 *The Data Used in This Study*   177
        Australia   181
        Canada   190
APPENDIX
    8.3 *The Distribution of Activity in Australian and Cana-*
        dian Manufacturing   201
APPENDIX
    9.1 *Discriminant Analysis: Some Theoretical Considerations*   207
BIBLIOGRAPHY   210

1. Introduction: The Scope of the Study

This study seeks to analyse and empirically assess the significance of transport costs and tariff policy in affecting trade and industrial structure in the manufacturing sectors of Australia and Canada. While tariffs have been the subject of much theoretical and empirical research, the same is not generally true of geographic isolation and the associated costs of transportation. In many ways this is hardly surprising. Theoretically, tariffs and transport costs may be treated as being conceptually identical. Tariffs are a "man-made" barrier to trade and may therefore be manipulated to achieve certain policy objectives. The natural barrier of transport costs is largely outside the influence of policy makers and thus has tended to be overlooked by economists.[1] Nevertheless, it should be recognised that international transport costs, like tariffs, may significantly affect the competitive position of industries.

Here, the transport costs and tariff barriers to trade are examined from two points of view: as a disadvantage to exporters and potential exporters; and as a possible advantage to import-competing producers. A major contribution is to provide estimates of transport costs and tariff protection available to Australian manufacturing industries, and to compare them with the corresponding barriers sheltering similar Canadian industries. Australia and Canada share many characteristics, including long histories of tariff protection. However because of Canada's proximity to, and the relative importance of its trade with the United States, in respect of transport cost protection, Canadian industries are likely to face quite different circumstances. Not only are transport costs between Canada and the U.S. likely to be significantly lower than between Australia and its trading partners, the proximity of both combined with their long internal distances may well promote trade across the border.[2] This, then, provides an opportunity to compare the Australian manufacturing sector which has developed behind high barriers of artificial and natural protection, with the Canadian manufacturing sector which has developed mainly behind the artificial barriers of tariffs and other measures of trade control.

---

1. That there may be an element of "man-made" protection in transport costs is discussed in Chapter 6, footnote 5, and in Chapter 10.4.

2. For example it is possible that a commodity (eg. farm machinery) may be exported from "eastern" Canada to the "eastern" U.S., while "western" Canada imports it from the "western" U.S.

This study finds that for many exporters in both countries, international transport costs may well be higher and provide a greater barrier to trade than tariffs. For import-competing producers, those in Australia shelter behind significantly higher tariff and transport cost barriers than those in Canada. While on average, tariffs are higher in Australia, the structure of tariff rates in the two countries is remarkably similar. As well, despite the proximity and importance of the United States to Canada's trade, for many industries of both countries transport costs comprise a significant element of the total protection available to them.

While it is apparent in both countries that there are advantages to local industries conferred by barriers to imports in sheltering them from foreign competition, and all else being equal, increasing the sizes of domestic markets, there is evidence that the advantages may well be overshadowed by the sum of two other broad influences. First, tariff barriers to imports are associated with industry structures which are inimical to efficiency, providing, for example, apparent encouragement of "excess" entry of firms, and output diversity within industries, both of which may inhibit the exploitation of scale economies.[3] Second, the foreign trade barriers considered here — transport costs for exports, and foreign tariffs — in inhibiting exports, tend to restrict the sizes of available markets and to reinforce these adverse effects.

1.1 Protection in Australia and Canada

Australia has a long history of tariff protection. Protective tariffs were adopted in 1865 and the common external tariff dates from late 1901. This history of protectionism and its political and economic importance has led the theoretical and empirical analysis of tariffs to be a key area of study for Australian economists. For much the same reasons a similar long-standing interest has been shown by economists in Canada. There, the beginnings of industrial protectionism can be discerned with the introduction of the Cayley tariff of 1858[4], though overt protectionism is usually considered to have begun with the "National Policy" of the Macdonald government in 1879.

That Australian levels of protection of manufacturing are high by world standards is well known. In 1970, Australian tariffs on industrial products

---

3. Throughout this study tariffs and transport tests are considered as analogues. Of interest is the effect of transport costs on comparative industry structure/efficiency as a result of Australia's comparative isolation from world markets, and the "extra" transport costs that this entails. It should be recognised that transport costs in principle do not permit inefficiencies, and the fact that everything cannot be produced in the one place involves inefficiency no more than the fact that everything cannot be produced at the same time.

4. Named after the then Finance Minister.

were two to three times the world average, and more specifically, were higher than those of Japan and of any of the western European countries with which Australia is usually compared. Only New Zealand's tariffs were higher (Industries Assistance Commission, 1976). Despite the 25 percent tariff cut in July, 1973, Australian manufacturing industry still had higher average tariff protection in 1975 (the latest year for which comparable data are readily available) than the industries of Japan, the European Economic Community, Sweden, Canada and the United States, its major trading partners. Since then Australian trade barriers, mainly in the form of quantitative restrictions, have been raised to higher levels.

Tariff protection has been recognised by a succession of Australian governments as an important influence on industrial structure. In introducing the first overtly protectionist Australian tariffs in 1921, the Honourable Massey Greene, Minister for Trade and Customs, stated:

"I believe it will protect industries born during the war, will encourage others that are desirable, and will diversify and extend existing industries." (Brigden, 1929, p. 149).

By 1965 the aims of tariff policy expressed by Greene had apparently been achieved when the Vernon Committee declared that in its opinion,

". . . the tariff has been important in the expansion and increased diversity of Australian industry . . . " (Vernon, 1965, p. 38).

Since the middle 1960s however, there has been an increasing recognition of the cost of protecting Australian manufacturing. The misgivings expressed by many concerning the effects of the Australian tariff are well represented in the Jackson Committee Report of 1975:

". . . [Tariff policies have] led to a very diverse and rather fragmented industry structure. [As a result] factories opened proudly in the early post-war years have become today's structural problems . . ." (Jackson, 1975, p. 34).[5]

Similar concerns have been voiced in Canada. For example, the Economic Council of Canada has stated that ". . . commercial policy has contributed to a deterioration of Canada's capacity for sustained, dynamic, autonomous growth . . ." (1975, p. 37). Consequently, the Council has suggested that tariff reform be used to assist the Canadian economy to adapt smoothly to an increasingly competitive international environment (Economic Council of Canada, 1975, pp. 3, 8 and 172-173).

While tariffs have apparently been of major importance in the development of Australia's present manufacturing industry, it is suggested that

---

5. Of course industries unprotected by tariffs may be affected by changes in demand and this can also give rise to structural problems.

greater recognition should be given to the transport costs which are associated with geographic isolation. These are an inhibiting influence on trade and, consequently, are likely to be an important influence on industrial structure. To the extent that distance directly influences international transport costs,[6] both exports and imports are lower than they would be if Australia were geographically closer to the countries with which it trades. By contrast, Canada's trade which in great part is conducted with the United States is unlikely to be inhibited to the same degree.

Not all sectors of the economy are effected in the same way, however. Exporters are disadvantaged by distance. In addition to foreign trade barriers, the barrier of freight costs determined partially by isolation must be surmounted before exporters can compete on overseas markets. The other important aspect of the influence of distance from foreign markets is often overlooked: the advantage it confers on import-competing domestic producers. It provides a margin of protection which is an addition to artificial barriers to trade; one which is by no means insignificant for many industries. Indeed, it will be shown in this study transport costs (which are generally directly related to distance from markets) are a more important source of protection than tariffs in the case of some Australian and Canadian manufacturing industries. It is not an unambiguous advantage for all import-competing manufacturing industries, however. Transport costs also affect the cost of inputs and in this respect they are a burden both on manufacturing and on other sectors of the economy.

1.2 Comparison of Australian and Canadian Manufacturing Industries

The comparisons of the protective structures of Australia and Canada, and of various characteristics of industries comprising the respective manufacturing sectors have been made because of the similarities in the two economies, particularly the presence of:
(a) domestic markets which for some industries, may be small compared with their minimum efficient scales;
(b) similar consumption patterns;
(c) similar geographic concentrations of industrial capacity, sparsely distributed populations, and the transport costs and communication problems associated with long internal distances;
(d) similar federal systems of government with consequent problems of achieving co-ordinated and consistent economic strategies; and
(e) similar histories of protectionism.
   Tables 1.1, 1.2 and 1.3 compare some relevant characteristics of the

---

6. Hereafter, unless otherwise specified, the term, "transport costs" refers to international transport costs.

Australian and Canadian economies. Table 1.1 shows the similar distribution of gross product in the two economies, with manufacturing sectors contributing about one-quarter of the respective totals. Table 1.2 compares the trade performances of the two countries' rural and mining sectors. In Australia the rural sector makes a greater contribution to total exports than its Canadian counterpart, but otherwise the sectoral data are much the same for each country.

The major differences lie in the trade characteristics of the two manufacturing sectors. The export performance of the Australian manufacturing sector is markedly worse than the Canadian sector by the criteria of Table 1.3, while the proportion of imports comprising Australian supplies of manufactures is only half that of Canada. According to these data, the Australian manufacturing sector is much less open to international trade than its Canadian counterpart. The proportion of intra-industry trade is also lower in Australian manufacturing, and suggests a relative lack of specialisation in the sector.

TABLE 1.1:

AUSTRALIA AND CANADA, 1973 (b)
GROSS PRODUCT AT FACTOR COST

	Australia (b)	Canada
Rural (a)	8.0	5.3
Mining (a)	3.8	4.2
Manufacturing (a)	23.8	23.1
Services (a)	64.6	67.1
Total	100.0	100.0
(May not add owing to rounding)		

Source: Industries Assistance Commission, 1976, p. 73.

TABLE 1.2:

TRADE PERFORMANCE OF RURAL MINING SECTORS (a)

	Rural		Mining	
	Aust. %	Can. %	Aust. %	Can. %
Exports/total exports (c)	26.7	10.6	16.5	14.0
Imports/total imports (d)	3.4	4.2	3.2	6.3
Exports/sector gross product (f)	53.7	46.2	69.5	75.1
Sector gross product/GDP (g)	8.0	5.3	3.8	4.3

Source: Industrial Assistance Commission, 1977, p. 96.

TABLE 1.3:

TRADE PERFORMANCE OF MANUFACTURING (a)

	Aust. %	Can. %
Exports/total exports (c)	56.7	75.3
Exports/domestic production (i)	13.0	23.9
Exports/sector gross product (f)	38.4	75.3
Imports/total imports (d)	93.4	89.4
Intra-industry trade (j)	31.0	50.0
Sector gross product/GDP (g)	23.8	23.1

Source: Industries Assistance Commission, 1977, pp. 96-97.

(a) Divisions of the International Standard Industrial Classification.
(b) Data for Australia are for 1972-73.
(c) Value of exports of the sector as a percentage of total exports of goods from rural, mining and manufacturing sectors.
(d) Value of imports of competitive goods produced by the sector as a percentage of total imports of competitive goods produced by the rural, mining and manufacturing sectors.
(f) Value of exports expressed as a percentage of gross product at factor cost for the sector.
(g) Gross product at factor cost of the sector as a percentage of gross domestic product at factor cost.
(h) Value of imports as a percentage of domestic supply. Domestic supply is defined as the value of domestic production, plus imports, less exports.
(i) Value of exports as a percentage of domestic production.
(j) For definition see Grubel and Lloyd, 1975; and variable INTRA in Appendix 8.2.

These differences are a major concern of this study. A possible influence lies in one important characteristic of the Canadian economy not shared by Australia: its proximity to the United States. The dominance of the U.S. as a source of Canada's imports and as a market for Canadian exports is particularly important here. In 1973 approximately 70 percent of Canada's foreign trade (both imports and exports) was conducted with the United States (Economic Council of Canada, 1975, p. 98). Canada's two most important manufacturing provinces, Ontario and Quebec, are within 24 hours by road of many major U.S. centres. For a wide range of commodities, Canadian international transport costs may therefore be expected to be relatively low when compared with those of Australia. Isolation will also tend to result in higher inventories, and, at positive interest rates, goods in shipment for longer periods will have higher capital costs. Thus, the comparison in this study is between the Australian manufacturing sector, which has developed behind high barriers of transport and related costs, tariffs and other measures of trade control, and Canadian industry, which in great part may be considered to have developed behind the artificial barrier of trade protection alone.[7]

There is another important and obvious difference between the two countries: Australia has a population of about 15 million people, while Canada's is around 25 million. No explicit account is taken of this influence other than to include, at appropriate stages in the empirical analysis, variables which seek to measure the size of the markets available to the respective industries, or which attempt to measure aspects of economies of scale. In respect of the analysis of industry structures, the objective is the limited one of seeking to ascertain if there are relationships between variables which reflect relative industrial structure and performance, and the protection afforded by tariffs and transport costs.

1.3 Scope and Aims of the Study

This is a cross-sectional study[8] using data drawn (where possible) from the period 1 July, 1973 to 30 June, 1974 for Australia, and 1974[9] for Canada.[10] The time period chosen is a product of the Australian transport cost data available to the study[11], and the increasing use of nontariff barriers (which are not analysed here) by Australia since July, 1974[12].

The analysis of this study is in seven parts. Chapter 2 examines the development of commercial policies in Australia and Canada until 1974, and draws parallels between the application and the effects of such policies in the two countries. The primary objective of Chapter 3 is to provide a brief review of the theoretical literature on trade barriers, with emphasis on

---

7. It is interesting to note the data of Tables 1.1 and 1.3 in the case of Sweden. In 1975 Swedish manufacturing sheltered behind lower average nominal tariffs than manufacturing in Australia or Canada (IAC, 1978, p. 78) and like Canada, is close to large foreign markets. The Swedish sector had better export performance by the criteria of Table 1.3 (95.0, 37.3 and 85.1 per cent, respectively) and a much higher proportion of intra-industry trade (63.0 per cent) than those of both Australia and Canada. The proportion of manufactured exports of total exports in Sweden (91.5 percent) was similar to those of Australia and Canada. The contribution of manufacturing to gross product at factor cost (30.3 percent) was higher in Sweden than in Australia and Canada, with relatively small contributions by rural and mining (4.4 and 0.8 percent, respectively) (IAC, 1976, p. 73; IAC, 1977, p. 98).

8. Some of the assumptions made and problems which may arise in a cross-sectional analysis of the present type are discussed in Chapter 9.2.

9. The report period for Canadian data is the fiscal year ending as late as 31 March of the calendar year following the reference year (Statistics Canada, 1979b, p. 18).

10. The descriptions of the variables used in this study, their sources, and the time periods from which they are drawn may be found in Appendix 8.2. Where data are drawn from other than 1973/74, there is the implicit assumption that such data are representative of the study period.

11. See Chapter 7.1.

12. See Chapter 2.1.

international transport costs and their role in international trade theory. It should be stressed that this is not a formal study of industry location. Rather, Chapter 3 establishes that transport costs may be considered as analogues of tariffs and as one component of the total barrier to international trade; and further, that both domestic and foreign trade barriers are likely to affect the range of commodities produced, the size of markets, the number and size distribution of firms; and by implication, the ability of firms to exploit economies of scale. This provides a background for Chapter 4 which examines the empirical literature concerning the effects of trade barriers on the structures and performances of Australian and Canadian manufacturing industries, and considers some international comparisons of Canadian manufacturing with the manufacturing sectors of Australia and the United States.

Given the importance of barriers to trade as influences on industry structures, Chapter 5, 6 and 7 look at different aspects of these barriers. Chapter 5 reviews empirical evidence linking distance, international transport costs and tariffs; and their effects on trade flows. The formal empirical analysis of this study beings in Chapter 6, with an examination of the heights of trade barriers which disadvantage Australian and Canadian exports. As distance and the cost of transportation are linked, estimates are made of the "cost" of distance contributing to liner shipping freight rates facing exporters of Australian manufactures. While transport cost barriers to Australia's exports are significant and are often higher than corresponding tariff barriers faced by such exports, evidence is also presented which suggest that for Canada, the same may be true; and moreover, for some commodities transport costs may be more important influences in inhibiting Canadian exports than foreign tariffs. Chapter 7 examines trade barriers from the opposite perspective. In estimating nominal and effective rates of tariff and transport cost protection for 85 similarly defined manufacturing industries in Australia and Canada, it looks at the advantage that such barriers may provide to import-competing industries.

Having examined the evidence concerning the effects of trade barriers on patterns of trade, and through them, on aspects of industry structure; and having estimated the heights of these barriers, Chapters 8 and 9 examine, *inter alia*, the possible effects of the protective structures on various characteristics of the industries comprising the Australian and Canadian manufacturing sectors. Chapter 8 compares means and distributions of certain variables for the two countries, and then uses simple bivariate correlation techniques to analyse relationships between variables reflecting aspects of industrial structures and performances in each country. Chapter 9 uses two multivariate techniques. First, discriminant analysis is used in an attempt to establish if it is possible to accurately distinguish between Australian and

Canadian industries using variables measuring various characteristics of the two manufacturing sectors. Second, regression analysis is used to examine the roles of tariffs and transport costs as possible determinants of some important facets of industries in the two countries.

2. Austrialian and Canadian Commercial Policy

This Chapter outlines the development of the commercial policies of both countries. It is not specifically concerned with the determinaiton of tariff rates, but rather with the overall effect of the major policies and events. The term "commercial policy", rather than "tariff policy", has been used to convey the fact that protectionist policies in both countries have been, and remain, not restricted to the manipulation of tariffs alone. Non-tariff barriers of various types have at times played an important, and even a dominant part in the overall protective structures of both Australia and Canada. However in both, over the last century, the tariff has been the major influence on their levels of protection, and consequently a far greater stress on this aspect of commercial policy is given here. An understanding of the changing role of the tariff, and particularly its part in providing a framework for, and assisting industrial growth is essential for an understanding of the development and present structure of the two manufacturing sectors.

2.1 The Development of Commercial Policy in Australia
Australian Commercial Policy to 1900

Import duties have played a prime role in the Australian fiscal system since shortly after the establishment of the first permanent settlement at Port Jackson. The first suggestion of customs duties was made by Governor Phillip in 1791, though it was not until 1800 that Governor Hunter imposed "assessments" on imported spirits in the colony of New South Wales (Reitsma, 1960, p. 1). Until 1810, the Australian colonies of New South Wales and Van Dieman's Land (which later became Tasmania) had a large degree of autonomy in matters of fiscal and commercial policy. However, two Acts of the British Parliament, in 1819 and 1822, while authorising the existing duties, also imposed limits on the power of the colonies to levy or alter tariffs. In New South Wales these limits lasted until 1842 when the newly created Legislative Council was given, subject to Royal Assent, greater powers in formulating tariffs. In Van Diemen's Land the limits lasted until 1850. Meanwhile, the more recently established colonies also imposed tariffs. Western Australia imposed duties on imported spirits in 1832, and in 1838 South Australia passed a Wine and Spirits Duty Bill (Reitsma, 1960, pp. 1-3). Though the early duties were imposed primarily to raise revenue, there were growing pressures for protection. The middle 1840s were witness to New South Wales, Van Diemen's Land and South

Australia imposing measure and counter-measure designed to encourage local industry at the expense of the other colonies (Allin, 1907).

The Australian Colonies Government Act of 1850 provided the basis for responsible government in the colonies and also marked the beginning of a new phase in Australian tariff policy in the nineteenth century. The Act left the colonies essentially free to legislate on tariff matters. In accordance with the free trade ideas which held sway in Britain at the time, the three colonies — New South Wales, Victoria and Tasmania — developed generally similar tariff schedules, which, while providing for certain revenue-raising duties on such goods as wine, spirits and tobacco, allowed the importation of virtually all remaining commodities free of duty.

Free trade however, was not to last. January 1865 brought the introduction into the Victorian Assembly of the first protectionist Australian tariff. Victoria's example was later followed in varying degrees by the smaller colonies, Queensland, South Australia and Tasmania. The Victorian tariff was a result of the end of the gold rushes, which had attracted a vastly increased population. In the eight years to 1860 the Victorian population increased from 150,000 to 540,000 and with run-down in the gold rushes, the idea that employment could be maintained by means of a protective tariff gained acceptance. Circumstances in New South Wales were fundamentally different. There, pastoral interests held sway, and were concerned mainly with keeping down production costs of goods destined for export.[1] As well, the relative abundance of coal and other resources gave New South Wales industries certain natural advantages, while the Government's policy of Crown land sales provided it with sufficient revenue for it not to be dependent upon Customs duties. Though there was strong support of protection in New South Wales during the 1860s, such sentiment declined just as it gained increasing strength in Victoria. The remainder of the nineteenth century saw, under the influence of Henry Parkes among others, the maintenance of free trade in New South Wales (though support for protection was increasing towards the end of the century), and the increasingly protectionist policy of Victoria.

Commercial Policy from Federation to War's End, 1901-1920

The Federation of the Australian colonies on 1st January 1901, was followed some ten months later by the introduction of the first uniform Australian tariff to the national Parliament. While trade between the States became free, the structure of the common external tariff attempted to

---

1. Agricultural interests in the 1840s however had advocated protection for farm products, particularly in New South Wales and Western Australia, to guarantee "home markets" (Goodwin, 1966, pp. 6-7).

accommodate the divergent views held by members at that time concerning the issue of free trade versus protection. The tariff was a "compromise tariff" and reflected the recognition that "at this time in our history neither free-trader nor protectionist can have his way entirely".[2] The prime objective of the tariff was the raising of revenue, "but protection, to existing industries at least, must accompany it".[3] From that time the protectionists gained increasing ascendancy. The support given the protectionists in the 1906 election from an electorate which saw its jobs threatened by the import of American products at "dumped" prices, encouraged the first general revision of the tariff. The revised tariff received assent in June 1908 and provided for a general increase in the rates of duty and for preferential rates of duty favouring goods produced or manufactured in the United Kingdom. Tariffs were further raised in 1911 and again in 1914 when the system of Imperial Preference was extended. Further development, however, had to await the end of the war.

The Tariff Board and Tariff Policy, 1921-1939

While the inter-war period brought a number of major developments in tariff policy, of major concern to this study was the creation of the Tariff Board in 1921 as an independent advisory body to the Government on matters of protection policy. It comprised people drawn from government, manufacturing and importing, and, after 1923, primary production (Goodwin, 1966, p. 35). Its prime functions were, upon reference from the responsible Minister, to enquire and report upon:

(a) the necessity for new increased, or reduced duties, and the deferment of existing or proposed deferred duties ;

(b) the necessity for granting bounties for the encouragement of any primary or secondary industry in Australia; and

(c) the effect of existing bounties or of subsidies subsequently granted.[4]

However, by 1928 the Board had on a number of occasions expressed concern about "the danger of the tariff being used to bolster up the ever-increasing cost of production", and instances of the "abuse" of protection where "a highly protected industry returns to its share-holders dividends considerably in excess of commercial rates . . ." (Tariff Board, 1927, p. 18). This disquiet, together with the recognition by the Board and others of the need for a comprehensive survey of the protective structure, led the Prime Minister of the day, Mr. Stanley Bruce, to set up an informal committee of enquiry under Professor J.B. Brigden. Its terms of reference

---

2,3. The Right Honorable C.C. Kingston, (Minister for Trade and Customs) Hansard, 8th October, 1901, quoted in Brigden (1929, p. 148).

4. Tariff Board Act 1921, Section 15 (1) (d) (e) and (f).

were "to inquire into the methods by which we are striving to apply . . . [protection] policy in order that we may satisfy ourselves that it is achieving its objects" — "to accelerate our development and to increase our national prosperity".[5]

The Bridgen Committee reported to the Prime Minister in 1929. While it heavily discounted the infant industry argument and the effect of tariffs as a short term full-employment measure (Goodwin, 1966, p. 37), the Committee was of the opinion that, ". . . without the tariff [Australia] could not have offered the same field for immigration and would not have been able to maintain [its] growth of population". As well, ". . . it appears very unlikely that under free trade conditions any form of alternative production could have been found to take the place of protected industry which would give the same national income as at present"[6] (Brigden, 1929, pp. 84 and 87). Thus in the main, the Committee supported the operation of protection policy to that time, but suggested that ". . . the tariff may be likened to a powerful drug with excellent tonic properties, but with reactions on the body politic which make it dangerous in the hands of the unskilled and the uninformed" (Brigden, 1929, p. 99). It concluded that the total burden of the tariff had reached its "economic limits" and "that no further increase in, or extensions of the tariff should be made without the closest scrutiny of the costs involved " (Brigden, 1929, pp. 6-7).

Events, however, overtook the Brigden recommendations. The Great Depression, which had begun in the year of the Report's publication, provoked the erection of protective barriers throughout the world. In Australia, as in most other countries, protective measures were aimed at improving the balance of payments and stimulating employment. Between 1929 and 1932 the Scullin administration, by-passing the Tariff Board machinery, steeply increased tariff rates, imposed primage duties as a "temporary" means of raising revenue (this "temporary" device existed until 1982), and imposed direct controls on imports. However, the devaluation of the Australian pound and the Ottawa Agreement[7] exerted a moderating

5. S.M. Bruce in his foreword to Brigden, 1929.

6. In a review article Viner (1929), criticised the implicit assumptions by the Committee that total income rather than per capita income should be the correct goal of economic growth; and that Australian staple industries were limited fundamentally by geography and conditions in world markets from profitable continued expansion. He concluded that "I am not convinced that the authors have successfully established their central thesis, even on the basis of their statement as to what Australia regards as desirable objectives for itself. I must admit, however, that they have made out a stronger case for their position than I would have supposed possible before reading their report, and I not only regard their investigation as well worth the great amount of effort which it must have cost, but deserving further extension and refinement" (Viner, 1929, p. 314)

7. In essence, this agreement provided that duties should be set at a level which would enable economic and efficient U.K. producers to reasonably compete on the Australian market.

influence on pressures for still more protection. These events, together with the government action in authorising the Tariff Board to review the new tariff structure, resulted in the reduction of many of the excessively high protective rates.[8] Nevertheless, by 1939 the average level of general tariff rates was still about 50 per cent above the level existing before the Depression (Jackson, 1975, p. 27).

The Post War Period, 1945-1971

During the fifteen years following World War II, the influence of the tariff as the predominant protective device was eroded. The war had stimulated the development of an integrated and almost autonomous Australian manufacturing sector; one which, though substantially different in structure from that existing before the war, was nevertheless protected by the high pre-war tariff. In the years immediately following the war, owing to the initial general improvement in Australia's competitive position, many industries no longer required all the protection which was available to them under the tariff. Later, import restrictions of one kind or another provided a further cushion for Australian manufacturing industry. In 1949, dollar shortages provoked controls upon goods imported from the United States and, more generally, chronic shortages of foreign exchange after the Korean War boom[9] in 1950-51, led to the imposition of general import quotas,[10] which were not abolished until 1960.[11] Thus, during this period, Australian manufacturing industry was substantially insulated from the rigours of overseas competition by direct quantitative restrictions. Following the abandonment of import licensing, the tariff once again asserted its dominance, and quantitative restrictions faded from the scene for nearly 15 years — until the second half of 1974, and fortunately, after the present study period.

Despite the period of apparent quiesence on the tariff front until the early 1960s, there had been periodic rumblings concerning the anachronistic

---

8. There was however, some back-sliding. Between 1936 and 1938, again without reference to the Tariff Board, the Government increased tariffs and introduced quantitative restrictions. This was part of a deliberate policy of trade diversion with the aim of improving Australia's balance of payments position. The quantitative restrictions were abandoned in 1938 though "the protective effect of the measures was consolidated by the tariff legislation" (Reitsma, 1960, pp. 24-25).

9. These shortages were caused mainly by the loss of many of Australia's traditional rural export markets.

10. In March 1952, all but two per cent by value of Australian imports became subject to import licensing (Lloyd, 1973, p. 11).

11. In February 1960, 90 per cent of imports were freed from quantitative restrictions and, but for a few lines, the remainder has been freed by 1963 (Lloyd, 1973, p. 11).

14

structure of the tariff and the high levels of protection available which, in many cases, were not needed by the industries concerned. On at least two occasions during the second half of the 1950s, the Tariff Board called for an enquiry into the overall structure of the tariff (Tariff Board, 1955, 1956), while the import lobby of the Associated Chambers of Commerce of Australia was persistently calling for a tariff review.

These calls gained impetus in the early 1960s until, in its 1964-65 Annual Report, the Tariff Board came out strongly for a systematic review of the Tariff protecting all major Australian manufacturing industries. This call, together with the Vernon Committee's suggestions for changes in the tariff making process (Vernon, 1965, Ch. 17) went towards creating the necessary climate for reform. In its succeeding reports the Board developed its position. In its 1966-67 report it proposed ". . . a progressive and systematic review of the Tariff consisting of an internal examination by the Board of the structure and levels of protection in the Tariff, together with public enquiries into the main areas of production where there has been no recent public enquiry . . ." (Tariff Board, 1967, p. 8). The Board stated that the sequence of its enquiries into the various industries would be determined by the level of protection available to them, and in its next report stated its points of reference in terms of the effective rate of protection. Industries whose effective rate was greater than 50 per cent were designed "high cost" and would be examined first in the review programme. Those in the "medium" range, having effective rates between 26 and 50 per cent, would be "watched", while low cost industries having rates no greater than 25 per cent would, in normal circumstances, not be included in the review. The report of 1969-70 finally contained estimates of industry effective rates of protection and in early 1971 the Government accepted the Board's proposals. The tariff review was to take place over seven years ending 1978, and the scope and method of review were that proposed by the Board.

Australian Commercial Policy, 1971-1974

There were three major developments in Australian commercial policy during the period 1971 to 1974. The first was the government's acceptance in early 1971 of the Tariff Board's proposal for a comprehensive review which was mentioned briefly above. The second was the 25 per cent tariff reduction of July 1973, and the third was the replacement of the Tariff Board, on 1st January 1974, with the Industries Assistance Commission, which has a much broader field of enquiry than its predecessor. The first and the third will not be dealt with in detail here. By July 1974 the tariff review was still in its early stages and its effect on overall levels of protection was not yet significant. While average nominal tariffs for the manufacturing

15

sector fell from 22 per cent in 1972-73 to 17 per cent in 1973-74, the reduction was almost solely a result of the 25 per cent tariff cut (Industries Assistance Commission, 1976b, p. 59). As this study concentrates on manufacturing, the broadened sphere of interest of the Commission which includes the rural, mining and services sectors is not of present relevance.

The 25 per cent tariff cut however occurred at the beginning of the main study period. It had its origins in the growth of Australia's overseas reserves during 1971 and 1972. By December 1972, reserves had grown to $4750 million from a level less than a third of that two years earlier. When combined with the growing pressure on domestic industrial capacity, and the ambitious social objectives of the new Labor Government, the build-up in reserves made the policy of increasing imports an attractive alternative for increasing domestic supplies without a corresponding increase in locally generated inflationary pressures. The Government set up a committee under the Chairman of the Industries Assistance Commission, Mr. G.A. Rattigan, to explore policies to stimulate imports. The Committee recommended a 25 per cent reduction in tariffs, a recommendation which was accepted and implemented by the Government on 18th July, 1973.

Evidence presented by Gregory and Martin (1976), and by Gruen (1975) suggests that the effects on manufacturing industry of the 25 per cent tariff cut were overshadowed by the series of currency appreciatons which took place over the period 1972-74. Estimates suggest that the tariff cut was the equivalent of a 4 to 6 per cent revaluation,[12] which compares with an overall appreciation in the effective exchange rate[13] exceeding 20 per cent over the period 1973-74 (Gruen, 1975, p. 11), and had its major effect on import volumes between 9 and 15 months after the event (Gregory and Martin, 1976). The tariff cut, at least over the period relevant to this study, apparently had a negligible effect on the level of imports, profitability or employment (Gruen, 1975, p. 14; Industries Assistance Commission, 1975, pp. 13-17; Gregory and Martin, 1976).

The Tariff and Industrial Development: A Summary

Aside from the stimulus provided by World War I, the development of manufacturing over the period 1908 (when the Lyne Tariff was introduced) to 1939 was primarily dependent upon the tariff (Jackson Committee, 1975, p. 26). In particular, the Greene Tariff of 1921 saw what could be conceived

---

12. See Report of Possible Ways of Increasing Imports (Rattigan, 1973); Industries Assistance Commission (1974, Appendix 5.7); Gregory and Martin (1976).

13. i.e. A weighted average of Australia's exchange rates with the currencies of its trading partners. A detailed description of its computation appears in Industries Assistance Commission (1973, Appendix 2).

as the first overtly protectionist Australian tariff. In introducing the Bill, the Hon. Massey Greene stated:

"I believe it will protect industries born during the War, will encourage others that are desirable, and will diversify and extend existing industries" (Brigden, 1929, p. 149).

By 1929 the Brigden Committee had concluded, *inter alia*, that the "evidence available does not support the contention that Australia could have maintained its present population at a higher standard of living under free trade", but added that "the policy of protection has not had very great effects upon the prosperity of the community as a whole" (Bridgen, 1929, pp. 1,6). The 1930s saw Australia, like most western countries, adopting significantly increased protection in an attempt to preserve employment and balance of payments stability.

Like the Great War before it, World War II provided a direct stimulus to virtually all facets of Australian secondary industry. The end of wartime controls and world scarcity of resources created transitional problems which were eased by pent-up wartime demand. The war had brought the realisation of Australia's vulnerability "and the consequent need for increase in population and production, particularly in manufacturing" (Vernon, 1965, p. 2). Despite initial problems created by immediate postwar shortages, the manufacturing sector expanded in the 10 years to 1962-63 at a rate faster than all other sectors combined. Expansion was most marked in the "new" post-war industries : oil refining, motor vehicles, iron and steel, electrical and manufactured goods. "Old" industries, including textiles and food processing, expanded relatively slowly (Vernon, 1965, p. 4). Of particular importance was the motor vehicle industry, which during the post-war period assumed a special place in the development of the Australian manufacturing sector. In providing a market for components from the glass, paints, rubber and fabricated metal industries, its expansion in turn provided an impetus for these dependent industries. The immigration programme provided both a supply of labour, and a major contribution to the expanding size of the domestic market. Import licensing during the 1950s, a result of balance of payments problems, had, until its substantial abolition in 1960, the incidental effect of guaranteeing the major portion of the local market to domestic firms and encouraging expansion of a wide range of industries. This, combined with the policy of "giving adequate tariff protection to economic and efficient industries . . . continued to promote expansion " (Vernon, 1965, p. 4).

In noting the rapid development of manufacturing in the 30 years to 1963, the Vernon Committee found that the tariff had, among other influences, been an important factor in this development. Its major benefits were seen to be the promotion of diversification from which resulted both social and economic advantages. In the words of the Brigden Committee, 36 years earlier, the social advantages were the development of ". . . greater versatility . . . of various aptitudes in the population and generally promoting a fuller and richer national life" (Brigden, 1929, p. 18). The economic benefits were seen as its contribution to economic stability through lessening the importance of fluctuations in the prices of rural products, and the provision of external economies arising from the development of a complex of industrial skills, facilities and services, and investment opportunities. The tariff was also given support in terms of the infant industry argument:". . . the case for tariff protection or other assistance in the early stages of industries which are likely to benefit from large scale production is strong" (Vernon, 1965, pp. 361-362).

In summary, the Committee strongly suggested "that despite the difficulty of isolating [its influence], the tariff has been important in the expansion and increased diversity of industry, the development of labour skills, the advance of technology, the ability to absorb a rapid increase in population, involving a high rate of immigration and the steady increase in capital investment essential to all these achievements" (Vernon, 1965, p. 368). The evidence upon which these conclusions are based is difficult to discern however. Despite its apparent faith in the efficacy of tariff policy, and like the Bridgen Committee before it, the Vernon Committee saw the limitations of tariffs and though it believed that they had not unduly impaired the ability of primary and secondary industries to expand their export activities, it was "satisfied there is no case for the indiscriminant application of tariff protection" (Vernon, 1965, pp. 366-367).

Ten years later the Jackson Committee examined a manufacturing sector which for the preceding 15 years had been subject to an industrial policy centred almost solely on the tariff. In the main, during that period provided an established activity could demonstrate technical efficiency, the Tariff Board was willing to grant "made-to-measure" protection. The made-to-measure approach, together with the earlier import control ". . . had led to a very diverse and rather fragmented industrial structure. [One where] factories opened proudly in the early post-war years have become today's structural problems . . ." (Jackson, 1975, p. 34). The tariff review initiated by the Tariff Board in 1971, and taken over by its successor, the Industries Assistance Commission in 1974, was a response to the problems which had accumulated from a tariff system built up, and in approach, largely unchanged for over 70 years. It is with its legacy that an important part of this study is concerned.

2.2 The Development of Commercial Policy in Canada
Canadian Commercial Policy to 1879

During the period of French control of the St. Lawrence colony and later, with the coming of British administration in 1763, the main revenues for the colony's administration were derived from duties on wine, rum and brandy, import taxes (mainly on "luxury" goods) and export taxes (mainly on the fur trade). Establishment of free trade between the provinces was provided by the Constitution Act of 1791 and two years later the colonies of Upper and Lower Canada imposed revenue-raising tariffs on wines. The Canada Trade Act in 1822 established substantially common tariffs for both Canadas, provided for the division of customs revenues, and extended the provincial policy of selectively admitting products from the United States.[14] It did, however, continue previous restrictions on foreign imports via that country.

The end of the 1830s saw both provinces still substantially dependent on customs duties, which even in prosperous times were inadequate. These financial problems, however, especially those of upper Canada, assisted in providing a climate conducive to the union of the two Canadas. The Union took place in July 1840, and in September of the following year the new Canadian Legislative consolidated the separate, but virtually identical Customs Acts of the two provinces and provided for a general rate of duty of five per cent on goods not otherwise specified (twice the old rate) to alleviate the colony's financial difficulties. The 1820s and the 1830s also saw the emergence of arguments for protective tariffs on manufactures as a stimulus to the growth and diversification of the economy. The infant industry argument appeared together with arguments stressing the need for tariffs to alleviate unemployment, and that "temporary" protection was required to strengthen the Dominion by fostering trade between the provinces (Goodwin, 1961, pp. 45-46).

With the abolition of British corn laws in 1846, and the news that within three years Canadian preference in British markets would be lost, came a major watershed of Canadian commercial policy. In addition, preference accorded by the colonies to British imports was, at Britain's instigation, relaxed. With the end of preference (albeit temporarily) and of the prohibition of imports via the United States, came a substantially autonomous Canadian tariff policy, though one which had still to balance the views of the agricultural protectionists, the emerging manufacturing protectionists and those of the free-trading merchants and shippers.

---

14. Trade with the United States which had been the subject of much bitterness on both sides, had been regulated in 1819.

Increasingly however, the balance was tipped against the free traders. Despite the negotiation of the Reciprocity Treaty with the United States in 1854,[15] protectionist opinion was gaining ground with the building of the first rail links and the consequent beginnings of industrialisation. The Cayley Tariff of 1858 (named after William Cayley, the Finance Minister), increased duties on manufactured and processed goods ; rates imposed on raw materials were substantially lower. The Galt Tariff (after Sir Alexander Galt, Cayley's successor) implemented the following year, provided for further increases in duties. Though the raising of revenue was professed as the main motive for the increase, they were also seen as "[encouraging] . . . commerce and [providing] incidental protection [to] manufacturers".[16]

Confederation in 1867 may be considered to mark the beginning of Canada's industrialisation. The first Dominion Tariff, however, though it continued the basic rates of the previous provincial tariff, had as its main objective the raising of revenue, particularly in view of the assumption by the Federal Government of the provinces' developmental debts (railways, canals, and municipal) to the extent of $88 million. Nevertheless in his provincial budget speech in 1866, Alexander Galt could be seen to recognise the tax effect of duties on inputs which is central to the concept of the effective rate of protection:

"The policy of this country has been to make every article of natural production imported into the province free and for revenue purposes to impose duties on all those manufactured articles which it was thought were able to bear the burden, affording at the same time an incidental amount of protection to our manufacturers. Now we propose to decrease the duties on the largest class of manufactured goods entering the country, *and to take them off altogether from those articles which, to a great extent, enter into the manufacture of other articles in this country*".[17]

While it was possibly true at this time that protection was of only secondary importance in the formulation of tariff policy, the overall effect of the policies of 1858 and 1859 and of the first Dominion Tariff, provided an environment conducive to industrialisation and which led to a situation where, by 1878, "the manufacturer and the industrial worker were political forces of the first rank" (McDiarmid, 1946, p. 130). Indeed, Neill suggests directly that Galt's 1859 tariff, "was more than secondarily protective"

---

15. This provided for the free exchange of a relatively limited list of national products between the United States and the British North American Colonies. The treaty was abrogated by the United States, and came to an effective end in March 1866, following the Cayley and Galt tariff increases of 1858 and 1859, and the bitterness caused by the American Civil War.

16. William Cayley, Montreal Herald and Daily Commercial Gazette, June 22, 1858, in McDiarmid (1946, p. 77).

17. Budget Speech, 1866, quoted in McDiarmid (1946, p. 136), emphasis added.

(Neill, 1979, p. 3). He makes the point that as its incidence was on finished goods rather than inputs, this shows a clear protective interest.

The "National Policy", 1879-1913

The "National Policy" implemented by the newly elected Conservative government under Sir John A. Macdonald in 1879 had been advocated by representatives of the party during the latter half of the 1870s. It was in great part a response to the serious depression in world economic activity which began to affect Canada during 1873. Macdonald first introduced the proposal to Parliament in 1878 prior to his party's successful election to government. He saw a "judicious re-adjustment of the tariff"[18] as leading to a restoration of prosperity, fostering agriculture, mining, manufacturing and other interests, retarding emmigration to the United States, providing a bargaining weapon in tariff negotiations with that country, preventing the dumping of foreign goods in Canadian markets and encouraging interprovincial trade (Young, 1957, p. 44).

The period of the middle 1870s saw much debate on the tariff issue and the organisation of a manufacturer's lobby — the Manufacturers' Association of Ontario. It aimed "to secure by all legitimate means the aid of both public opinion and governmental policy in favour of the development of home industry and the promotion of Canadian manufacturing enterprise . . ." (Clark, 1939, p. 5). These lobbying pressures, the depression, and the tendency for protectionism on the Continent led to the adoption of the "National Policy" as a significant plank in the Conservative platform and in no small way, to their success in the 1878 election. The National Policy tariff, when introduced, adopted a "made-to-measure" approach mainly based on specific duties. The principle of tariff-making at this time was put simply by Macdonald: ". . . let every manufacturer tell us what he wants and we will try to give him what he needs".[19] In drafting the new tariff, apparently this principle was followed closely. The government, upon receipt of advice on rates required by industry from ". . . those who were interested in the general interests of the country, or interested in any special interests",[20] introduced a tariff schedule which corresponded almost entirely to the advice it received.

Though the introduction of the National Policy is usually considered to have begun overt Canadian protectionism, it was not until 1887 that the tariff reached its height when protection of iron and steel, farm machinery

---

18. Quoted in Young (1957, p. xx).
19. Quoted in Porritt (1908, p. 317).
20. Sir Leonard Tilley, House of Commons debates, March 1879, p. 411, quoted in Young (1957, p. 46).

and textiles was further increased. In the interim, changes in the method of valuation and certain administrative changes[21] had already increased the protective effect of the initial National Policy tariff. Revenue derived from the tariff still provided the major proportion of federal receipts, however. In the decade of the 1870s, roughly three-quarters of total federal revenues were provided from this source (McDiarmid, 1946, p. 165), and this lends some support to Neill's (1979) contary view that the National Policy tariff was mainly a revenue raising device.

While the thrust of the National Policy remained unchanged until World War I, there were some significant developments in tariff policy. Crop failures and a decline in agricultural prices brought about the organisation of the wheat farmers of Western Canada who sought successfully, the reduction of tariffs on certain agricultural inputs, while the assumption of office by the Laurier government in 1896 saw the unconditional introduction of British Preference and the offering of similar preference to other countries, provided they offered equally favourable treatment to Canada. Further innovation occurred in 1907 with the addition of a third column in the tariff to act as a basis for trade bargaining with non-British countries. Finally, in July 1911, following protracted negotiations, came the successful passing of another reciprocity treaty through the United States' Congress.[22] In Canada however, the Opposition were able to force the Laurier government to an election on the issue. The defeat of the government in that election brought an end to the issue of reciprocity until the middle 1930s.

The Economic Consequences of the National Policy

The National Policy tariff was introduced in conjunction with the proposal for a transcontinental railway. Such policies sought to create an integrated industrial economy by providing stimulus to interprovincial trade and trade with Britain and the Continent rather than with the United States. While the two policies were witnesses to industrial expansion, it is interesting to speculate if the expansion may have been greater had trade with the U.S. been free. In the 10 years to 1891 the number of establishments in the manufacturing sector, wages paid and gross value of product, all increased by over 50 per cent, while the value of capital employed increased by over 100 per cent, despite the experience of worldwide deflation during the period. Employment increased by nearly 45 per cent. The period of the National Policy's operation, particularly the 18 years preceding World War I, was characterised by significant increases in all the major indices of

21. e.g. Inland transport costs became dutiable.
22. Like the 1854 treaty, this too, by today's standards, applied to a relatively limited range of goods.

national growth. In the first 10 years of the century manufacturing industry expanded more rapidly than at any peace-time period in Canadian history (McDiarmid, 1946, pp. 239-242).

Nevertheless, not all interpretations of the evidence are favourable to the national policy. W.J. Donald, for example, suggests that "practically all the successful pig iron and steel plants were started because of fundamental technical conditions that favoured their development rather than because of the application of the National Policy . . ." (in McDiarmid, 1946, p. 193). As well, evidence in both the United States and Canada suggested that tariffs were associated with the formation of trusts and other restraints of trade.[23] Whether the economic growth described can be attributed to the delayed effect of the national policy tariff cannot really be ascertained, though certainly the development of natural resource based industries,[24] contributed importantly to the overall rate of growth. As a balance to the favourable interpretations of the national policy outlined earlier, perhaps the case against it is best summed up by Dales.

". . . To the extent that the national policy was intended to reverse, or even reduce, the disparity in Canadian and American growth rates it was clearly a failure. After 1900 the Canadian economy, including Canadian manufacturing, grew more rapidly than the American economy for a dozen years, and Canadian historians have not hesitated to attribute this surge to the beneficial, if somewhat delayed, effects of the National Policy. As Careless wrote, it was 'the age that had failed' before 1900 and the rise of a prosperous age after 1900 that '. . . spelt success at long last for the National Policy . . .' Careless, 1953, pp. 295-312). In Canadian history it is heads the national policy wins and tails the age loses" (Dales, 1966, p. 151).

The Inter-War Period 1919-1939

The removal in 1919 and 1920 of the revenue-raising duties imposed during wartime left a tariff structure virtually unchanged from that existing in 1911. While in response to farm pressure, token reductions were made on a range of agricultural machinery, the tariff for the period of the 1920s remained relatively stable.[25] However, like many other countries, including

---

23. Though nothing came of it, a reduction in the tariff was even mooted as a potential anti-trust weapon in Canada, (McDiarmid, 1946, pp. 188-190).

24. Iron and steel, flour and grist mills, and pulp and paper.

25. One policy measure is worthy of note, however. An excise duty of 5 per cent on passenger cars, which has applied to both imports and domestic production, was removed from locally-produced motor vehicles with a retail price of less than $1,200, provided a 50 per cent Canadian content qualification was met. This scheme illustrates at an early stage, the special place the motor vehicle industry has assumed in Canada. Indeed, the industry has been seen in both Australia and Canada as the key to industrial development, and this scheme was apparently the first of many variants of local content scheme adopted by both countries over the succeeding years.

Australia, with the coming of the Great Depression Canada used commercial policy as an instrument to protect domestic activity and to assist recovery. A wide range of duties were increased in the Liberal Government's 1930 budget, together with the implementation of retaliatory policies against the agricultural protectionism of the United States embodied in the Hawley-Smoot bill passed by the Congress in 1930. These policies included the introduction of countervailing duties on United States' produce, and the extension of preferences to the United Kingdom and Empire countries, and to most-favoured-nations.

Nevertheless these moves toward protectionism and retaliation were not enough to preserve the Liberals in government at a time of deepening depression. Upon coming to office in July 1930, the new conservative Prime Minister, R.B. Bennett, began implementing a policy over the succeeding 12 months which was aimed at excluding the importation of goods which could be produced in Canada. Included were general tariff increases, and more subtle, were certain administrative procedures mainly concerned with the valuation of imports which "alone raised the actual tariff level as much as 10 per cent" (McDiarmid, 1946, pp. 275-276).

The Ottawa Conference held in mid-1932 produced a series of predominantly bilateral agreements to extend preferential tariff treatment to trade between Commonwealth countries, including Canada and Australia. While the conference was a stimulant to intra-Empire trade it exacerbated Canada's already strained trade relations with the United States. The passing of the Reciprocal Trade Agreements Act by the U.S. Congress in 1934 brought the first Canadian efforts at reconciliation and led to the trade agreements of 1935 and 1938. In return for most-favoured-nation treatment of the United States and, for certain commodities, specific reductions below M.F.N. rates, under the provisions Canada received tariff concessions on a wide range of commodities. By the outbreak of World War II the inward-looking protectionism of the early 1930s had given way at least in part, to the realisation of the role played by international trade in assisting recovery. During the latter stages of the 1930s, increasingly it was perceived that protectionism as a

". . . policy of fighting depression [had] met with limited success, owing to shrinkage of income from export sales and the collapse of investment in raw material industries which the tariff could not protect. In fact, tariff induced rigidities in manufactured goods prices impaired the lot of those engaged in such industries. Changes in the distributive shares of the shrunken national income were a joint result of the fall in export prices and rigid prices for protected manufactured goods while . . . investment in protected industries was inadequate to take up the slack" (McDiarmid, 1946, p. 339).

24

During the years of World War II the volume and direction of trade were largely independent of tariff policy. The end of the war, however, brought to Canadians the realisation that through the war effort their dependence upon the United States was probably stronger than at any stage in their history. Previous response to this perceived dependence centred on improving trade flows with the Empire and especially Britain. The post-war Canadian response showed a fundamental change in emphasis from the narrow, primarily bi-lateral, Empire-Europe orientation, to a multilateral approach to the reduction of trade barriers, through the General Agreement on Tariffs and Trade (GATT) negotiated in 1947. Under GATT, of which Canada was a primary initiator, signatories agreed with the principle that no new bi-lateral preferential arrangements should be exchanged,[26] and that commercial policies should promote international specialisation and trade.

The first large scale GATT negotiations took place in Geneva in 1947 and were followed three years later by further negotiations in Torquay, in England. Both rounds of negotiations resulted in an exchange of reductions in tariffs among participants. Under these two agreements the depression-created tariffs erected in the 1930s were largely dismantled by Canada in return for similar reductions by its trading partners. Young, however, has suggested that the effect of these tariff reductions on the protective effect of the Canadian tariff was relatively insignificant when he commented, "Many of the changes in the Canadian tariff, as in the tariffs of other countries, have had some element of window dressing about them" (Young, 1957, p. 52).[27] Nevertheless some Canadian protection had been reduced under the negotiations.

The remainder of the 1950s and the early 1960s were a period of relative stability in most tariffs outside the European Economic Community, until the Kennedy Round of negotiations during 1964-67. Under the Kennedy Round, Canada agreed to reduce rates on 56 per cent of its dutiable imports

---

26. Preferential arrangements creating unions or free trade areas, however, are not prohibited under GATT.

27. Unless tariff reductions lower prices, affect resource allocation and/or productive techniques, the change does not reduce the protective effect of the tariff. Prior to the GATT tariff negotiations in 1947 and 1951, there were significant elements of "water" (ie. unused protection) in the Canadian tariff. The process of squeezing water from the tariff obviously cannot go on forever. "Easy" tariff reductions became harder to find until "[in the views of some people], the pre-war agreements and the two major GATT negotiations at Geneva and Torquay largely exhausted the easy tariff reductions . . . by 1951 the Canadian tariff was beginning to approach a point where most reductions would have a significant impact on protected industries" (Young, 1957, p. 59).

(Economic Council of Canada, 1975, p. 86). While at first glance this is impressive, empirical evidence suggests that the effect of the Kennedy Round on Canada's overall tariff levels was not significant.[28] For example, Melvin and Wilkinson found that while for 32 selected industries, nearly all nominal rates were reduced, "in only about a tenth of the industries . . . [did] the absolute reduction exceed 10 percentage points in the effective rates. For about one-third of the industries, the levels of effective rates . . . actually increased" (Melvin and Wilkinson, 1968, p. 4).

The Tariff and Canadian National Development

Canadian governments for well over 100 years have used the tariff for furthering their political goals: the derivation of revenue, trade bargaining and the protection and development of Canadian industry. An overt statement of the protective aims of Canadian tariff policy and its implementation, however, primarily date from the National Policy tariff of Sir John Macdonald of 1879. The tariff was one part of a three-pronged policy, the others being the development of the trans-continental railway and the fostering of immigration. All three elements were a response to pressures from the south. The threat of the United States to Canada's independance has never been far from Canadian minds and the inward-looking national policy largely followed Canadian failure to gain preferential access to the British and the highly protected American markets. The rapid western expansion of the United States was also an important influence in the decision to stimulate Canadian east-west trade. Nevertheless "reciprocity" (i.e. the reciprocal dismantling of north-south trade barriers) has been an important element in Canada's tariff history, particularly in the early 1890s and just prior to World War I.

The National Policy remained the basis for Canadian commercial policy until the defensive, depression-created tariff barriers of the early 1930s, which were moderated towards the end of the decade. The end of World War II, which had brought with it increased dependance on the United States, saw Canada begin the pursuit of a policy of multi-lateral tariff reductions through GATT. In the same period, two important post-war developments have brought about a measure of Canadian-United States integration: the renewal of the defence production sharing programme, and the Canada-United States Automotive Agreement.

What has been the effect of protection on the Canadian economy? The Economic Council of Canada has made the following assessment:

"The lingering protection in Canada and foreign countries still largely confines

---

28. See Melvin and Wilkinson (1968); and Officer and Hurtubise (1969).

Canadian secondary industry to a relatively small market, and this has adverse effects on the growth of productivity and real incomes, as well as on the extent and pattern of foreign ownership, the pace of technological advance, and the development of innovative capability . . . commercial policy has contributed to a deterioration of [Canada's] capacity for sustained, dynamic, autonomous growth . . . Thus the results of a long evolution of trade policies can hardly be viewed as a contribution to independent national decision-making in Canada" (Economic Council of Canada, 1975, p. 37).

2.3 Australian and Canadian Commercial Policies: A Summary

To those familiar with the history of commercial policy of either country, an examination of the history of the other gives one a decided sense of *deja vu*. Both countries (or colonies as they then were) first introduced tariffs solely as a means of raising revenue. Both countries were witnesses to the gradual emergence of protectionist sentiment in the mid-1800s; in Australia, mainly as a result of the running-down of the Victorian gold rushes and of the resulting unemployment there; and in Canada, as a result of the building of the first rail links and the perceived need for, and the development of industrialisation.[29]

The success of those advocating national protectionist policies, first in Canada, with the introduction of the National policy in 1879, and later in Australia, with Federation in 1901, was a victory for manufacturing over agriculture. In both countries it laid the foundation for the resentment of farmers, placed as they were, in a position of relative disadvantage. The resentment still persists. In both countries, not only has the tariff divided farmer and manufacturer but it also has aligned region against region. In Australia there persists dissatisfaction, particularly in the minerals and primary producing states of Queensland and Western Australia, because of the disadvantage they suffer by a tariff protecting mainly New South Wales and Victoria, the populous, manufacturing states. In Canada, the Atlantic provinces and the West are similarly disadvantaged by a tariff structure primarily protecting Ontario and Quebec.

While the tariff in both countries was initially a means of raising revenue and then later mainly an instrument for the creation and maintenance of a manufacturing sector, in Canada the role of the tariff as a bargaining device has at various times, been extremely important. The issue of reciprocity of trade preferences with the United States has been a fairly constant thread running through the history of Canadian commercial policy from the middle 1850s, though its importance has varied. This has been virtually the

---

29. Agricultural protectionism in Canada had been an important issue in the first half of the nineteenth century but gradually faded with the increasing political dominance of manufacturing.

only issue where there has been no significant parallel in Australia, at least until the Fraser government's trade war of words with the European Economic Community in the late 1970s and early 1980s.

It is apparent that in both countries there is some disenchantment with long-standing tariff policies. In both countries it is now seen by many that such policies, while initially providing an environment conducive to industrial growth, are now contributing to the maintenance of industrial structures inimical to industrial efficiency, and the inhibition of needed structural change.

In assessing the need for a more outward-looking trade strategy, the Economic Council has implied that the National Policy of a century ago is no longer suited to Canada's needs, if indeed it ever was. As part of a more outward-looking strategy, the Council has suggested tariff reform as an important element in assisting the Canadian economy to adapt smoothly to the increasingly competitive international environment (1975, pp. 3, 8 and 172). The earlier discussion in this chapter has shown that in Australia since 1967, a similar strategy has been proposed and partially implemented (with many setbacks) by the Tariff Board and its successor, the Industries Assistance Commission. It should be apparent that there is a clear parallel between the perceived inward-looking strategy of Canada and many of the policies pursued by successive Australian governments since Federation.

Therefore in part, the later empirical analysis of this study attempts to assess the contribution of the respective tariff regimes to the relative structures and performances of the manufacturing sectors of the two countries.

3. Trade Barriers and Industrial Structure and Performance: Some Theoretical Considerations

Given the importance of protection to the development of manufacturing in both countries, this chapter first considers in summary, some theoretical aspects of protection which are of relevance to the present study. The discussion is confined to a brief examination of the role of tariffs in determining the division of a domestic market between local producers and importers, and their effects on "X-efficiency" — the possible under-utilisation of resources (Liebenstein, 1966). The concept of the effect rate of protection and its implications for resource allocation is also considered.

Not so well known as the literature on tariffs, nor so comprehensive, is the theoretical literature on international transport costs and their role in trade theory. The second part of this chapter gives special emphasis to two studies which consider international transport costs and tariffs as analogues, and examines their effects on the diversity of goods produced behind these barriers to trade. Some possible effects of protection on industrial structure and performance are considered in part three.

3.1 Some Aspects of the Theory of Tariff Protection
Nominal Tariffs and Efficiency

The effects of the imposition of a nominal tariff on price and output can be approximated using partial equilibrium analysis, by representing the demand and supply schedules for a given commodity in two countries, initially in the free trade case, and then with the imposition of a tariff. The tariff will generally affect the price received by domestic producers, the size and their share of the domestic market, and by inference, the economies of scale open to them. Partial equilibrium analysis is also used to assess the welfare effects of losses and gains from changes in production and consumption associated with the imposition or removal of tariffs (Corden, 1957; Johnson, 1960).[1] However, of prime interest here are not the effects of a tariff on allocative efficiency, but rather the possible "X-efficiency" effects when firms are not subject to strong competitive pressures. These effects include the failure to minimize costs, not because of plant size or factor

---

1. Most estimates of the allocative gains from trade liberalisation are relatively small, both absolutely and in relation to a country's G.D.P. (Stern, 1973, p. 866). See Chapter 4 for a brief discussion of the "costs" of protection

prices, but perhaps through the retention of obsolete technology or, more generally, because of the under-utilisation of resources.

Corden (1970) has shown that the X-efficiency gains to be realised as firms respond to increases in competitive pressures are by no means theoretically guaranteed.[2] However, in economies characterised by industrial concentration and by inference, monopoly power, ". . . protection may increase the degree of monopoly, raise monopoly profits . . . and the 'intensity of competition' in the economy may fall. For a given efficiency level, this will then raise the rate of profit and shift income distribution from labour to profits . . . assuming that labour and other factors that have lost real income have no scope for varying efficiency-creating inputs, there will be a fall in the general level of efficiency, or at least in the 'pockets' of monopoly concerned" (Corden, 1970). Also of relevance in Australia and Canada may be the case where tariffs are made-to-measure, so that poor management is rewarded by higher tariffs. A made-to-measure tariff system ". . . will encourage firms to avoid profit increases resulting from extra tariffs for fear that they will lose the tariff increases ; it pays them to be inefficient" (Corden, 1970, p. 7).[3]

Effective Protection and Resource Allocation

In addition to tariffs on final outputs — nominal tariffs — it is common in most countries for duties also to be imposed on intermediate inputs. This "antiprotection" constitutes a disadvantage to firms using tariff-affected inputs unless they are otherwise compensated. The common form of compensation is for countries to "escalate" their tariff structures: to impose higher tariffs on final products than on intermediate inputs.

The first analysis of the concept of effective protection and its application to policy issues is usually attributed to a Canadian, Clarence Barber (1955). The concept is designed to show the net effects of protection on final product and inputs, and may be defined as the percentage increase in value added per unit of output made possible by the tariff structure (Corden, 1966). The basic argument of the effective protection concept is that nominal tariff rates do not give an accurate indication of the extent to which the tariff structure protects value added in a given industry. A nominal tariff on the final output of an industry permits the producer to raise the price at which he sells his product on the home market while at the same time

---

2. "All that one can really say in general is that a protective structure may well have effects on efficiency, but the sign of these effects need not be uniform throughout the economy" (Corden, 1970, p. 7).

3. Not discussed here is the obvious case of the pursuit of higher tariffs by rent-seeking producers.

remaining competitive with imports. The existence of tariffs on inputs of materials or components raises the cost of the inputs to the producer whether or not he imports them or obtains them locally. "'Effective protection' is the net effect of the nominal tariff structure on the price the producer can charge domestically for his output compared with the prices he pays for intermediate inputs" (Melvin and Wilkinson, 1968, p. 4), and these rates are supposed to predict the movement of domestic resources as a consequence of a change in the tariff schedule.

Their estimation is typically undertaken in a partial equilibrium framework under highly restrictive assumptions.[4] In the literature particular comment has been provoked by the assumption of zero substitution elasticities between material inputs and primary factors, the relaxation of which may affect the ranking of industries by effective rates (Balassa, 1971, p. 253). Indeed, Bhagwati and Srinivasan have concluded, ". . . somewhat nihilistically, that a measure of [the effective rate of protection] which will *unfailingly* predict the domestic resource shift consequent on a change in the tariff structure does not exist in general. Even in the highly restrictive situations where a measure can be shown to exist, the information required for its computation generally subsumes the answer to the prediction problem which [effective rate] computations is supposed to provide" (1973, pp. 25-26).

Fortunately, the application of the effective rate concept does not appear to be fraught with quite the degree of difficulty implied by Bhagwati and Srinivasan. For example the sensitivity of effective rates (ERP) to the variability of input coefficients has been investigated by Balassa *et al* (1971). In studying the structure of protection in seven countries, they found that ERPs themselves, and their rankings by industry group did not differ materially when first calculated by the national input coefficients, and then by coefficients adapted from the Netherlands and Belgium, taken as approximations of free trade coefficients. In Australia, the Industries Assistance Commission has also conducted tests of the sensitivity of industry ERPs to small changes in their determinants. "The analysis showed that for almost all industries, changes of 1 percent in each of the determinants would not combine to change the average effective rate by more than 2 percent" (1974, p. 56).

Effective rates still enter importantly into tariff policy discussions in both Australia and Canada and perhaps current attitudes to the effective rate of protection are still best summarised by Grubel.

"At the present, it is an essentially unresolved question whether the neglect of general equilibrium repercussions in the calculation of effective rates leads to

4. For an excellent survey of the issues, see Grubel (1971).

highly misleading results which can produce harmful economic policies. . . . in practice, the answer to the basic questions depends decisively on the following two factors.

First, how significantly are industry rankings influenced when factor substitution and general equilibrium repercussions are considered? There is some evidence that for countries with large and non-uniform tariffs the influence on rankings is likely to be small. Second, how do policy makers use the information of effective tariff rates? It is not unreasonable to assume that this information is only one of many types of information used in arriving at policy decisions. Thus, knowledge about effective protection rates is constantly checked for consistency with other information. If it turns out to be grossly misleading, policy makers will find out this fact and stop paying attention to effective rates. At the same time, policy makers' apparent interest in knowledge about effective rates suggests that they consider it to be useful added information for their decision making process" (1971, p. 12).

While the later empirical analysis makes use of the concept of effective rates of protection (both effective tariffs and effective transport costs), criticisms of the concept should be kept in mind.

3.2 Transport Costs, Tariffs and the Range of Commodities Produced

In the literature of the pure theory of international trade, explicit analysis of the role of transport costs is relatively uncommon. This is not surprising as such costs may be treated as being conceptually identical to tariffs. Thus, the latter, as a "man-made" barrier to trade and subject to manipulation to achieve certain policy objectives, has naturally received most attention, while the former, "natural" barrier is considered to be largely outside the influence of policy-makers and has tended to be overlooked. However, in the absence of other influences, the existence of international transport costs has obvious implications for industrial structure. The studies examined here suggest that the closer is a given country to potential markets, and assuming there is a direct relationship between distance and transport costs,[5] the greater will be the tendency towards specialisation in production. If, on the other hand, a country is geographically isolated like Australia, it is likely that the pattern of production will be more diversified. Within the context of the present study which analyses the determinants of the relative structures of Australian and Canadian manufacturing industries, *ceteris paribus*, it may be expected that Canadian industry would be more specialised in production than Australian industry.

This study does not seek to provide a comprehensive examination of the literature concerning the role of transport costs in the body of international trade theory. Rather, it concentrates on two works which explicitly estab-

---

5. While this is generally the case, the relationship is not linear. See Chapter 6 for a discussion of distance and transport costs.

lish that transport costs may give rise to a range of non-traded goods. The first is by Haberler (1936) and the second, the joint study of Dornbusch, Fischer and Samuelson (1977), both of which are concerned with the establishment, within a range of goods, of boundaries determining those which are exportable, non-traded, and importable commodities. It will be shown that Dornbusch, Fischer and Samuelson (DFS), in extending the development of the two-country, many commodity model of comparative advantage, owe a debt to Haberler's work 44 years earlier, which is perhaps more significant than may at first be realised.

Transport Costs and Non-Traded Goods

It is apparent that transport costs affect commodity trade and thus production patterns, and Haberler (1936) has specifically noted the effect of transport costs in giving rise to a class of goods which enter only into domestic trade. "A commodity does not pass directly from the export class into the import class; it first must enter this [non-traded] class and be produced simultaneously in both countries for their home markets"[6] (1936, p. 141). The class of non-traded goods is determined in the following way. The relative cost of commodity A, in two countries, I and II, is determined by relative labour inputs a_1/a_2. If the cost of transporting that commodity from country I to country II is t_{12}^a, and if the cost is borne by the supplying country, then if $(a_1 + t_{12}^a)/a_2 < W_2/W_1$, the ratio of money wages expressed in common currency units, the commodity will be exported by I. On the other hand, if $W_2/W_1 < a_1/(a_2 + t_{21}^a)$ where t_{12}^a is the cost of transporting A from II to I, then country I will import that commodity. It is evident that $a_1/(a_2 + t_{21}) < (a_1 + t_{21}^a)/a_2$. If, therefore, W_2/W_1 lies between these values, the good will be neither imported nor exported. Thus, a good will not be traded unless the difference between its cost of production in the two countries is greater than the cost of its transportation. Though Haberler, using simple arithmetic examples examines the case of many discrete goods (1936, p. 138), his analysis may be stylised in the following manner (fully realising the schedule is not continuous), assuming first that transport costs are zero.

Figure 3.1 uses notation which is different from Haberler, but which is consistent with the later examination of the DFS model. It is hoped that the analysis of the diagram will clearly show how Haberler's work in 1933 provided the basic framework for DFS 44 years later. In Figure 3.1, commodities z_1, z_2, z_3, are ranked according to increasing home country comparative (labour) cost,

---

6. The notion that goods pass from the export sector, to non-traded goods, to the import sector does not conform to the empirical observation of intra-industry trade (i.e. commodities of the same type which are both imported and exported). See Grubel and Lloyd (1975).

country comparative (labour) cost,

$$\frac{a(z_1)}{a^*(z_1)} < \frac{a(z_2)}{a^*(z_2)} < \frac{a(z_3)}{a^*(z_3)} < \ldots < \frac{a(z_n)}{a^*(z_n)}$$

where the asterisk denotes the foreign country and the $a(z_i)$ are unit labour requirements.

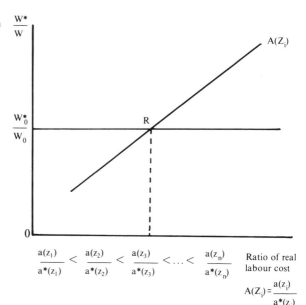

Figure 3.1

By construction, the relative unit labour cost schedule $a(z_i)/a^*(z_i)$ is upward sloping. For a given relative wage W_0^*/W_0, the home country has a comparative (labour cost) advantage in the production of commodities to the left of R where $a(z_i)/a^*(z_i) < W_0^*/W_0$. These commodities will therefore be exportables. The foreign country produces and exports commodities, to the right of R where $W_0^*/W_0 < a(z_i)/a^*(z_i)$.

Transport costs, t, are now introduced and are assumed to be the same for all commodities in either direction. Now, for a given relative wage W_0^*/W_0, the home country will produce and export commodities where $(a(z_i) + t)/a^*(z_i) < W_0^*/W_0$ and the foreign country will produce and export those where $W_0^*/W_0 < a(z_i)/(a^*(z) + t)$. The introduction of transport costs drives a wedge between the home country and foreign country schedules as shown in Figure 3.2

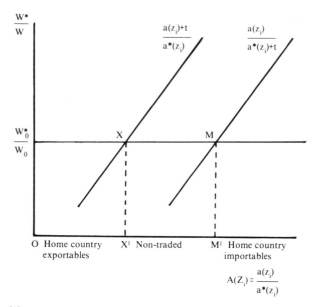

Figure 3.2

The home country will export goods to the left of X, while importing from the foreign country goods to the right of M. The range of commodities, XM, will be produced by both countries but will not enter trade. However, it has been left to DFS to "show precisely how tariffs and transport costs establish a range of commodities that are not traded ..." (1977, p. 829).

An Analysis of Transport Costs and Tariffs with a Continuum of Goods

DFS first establish the "real" model and *inter alia*, later extend it to non-traded goods, transport costs and tariffs. The real model differs from previous two-country, many-commodity models in that rather than "many" commodities, a continuum of goods is analysed. Below, portions of the model relevant to the present study are summarised using DFS's notation. For the purpose of reference, their equation numbers are included on the right hand side of the following pages.

The real model

Commodities are indexed on an interval (0, 1) according to diminishing home country comparative advantage in terms of unit labour requirements. The relative unit labour requirements are, by assumption, continuous and associated with each point on the interval is a commodity, z. For each commodity unit labour requirements in the home and foreign (denoted by *) country are a(z) and a*(z), with the relative unit labour requirement being:

(3.1) $$A(z) \equiv \frac{a^*(z)}{a(z)} \quad A'(z) < 0 \tag{1}$$

The model is based on the Ricardian labour theory of value, in which relative wages determine relative prices and thus the range of commodities produced at home and abroad. Therefore, a commodity z will be produced at home if

(3.2) $$a(z)w \leq a^*(z)w^* \tag{2}$$

Where w = wages measured in any common unit; and

ω = ratio of real wages is

(3.2') $$\omega \equiv \frac{w}{w^*} \leq \frac{a^*(z)}{a(z)} \equiv A(z)$$

The A(z) function is shown in Figure 3.3 and by construction is decreasing in z.

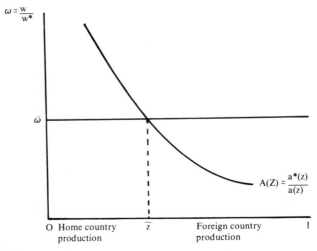

Figure 3.3

36

Thus, for a given ω, the home country will produce the range

(3.3) $\qquad O \leq z \leq \widetilde{z}\,(\omega)$ $\hfill$ (4)

while the foreign country will produce

(3.3') $\qquad \widetilde{z}\,(\omega) \leq z \leq 1$ $\hfill$ (4')

The equality of (3.2') defines the borderline commodity z.

Extensions of the model

(i). Transport costs

In common with Samuelson (1954), and Mundell (1957), transport costs are treated as a shrinkage of goods in transit. Thus upon exportation, a given quantity of a commodity z, has, by the time it is received at tis destination, shrunk by a proportion, $(1-g)(z)$. The proportion $g(z)$, which arrives is assumed to be the same for shipments in either direction and for all commodities.

Modifying (3.2') to take account of transport shrinkage for the home country

(3.4) $\qquad wa(z) \leq (1/g)w^*a^*(z)$ $\hfill$ (17)

or $\qquad \omega \leq A(z)/g$

For the foreign country

(3.5) $\qquad w^*a^*(z) \leq (1/g)wa(z)$ $\hfill$ (18)

or $\qquad A(z)g \leq \omega$

Thus the home country (foreign country) will produce those commodities for which domestic (foreign) unit labour costs adjusted for transport shrinkages are less than foreign (domestic) labour costs.

The respective home country and foreign country $A(z)/g$ and $A(z)g$ schedules adjusted for unit labour requirements are shown in Figure 3.4. The home country produces to the left of $A(z)/g$, exporting $O\bar{z}^*$, while the foreign country produces to the right of $A(z)g$, exporting $\bar{z}1$. The intermediate range $\bar{z}^*\bar{z}$ corresponds to XM in the analysis of Haberler's work in Figure 3.2, and represents goods produced by both countries but not traded. The commodities $\bar{z}$ and $\bar{z}^*$ are respectively, the borderline commodities between domestic non-traded goods and home country imports; and foreign non-traded goods and home country exports. Equilibrium $\bar{z}$ and $\bar{z}^*$ are determined by considering the trade balance equilibrium modified to account for non-traded goods which are endogenously determined, and through the determination of the equilibrium relative wage ω, which is

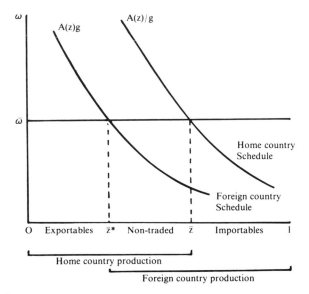

Figure 3.4

found to be a function of the relative sizes of the two countries, L^*/L,[7] and transport costs, g.

(ii). Tariffs

Tariffs are considered for the case where there is complete absence of transport costs. Each country is assumed to impose a uniform tariff, t, and t^*, respectively, on its imports. The proceeds of the duties are rebated in the form of lump sums. Just as transport costs lead to cost barriers to imports, and therefore to a range of non-traded commodities, so too do tariffs.

In this case the boundaries are defined by:

(3.6) $$\bar{z} = A^{-1}\left(\frac{\omega}{1+t}\right) \tag{23}$$

for the home country and

(3.6) $$\bar{z}^* = A^{-1}(\omega(1+t^*))$$

---

7. The DFS model is a "standard" Ricardian model with one factor of production and trade determined by comparative advantage. The sizes of countries is measured by the sizes of the respective labour forces. For the derivation of the B( ) schedule — the locus of trade balance equilibria — and the effects of relative size, see Dornbusch, Fischer and Samuelson (1977, pp. 825-827).

for the foreign country, where $A^{-1}(\ )$ is the inverse function of $A(\ )$. As $\bar{z} \neq \bar{z}^*$ there will be a range of non-traded goods. In this case, and analogously to the previous analysis of transport costs, the equilibrium relative wage is shown to be a function of relative size and tariffs; and importantly, that the range of non-traded goods depends on *both* home country and foreign country tariffs.

In terms of Figure 3.4, the analogy between the analysis of transport costs and tariffs is plain. In the former case, as $g(z)$ decreases (i.e. as transport costs $(1-g)(z)$ increase), the gap between the home country's $A(z)/g$ schedule and the foreign country's $A(z)g$ schedule becomes larger and so does the range of non-traded goods. In the latter case, the corresponding schedules are for the home country $A(z)(1+t)$, and for the foreign country $A(z)/(1+t^*)$. As tariffs increase, so too does the gap between the respective schedules and consequently, the range of non-traded goods.

The terms $(1-g)$ and $(1+t)$ have essentially the same effect on the range of goods not traded. The former is the fraction of goods "lost" to both countries in transit, the latter is the addition to income spent on home goods stemming from the rebate of the tariff on imports. An increase in either will enlarge the non-traded goods gap; a decrease will reduce it. Indeed, it may have rendered the DFS exposition clearer had transport costs been considered, not as $g(z)$, the fraction of goods arriving, but as $(1-g)(z)$, the fraction lost.

For present purposes, it is more useful to think of transport costs as a tariff equivalent. Thus rather than the shrinkage used by DFS, this study treats transport as an addition to the cost of importing in much the same way as Haberler. Within the DFS framework, if transport costs are paid by the foreign country and the proceeds are transferred to and spent by the home country, then the expression for transport cost $(1-g)$ becomes $(1+g)$. If both transport costs and tariffs are barriers to trade, then the total barrier is given by the expression $(1+g+t)$. Incorporating these changes, and assuming common uniform tariffs, Figure 3.4 now becomes: Figure 3.5

Obviously the higher are g and t, the larger is the range of non-traded goods, and the less specialised in production will both countries be. At the extreme, prohibitively high tariffs and/or transport costs will lead both countries to produce the full continuum of goods.

3.3 Some Implications for Industrial Structure and Performance

The highly restrictive two-country, single factor model of DFS provides an illustration of the method by which trade barriers may affect the *range* of goods produced by home and foreign countries. In small, protected economies like those of Australia and Canada which are characterised by oligopoly (Parry, 1977, p. 3; Eastman and Stykolt, 1967, p. 10), it may reasonably

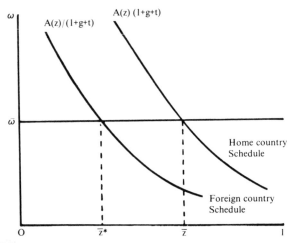

Figure 3.5

be expected that the greater the variety of goods produced, the greater is the probability that some of them will be produced by firms utilising plants of sub-optimal scale. Indeed, the relative diversity of firm output in Canada and its adverse effect on costs of production (when compared with a situation where there is no "excess" diversity) has been noted by a number of researchers (English, 1964; Eastman and Stykolt, 1967; Wilkinson, 1968; Berry, 1971; Caves, 1975), and in Australia by Grubel and Lloyd (1971; 1975).

As DFS have pointed out, *both* domestic and foreign tariffs affect the size of the total market available to a domestic producer. The possible effects of this may be considered in the context of the "Canadian model" of Eastman and Stykolt (1967, p. 22). Foreign tariffs, if there are non-zero foreign demand elasticities, lower the maximum price at which domestic producers can export and therefore tend to limit domestic firms to the local market and thus raise the barriers to any increase in capacity. A tariff protecting a local industry, however, increases the price which may be charged by domestic firms in the local market to the sum of the price of the lowest priced import and the tariff. The tariff increases the range of domestic prices available to local producers, within which they compete only with each other. Above this range, local producers are effectively in the world market competing with many firms; below it they may export, again competing on world markets with many firms.

Trade restrictions act as barriers to entry of imports to the domestic market and restrain domestic competitive pressures. In the opposite direc-

40

tion, however, trade barriers may induce direct entry of foreign firms in an effort to overcome these barriers. Within an industry, such barriers therefore affect the number[8] and the size distribution of firms, their competitive behaviour, their diversity of output, and their ease of entry (Eastman and Stykolt, 1967; Parry, 1977). In economies characterised by oligopoly, and in which there is collusion in some industries, it may be that the oligopolists are of the opinion that profits can be maximised by charging relatively high prices. These prices attract entry with the consequence that more plants become established than can be accommodated in the market at a price covering the maximum average cost of firms of optimum size. "The ensuing market structure is one in which the number of plants is large, the scale of plants is suboptimal, and average costs are high" (Eastman and Stykolt, 1967, p. 19). The effects may be even more far-reaching, however. While protection is likely to permit the entry of firms utilising plants which are often of sub-optimal size, this often entails the significant under-utilisation of installed capacity as well. "The dual problem frequently involves under-utilisation of sub-optimal size plant . . ." (Parry, 1977, p. 8). The characteristics described by Parry, and particularly the under-utilisation of capacity, are suggestive of Chamberlinian monopolistic competition. Indeed, Krugman (1979) has found that such a market structure will emerge when economies of scale are internal to the firm, and if such economies are limited, his results imply that protection will lead, *ceteris paribus*, to a larger number of smaller establishments.

The common thread running through many of the studies discussed here is the role of trade as a determinant of market structure and performance. For example, imports effectively increase domestic competitive pressures and reduce domestic barriers to entry, while presence of alternative export markets may also reduce the mutual interdependence of domestic sellers and lead to less collusive behaviour. Moreover, the presence of export markets may affect the scale and the utilisation of plant in the domestic market. Trade barriers, in turn, are crucial determinants of the flow of trade, and Chapter 4 which follows, examines the empirical evidence concerning the possible effects of protection on aspects of the structure and performance of industries.

---

8. The number of firms may have little to do with the degree of competition which characterises a market: duopolists may behave competitively; a large number of firms may not. Implicit in the work of Eastman and Stykolt is the apparent assumption that markets are characterised by a "given" degree of competition, and that the competitive pressures of "more" firms do not offset the apparent losses resulting from suboptimally sized plants.

4. Trade Barriers and the Structures and Performances of Australian and Canadian Manufacturing Industries

From the previous chapter it may be seen how trade barriers affect the borders between tradeable and non-tradeable goods, thus influencing the diversity of products produced and the size of the market available to local firms. The primary purposes of this chapter are to survey the main issues arising from the presence of these barriers, the empirical work on their effects, and the link between market size and aspects of industrial structure and performance in Australia and Canada. The framework of the chapter is provided by various empirical studies of Canadian industrial structure and performance, supplemented where possible by Australian empirical evidence. This evidence is sparse, and the paucity of Australian research in this area may indeed be described as an "industrial organisation vacuum" (Round, 1974).

4.1 Trade Barriers and Economies of Scale

The term "economies of scale" is often used as an omnibus term. While it often refers merely to the size of the market available to firms within a broad industry group, there are three more specific concepts of scale economies in common use, all referring to the operations of a given firm: firm-specific; plant-specific; and product-specific economies of scale.[1] The first of these refers to possible economies which may accrue to a group of plants operated by one company in the same broad product group. Thus for a firm comprising a number of plants, savings may be derived from certain non-production functions being undertaken by the firm as a whole, rather than each plant undertaking them separately. Advertising is perhaps the most obvious example. Plant-specific economies refer to costs of alternative plant sizes producing a particular product or group of products in the same industry (e.g. beer, cars, television sets). Product-specific economies are those which commonly refer to a product which is so narrowly defined as to be not distinguishable in the census of manufactures (e.g., a paper clip of a given size and design; a motor of a given capacity and for a specific use). All of these concepts may, of course, be interrelated. For convenience however, they are discussed separately.

---

1. The organisation of the following material owes much to Daly (1979).

Size of the Market

Market characteristics frequently depend on the nature of the commodity concerned. The size of the market for a producer of ready-mixed concrete, or for many of the service industries is generally restricted to a relatively small geographic area. Production of such commodities is typically localised owing to high transport costs; the notion of a national market in these cases is therefore a relatively meaningless concept. On the other hand, markets for many products are truly international and are not restricted by regional or national boundaries. Thus of prime importance in determining the size of the market for a product is the inhibiting influence of trade barriers.

Eastman and Stykolt (1967) found that while Canadian manufacturing costs usually exceeded the lowest level technically achievable, the reason was not Canada's ignorance of the best production techniques, which are generally available through its trade and cultural ties with other countries (and in particular with the United States), but relative commodity and factor prices arising from the separation of the U.S. and Canadian markets; and differences in market size. The separation of the markets stems both from the erection of tariff and other artificial barriers which impede trade, and international transport costs which act in a similar manner. The influences of trade barriers and the "natural" protection provided by transport costs, to the extent that they insulate Canadian industry from foreign prices in effect, largely determine the size of markets.[2] They create different competitive conditions and permit, and even induce, different behaviour by producers in the two economies, as suggested by the relative inefficiency of Canadian producers (Eastman and Stykolt, 1967, pp. 14-15). Consistent with this conclusion are Williams' findings that Canadian industries which were subject to high United States tariffs, high levels of protection on intermediate inputs purchased from the import-competing sector, and characterised by a high proportion of exports were the most likely to expand under free trade conditions. Those protected by high domestic tariffs were the most likely to contract (Williams, 1978, pp. 24-29). In the absence of other influences (and as suggested by Grubel and Lloyd's (1975) analysis of intra-industry trade), the lower are the barriers to trade, the larger is the size of the market, and ". . . the size of the market measured as a ratio of market size to efficient plant size is the principal determinant of the productive efficiency of an industry" (Eastman and Stykolt, 1967, p. 53).

---

2. Some evidence in this respect has been provided by Caves who found an inverse relationship between effective protection and the size of the Canadian market measured in average U.S. sized plants (Caves, 1975, p. 58).

However it may well be that in relatively small economies like Australia and Canada, the influence of the size of the domestic market as an inhibiting influence on a firm's ability to lower its costs to internationally competitive levels has been overemphasized. For example, English (1964), in his comparative study of the structures of Canadian and United States industries, found that the size of the Canadian domestic market was "no longer a significant restraint upon the competitive strength of Canadian manufacturing . . .", and that there was a tendency in Canada to exaggerate the volume of production required to bring costs down to internationally competitive levels. Such a finding is consistent with the estimate that a country provides a home market sufficient to support most types of manufacturing at some point when its population is between 10 and 15 million people (Robinson, 1960).

Nevertheless,

"The fact that there are too many producers seems fundamental in some industries. In other cases firms seem to diversify because access to adequate markets for their most appropriate specialties is restricted. The origins of such inadequacies of industrial structure are very often misinterpreted, primarily because of the tendency to put too much stress upon foreign ownership of industry as a factor and *too little appreciation of the implications of pricing by the Canadian tariff, and the extent to which foreign tariffs prevent Canadian producers from realising their potential"* (English, 1964, p. 40 emphasis added).

Firm-Specific Economies

It is generally expected that relatively large firms are able to achieve various types of economies at the firm, rather than the plant-level for certain essentially non-production costs. These may include a greater ability to exploit the possibilities of specialization in management, easier and cheaper access to finance and raw materials, and the ability to undertake firm-wide advertising, and research and development activities. The net results of these influences is difficult to gauge, however. Savings often tend to be offset by higher production costs which may be caused by physical product differentiation and the consequent output diversity of the firm. Additionally, while there is evidence of savings and greater flexibility in methods of obtaining funds in capital markets for large well established firms (Royal Commission of Corporate Concentration, p. 264), and possible economies to be derived from centralised research and development activities rather than such activities being dispersed between plants, the possible savings which are available may not be great. Advertising costs are rarely more than 5 per cent of sales for firms in the Canadian manufacturing sector, while in recent years, interest costs have been about 1 per cent of sales, and R & D costs have been slightly under 1 per cent of total costs. In this respect the evidence suggests that in a number of industries ". . . small firms were not too seriously handicapped by low expenditures on R & D in the relation to sales, in spite of high threshold expenditures on R & D" (Daly, 1979, p. 60). In the final analysis it should be recognised that the inefficiencies which may develop through management problems in large-sized firms may more than offset possible savings which may be made in the areas just discussed. The net influence of firm size on productivity and profitability is therefore uncertain.

Plant-Specific Economies

Eastman and Stykolt have found that it was common for Canadian industries to comprise a number of sub-optimally sized plants. The result was an inability to minimise costs by producing at optimum scale, and thus to achieve the lowest possible average costs for given input prices. They concluded that the prevalence of Canadian industries with sub-optimally sized plants, each duplicating the output of the others is a consequence of "excess" tariff protection (1967, p. 7). More explicit evidence of an association between high tariffs and plants of less than optimum size has been provided by Gorecki (1976). Based on the engineering concept of minimum efficient size, he found that in industries characterized by "high" protection, average plant size was less than one-half of efficient size; those characteristics by "low" protection were, on average, of greater than minimum efficient size.

These conclusions are consistent with the findings of a number of other researchers who have noted the relatively large number of plants characteristic of Canadian manufacturing, their smaller average size, and the smaller size of Canadian enterprises which usually also have fewer manufacturing plants than their United States counterparts (Rosenbluth, 1957; English, 1964; Scherer, 1973; Caves, 1975, Economic Council of Canada, 1975, Daly and Globerman, 1976). While it is possible, and indeed common in U.S. industries for a large number of small plants to be efficient and profitable in producing and supplying a small range of components to larger firms within the industry, the protected Canadian market is apparently too small to absorb the output of larger production runs of a small number of items (Daly and Globerman, 1976, p. 51). Length of production runs (product-specific economies of scale) and the degree of specialization within plants may be more important than their size, and consequently it has been suggested that the wide variation of plant sizes in the United States indicates that plant-specific economies are not large (Economic Council of Canada, 1967, p. 153). Daly has presented evidence that the higher costs incurred in producing in plants of less than optimum size are frequently "less than 5 or

10 per cent", and that of the 30 percentage points difference in productivity levels between Canadian and U.S. manufacturing observed during the 1960's ". . . perhaps 5 percentage points . . . can be explained by differences in plant size" (1979, p. 29).

Product-Specific Economies

In comparison with their U.S. counterparts, Canadian industries tend to be characterised by the manufacture of more diverse products and shorter production runs (English, 1964; Eastman and Stykolt, 1967; Wilkinson, 1968, pp. 109-131; Berry, 1971, pp. 402-426; Spence, 1977, p. 256), though Oksanen and Williams have presented some evidence to the contrary (1978, pp. 98-99).[3] A result of what could be termed "undue" diversity is the associated time required to change production from one product to another. The average speed of machinery is as a consequence, lower compared with speeds sustainable over long production runs; and there is reduced scope for specialization in labour functions.

Of particular interest is the possible relationship between protection and the relative diversity of Canadian output which has been the subject of work by Caves (1975). His finding suggest that when compared with equal-sized plants of large companies in the United States, the outputs of Canadian plants of a given size are much more diversified, and moreover, that the Canadian plants of multinational companies are more diversified than those belonging to Canadian owned companies. Within individual industries, Caves found that in practically every industry (but with the obvious exception of plants which are not diversified at all), Canadian plants operated by subsidiaries were more diversified than their parent's U.S. plants. This tendency was not so great in Canadian-owned plants, but the diversification which did exist tended toward vertically related activities (Caves 1975, p. 4).[4]

---

3. Oksanen and Williams' measure of output diversity (or intra-industry specialisation) is value added per dollar of payroll. The main subject of their study is not an explicit examination of Canada's relative output diversity, but rather the estimation of a discriminant function which, using variables reflecting certain attributes of Canadian and U.S. manufacturing industries, would enable the accurate classification of industries as Canadian or U.S. The interpretation of the coefficients of the function may be considered secondary to their work.

4. This study is interested in the role of protection as an influence of industrial structure and performance, and Caves explicitly considered both the effective rate of protection and a measure of *ad valorem* transport costs as possible determinants of output diversity. The *a priori* expectations were that effective tariffs encourage diversity ; transport costs inhibit it. His regression results however, found that although the independent variables were correctly signed, there was no significant relationship between diversity and either the tariff or transport cost variables.

Despite the evident disadvantages of product diversity, in some circumstances these may well be mitigated by other considerations. For example, a "... cost disadvantage arising from small scale of production may be offset by advantages of design for specifically Canadian production or consumption conditions, by ready access to technical advice and repair services and by lower transport costs in some instances" (English, 1964, p. 2). Other considerations have been advanced by Daly, Keys and Spence (1968). While evidence derived from interviews conducted in their survey of Canadian manufacturing suggested that short production runs were a major factor contributing to higher costs in Canada, it also suggested that even significant increases in productivity may have a relatively small effect on the *total* costs of the firm. This may therefore act as an inhibiting influence on the willingness of firms to move towards greater specialization in production. Moreover, if lower costs were passed on to buyers, the necessary reductions in price to sell the extra output may be greater than the reduction in cost due to greater specialization. Under certain circumstances it is therefore quite conceivable that prospects of reductions in costs through greater specialization may not be sufficient to encourage a firm from moving from a position of assured profits to one of possibly greater, but more uncertain profitability. In the absence of insulation from world competition through trade protection, the firm would have less choice in the decision.

While it is true that in some cases the disadvantages flowing from small scale (broadly defined) may at least to some extent be mitigated by these influences, the weight of evidence suggests that the disadvantages are important. It is now recognized that in addition to possible gains from inter-industry resource movements stemming from reductions in protection, that there are intra-industry effects which increase the efficiency of resource use *within* industries (Lloyd, 1978, p. 281). Grubel and Lloyd (1975) found in Australia for some commodities which are subject to economies of scale, the small size of the market and protection may have encouraged firms to produce a wider range of products, rather than greater outputs of a given set of commodities. The Australian Industries Assistance Commission has also noted the greater scope for exploiting economies of scale through intra-industry specialization. "Product differentiation, particularly in the manufacturing sector, may allow different firms, possibly in different countries, to produce differentiated products within the same industry category. The opportunities to reduce unit costs of production through longer production runs and spreading overheads would be increased by such specialization" (1976, p. 72).

The likely importance of reductions in production costs owing to increased length of production runs has also been observed in Canada by the Wonnacotts (Wonnacott and Wonnacott, 1967, p. 336) and Williams (1978), and is supported by European experience (Balassa, 1966 ; Grubel, 1967). According to Ronald Wonnacott, "The evidence is that most of the specialisation resulting from free trade between developed countries tends to occur within manufacturing industries rather than between them" (1975, p. 23). The gains from such product-specific specialisation in Canada, like those in Australia may well be extremely significant.[5] On the evidence of statistical studies, interviews and student research papers, Daly is of the opinion that product-specific economies are ". . . the most important single source of the differences in cost and productivity between [Canada and the United States]" (1979, p. 28).

4.2 Trade Barriers and the Structure and Performance of Industries : A Summary of Evidence

Market Size

The evidence suggests that domestic and foreign tariffs affect the size of the market available to domestic firms, and this turn may affect their ability to realise economies of scale. The interaction of domestic and foreign tariffs and its effect on the ability of domestic firms to achieve optimal scale has perhaps been best summarised by Scherer *et al* (1975).

> "For at least half the Canadian industries covered by our sample, tariffs charged by the United States, the nearest and most obvious export market, were sufficiently high that they discouraged most attempts to capture scale economies by building export volume. A vicious circle tightened the constraint, since the difficulty of achieving all scale economies within the relatively small Canadian market put Canadian producers at a cost disadvantage compared to firms in the United States, all else equal, and this cost disadvantage made it all the harder to surmount tariff walls and tap the large U.S. market. At the same time, Canadian tariffs, higher on the average than those of the United States, insulated many Canadian industries sufficiently to permit them to adopt a parochial view toward their domestic market". (Scherer *et al*, 1975, p. 137).

It seems likely that these influences obtain in Australia as well.

The effect of this "parochial view" is well summed-up by Daly, Keys and Spence (1968). They strongly suggested that tariffs contributed to ease of entry and that the size of plant and equipment which can be profitably used in a small, protected market is less than in a larger, more competitive one. The effects of tariffs, therefore, are likely to be manifested in lower output per unit of input in Canada than in the United States. This conclusion has been given support by West (1971) and Spence (1977).

---

5. The costs of protection and the gains from specialisation are further discussed in Section 4.3.

Output diversity

Many studies have stressed the relative output diversity of Canadian firms and their apparent inability to exploit product-specific economies of scale. Caves (1975) for example has tentatively found that the diversity of domestically owned Canadian plants appears to be related to non-production activities of the firm: when non-production employees are a larger proportion of total employment in Canada than in the United States, Canadian-owned plants are more diversified into both secondary manufacturing and other activities, including research and development.[6] A consistent thread running through a number of the studies discussed in this chapter is the relatively high proportion of non-production workers in Canadian industries (e.g., West, 1971; Spence, 1977; Oksanen and Williams, 1978), which may be symptomatic of their inability to exploit the firm-specific managerial and administrative economies of scale available to their United States counterparts. West's findings in particular, strongly stressed the "scale effect" and the association between relatively low productivity and high proportions of non-production workers (1971, pp. 8-9).

The question of a relationship between protection and relative output diversity is more clouded. In contrast with the findings of Daly, Keys and Spence is Caves' finding that "For neither subsidiaries nor domestic firms was there significant evidence that ill-chosen policies (such as tariffs) might be causing excess diversity". Though Caves qualifies his findings owing to "the deficiencies of data and statistical procedure . . ." (1975, p. 5), nevertheless it appears that the conventional view that trade barriers encourage diversity should be examined more closely. However, while the role of protection as a cause of output diversity is not clear-cut, the effect of relative output diversity is the subject of broad agreement.

". . . [Canadian] industries with a large gross output relative to the United States . . . [display] a high productivity relative to the United States. On the other hand, there is no relationship between relative productivity performance and relative gross output per establishment. This would suggest that the economies of scale realised with large volume output [are] most likely to emanate not from differences in size of establishment but from greater specialisation within particular establishments." (West, 1971, pp. 8-9).

While the possible effect of protection on output diversity is clouded, it seems likely that it plays an important role in the determination of other aspects of industry structure and performance. For example, Spence (1977) and Williams (1978) both attribute an important role to protection. Respec-

---

6. This result may be biassed as "head office" employees are excluded from foreign-owned Canadian firms.

tively, they found that high tariffs were associated with relatively high costs, and relatively low productivities (measured as relative value added per worker) (Spence, 1977, pp. 262-271); and that the Canadian industries most likely to expand under free trade are those facing high U.S. tariffs, while those most likely to contract are those protected by high domestic tariffs (Williams, 1978, pp. 27-29).

Foreign participation

There is evidence that trade barriers also effect the form and degree of foreign participation in domestic economies. In this respect, surveys by Brash (1966) and Johns and Hogan (1967) have indicated that the desire to bypass protective barriers is an important motive for direct investment in Australia; and in Canada a similar motive has been noted by Brecher and Reisman (1957, p. 117) and Eastman and Stykolt (1967, p. 107). Another important motivation for such participation may be in foreign firms' desire and ability to exploit firm economies of scale in R & D (Horst, 1972; McColl, 1972, Conlon, 1974). The effect of direct foreign participation on domestic efficiency is difficult to gauge, however. English, for example, has found that there is a tendency for foreign owned Canadian firms to be "miniature replicas" of their parents, with a consequent tendency for there to be a greater number of products than would otherwise be the case; that the financial support by foreign parents of their Canadian branches provides a deterrent to competitive rationalisation; and that the parent-subsidiary relationship may preclude, or at least inhibit Canadian exports. "However, all of these circumstances are only partly attributable to the fact of foreign ownership. The necessary conditions which underline these phenomenan are Canadian and foreign tariffs". (English, 1964, p. 40). Indeed, the available evidence strongly points to adverse effects of protection on trade performance (Baumann, 1974; 1976; Daly and Globerman, 1976), and the use and transmission of technology (Eastman and Stykolt, 1967; Daly, Keys and Spence, 1968; Spence, 1977; Oksanen and Williams, 1978).

Given the findings of the studies discussed in this Chapter it is evident that there are significant costs stemming from the isolation of small-country economies by trade barriers of all types. These costs are associated with an inability to exploit economies of scale at the firm-, plant-, and product-levels, and possible effects on the use and availability of best-practice technology. The reduction in competitive pressures from abroad also may reduce incentive to minimise production costs. Arising from these findings is the obvious question : "What are the costs of protection?"

4.3 The Costs of Protection

While this study is not directly concerned with the general equilibrium effects of protection it is nevertheless instructive to look briefly at some of the work which has been done in estimating the costs of tariffs in Australia and Canada. It is now generally recognised that protection has the effect of reducing the productive opportunities available to the protected country through its effects on resource allocation, reducing intra-industry trade, and encouraging product diversity with a resulting reduction in the ability to fully exploit product-specific economies of scale. The work of Evans (1970) has provided the inspiration for much of the subsequent work which has sought to estimate the costs of tariff protection, though Evans himself recognised that his model was unsuitable for their estimation, omitting as it does a consideration of intra-industry specialisation and economies of scale (1970, pp. 110-111). His model did however provide a starting-point in predicting for Australia under free trade ". an increase in consumption (which is an underestimate) of between 0.8 per cent and 1.8 per cent" (1970, p. 151). A formal consideration of a method by which costs of protection in small developed economies like Australia has been undertaken by Dixon (1978) who suggested that ". . . widely used theoretical simplifications . . ., and faulty techniques of empirical application, may have led to gross underestimates of costs of protection . . ." (1978, p. 63). Using a simple three-commodity model, he found that when product-specific economies of scale and intra-industry specialisation are introduced *simultaneously*, a 50 per cent tariff on one commodity generates a welfare cost of 24.5 per cent of national income (Dixon, 1978, pp. 72-73). Dixon's work clearly suggests that estimates of tariff costs based on the assumption of constant returns to scale, and of zero elasticities of factor substitution will be considerably understated.

Williams in his study of Canadian and U.S. tariff also recognised the shortcomings of studies such as his which did not include the realisation of scale economies by some industries which would expand under free trade. His work therefore, resulted in ". . . exceptionally conservative . . . [estimates] and therefore [represented] a reliable lower bound estimate of the cost of the tariff" (1978, p. 32). His "conservative" estimates were that the unilateral abolition of the Canadian tariff would make it possible to obtain only 1.4 per cent more consumer goods, but over 5 per cent more investment goods.[7] The creation of a Canada-U.S. free trade area increased these gains to 4 per cent (greater than the sum of the individual gains) and 9 per

---

7. Broadway and Treddenick using substantially the same restrictive assumptions obtained a result which suggests that, "The Canadian tariff structure seems to impose little deadweight loss on the Canadian economy" (1978, p. 445).

cent, respectively. Obviously both the Canadian and U.S. tariff affect Canadian investment more than consumption, both absolutely and relatively. To William's estimates of the consumption gains to free trade between Canada and the U.S., Wonnacott (1975) has attempted to assess the *additional* benefits accruing to Canada resulting from the exploitation of economies of scale. These were estimated to be the product of the difference between the real productivities of Canadian and U.S. manufacturing (which in 1974 was estimated to be 27 per cent higher in the U.S., and which are assumed to be eliminated under free trade (Wonnacott, 1975, p. 175)), and the ratio of Canadian value added in manufacturing to GNP (.22 in 1973). The result of the computation $((.27)(.22) = .059)$ implied an increase in productivity equivalent to 5.9 per cent of Canadian GNP as a result of the elimination of the productivity gap through the exploitation of scale economies with free trade. If this is added to Williams' estimated consumption gain from the creation of the free trade area (the increase of 4 per cent in real consumption was equivalent to an increase of approximately 2.3 per cent in Canadian GNP), there is a *total* gain of 8.2 per cent of Canadian GNP as a result of free trade between Canada and the United States.

Central to many of the studies examined earlier in this Chapter has been the role of trade in affecting the sizes of markets available to domestic firms, and their abilities to exploit the various concepts of economies of scale. The studies just discussed point to the inimical effects of the inhibition of trade on consumption, investment, and perhaps ultimately, on growth. That trade barriers affect the pattern of trade is obvious. In the case of artificial barriers, that is their very objective. All else being equal, domestic protection reduces imports; foreign protection reduces exports. By far the bulk of the empirical work which has been done concerning the effects of trade barriers on patterns of trade has been confined to the analysis of "manmade" barriers — usually tariffs. The literature concerning the effects of the "natural" barrier of distance, and the associated barrier of transportation costs is not so comprehensive nor so well known. The following chapter briefly surveys the available evidence in this respect. It first looks at distance which in itself may provide a significant trade barrier. For example, isolation from international markets by long distances may limit what has been called the "geographic horizon" of firms, and simple geographic distance has been used by some researchers to reflect the natural impediments to trade in the broadest sense. Distance is also a very important influence on the cost of transportation, and its full influence may be considered to be at least partially embodied in such costs. *Ceteris paribus*, the cost of transportation will be higher the further a commodity must be transported. Thus,

Chapter 5 examines the links between distance, and transport costs — the "natural" barriers to trade — and their effects on trade flows; and evidence concerning the relative heights of transport costs and the "artificial" barrier to trade provided by tariffs.

5. A Review of the Empirical Evidence Concerning Distance, International Transport Costs, and Tariffs as Barriers to Trade

In reviewing the empirical literature concerning international transport costs, emphasis is given here to work which has compared the protection afforded by the "natural" barrier of transport costs with the "man-made" barrier of tariffs (Waters, 1970; Yeats, 1976; Finger and Yeats, 1976; Yeats, 1977; and Sampson and Yeats, 1977). These studies have focussed upon trade flows to the United States for which there is readily available published data on both transport costs and tariff barriers.

Before examining transport costs directly as a barrier to trade, section 5.1 looks briefly at regression studies by Linneman (1966) and by Gruber and Vernon (1970), which analyse the contribution of distance alone to the determination of international trade flows. It then examines a regression study by Geraci and Prewo (1977) which, among other things, shows the contribution of distance to the determination of transport costs and then, in turn, the role of transport costs and tariffs in determining trade flows. This article, though more recent than others mentioned here, provides an important link between the studies of distance alone, and the direct examination of the heights of transport costs and tariff barriers to trade conducted in section 5.2. This lays the groundwork for the analysis in Chapter 7 of transport cost barriers (which may then be considered to embody the influence of distance) and tariffs protecting Australian and Canadian industries, the effects of which underlie much of the remainder of this work.

5.1 Distance and Transport Costs as Determinants of International Trade Flows

Distance and Trade Flows

The first major empirical study of distance as a determinant of international trade flows was conducted by Linneman (1966), and was based on earlier work with Tinbergen (1962). His regression analysis of trade flows during 1959 depended on the hypothesis that the degree to which potential trade is realised varies from country to country, depending on the height of trade obstacles (both "natural" and "artificial") which are faced. The natural barriers to trade were measured by the simple geographic distance between a given pair of countries. This distance and its effects on trade patterns may be thought of as a composite of three influences: of the costs of transportation directly; of time and its influence on such factors as perishability, regularity of supply and the possible necessity to carry large stocks; and what has been termed the "economic horizon" or "psychic distance". Distance is therefore used as a proxy for natural impediments to trade in the broadest sense. Artificial trade barriers may take such forms as tariffs, quantitative restrictions, exchange controls, quarantine restrictions, standards requirements, and so on. The only artificial barriers explicitly examined in his study however, were the preferential arrangements between three of the most important trading blocs at the time of the study.

Linneman's results showed that both natural and artificial barriers were statistically significant and relatively important inhibiting influences on trade flows. In examining the estimated regression parameters for individual countries there emerged a fairly consistent relationship between the relative isolation of a country and the (absolute) size of its distance coefficient. Of the 80 countries included in the study, Australia has the sixth highest value after South Africa, Indonesia, Congo, Burma and Angola. The inference of these results is not surprising; geographically isolated countries tend to have high distance coefficients.

Linneman has also demonstrated the importance of distance in affecting trade between countries by constructing an index of the distance effect for each of the countries studied. The index of the theoretical level of foreign trade for Australia resulting from the effect of the distance variable (average value of index = 100) is 45, which implies a particularly unfavourable location. An examination of the values of the index for each of the 80 countries showed Netherlands and Belgium at one extreme with "ideal" trade locations (I_i = 289 and 285 respectively) and New Zealand, Japan and Australia at the other extreme showing these countries as very poorly situated (I = 48, 48 and 45, respectively), and these countries (and such countries as South Korea and Hong Kong) must therefore overcome comparative high natural trade barriers to realise their potential for trade. Perhaps a better illustration of Linneman's broad results is obtained when the individual countries are combined into geographical regions, as in Table 5.1.

At first glance the "good" trade location of Canada and the "subnormal" location of the United States appears contradictory. However, the former probably stems from the importance of the United States as a destination for Canada's exports. For example, in 1974, 70 per cent (by value) were directed to the United States (Economic Council of Canada, 1975, p. 98). Canada's proximity to the U.S. yields a small influence of distance on trade, and thus a relatively high location index. Conversely, nearly 80 per cent of

TABLE 5.1

INDEX OF FOREIGN-TRADE LOCATIONS

Foreign Trade Location	Area	Average I_i
Best	North-west Europe	220
Good	European periphery, North Africa, Canada	130
Normal	Mediterranean, Middle-East, Caribbean and Central Africa	100
Subnormal	United States, South America, Tropica Africa	70
Bad	Southern Asia	60
Worst	Far East, Oceania	50

Source: Linneman, 1966, p. 187.

U.S. exports in that year were directed to countries other than Canada (Economic Council of Canada, 1975, p. 98), yielding a large distance influence and thus a relatively low location index. Of more immediate relevance, however, is the result from the table which suggests that Oceania, which includes Australia, is more handicapped by distance than any other trade area.

Linneman's findings have received strong support from Gruber and Vernon (1970). While their study is mainly concerned with the role of technology in determining international trade flows, they have also shed light on the importance of distance as an inhibiting influence on trade. Of the eight independent variables included in their regression analysis of bilateral trade between ten geographic areas, for each of twenty four industries, distance makes the greatest contribution in explaining the variation in the volume of exports in the case of nine industries and the second largest (significant) contribution in the case of ten others. Gruber and Vernon grouped the industries into two categories : eight "technology-intensive" industries[1]; and sixteen "other" industries.[2] Broadly, their results suggest that distance is a much less important inhibiting influence on trade of industries in the former category than industries in the latter.

In summarising their findings in respect of the distance variable and the association of long distance with low trade, Gruber and Vernon state:

"There is a temptation to equate the distance factor with some simple economic equivalent, such as transport cost. But the pervasive strength of that factor,

1. Aircraft, office machinery, dairy, chemicals, electrical machinery, instruments, agricultural machinery, petroleum and coal products.

2. Transport equipment (less aircraft), other machinery, nonferrous-metals rubber and plastics, ferrous metals, fabricated metal, non-metallic mineral products, paper, textiles, food, tobacco, furniture and fixtures, leather products, printing and publishing, apparel, lumber and wood.

including its appearance in such industrial categories as 'drugs' and 'agricultural machinery' suggests that more may be involved in this measure than mere transport cost . . . such as limitations on businessmen's knowledge about sources and markets." (p. 260).

While there is undoubtedly truth in this "psychic distance" hypothesis, nevertheless an examination of the industries analysed suggest that there is also an apparent relationship between unit-value (whether by weight or by volume) and the distance coefficient. The "technology intensive" commodities tend to have relatively high unit values; the "other" industries tend to be characterised by low unit values. In this respect, the inference is clear: distance is less of an inhibiting influence on high unit-value commodities. This finding will be further explored in Chapter 6.

Distance, Transport Costs and Trade Flows

An important step between the distance-related studies just examined and the studies of the transport costs directly which comprise the remainder of this chapter has been provided by Geraci and Prewo (1977). In the present context, the importance of their work lies in the linking of distance with the cost of transportation ; and in the subsequent linking of the cost of transportation with international trade flows. As a sidelight, Geraci and Prewo's approach enables the problem of measurement errors which are common in estimates of f.o.b. and c.i.f. values to be overcome.

They specify a model in which for a given country, the true transport cost factor T_{ij}^* (i.e. the true c.i.f./f.o.b. ratio), which is not actually observed, is represented by a proxy, T_{ij}, which is the observed transport cost factor (and which is subject to possible errors in measurement). In turn, T_{ij}^* is specified as a function of the geographical distance between country i and country j, D_{ij}, and the average unit value of exports from country i, V_i. These functional relationships are expressed in equations (5.2) and (5.3) respectively. The aggregate value of exports from i to j (X_{ij}) is a function of the countries' gross domestic products (Y_i, Y_j) which represent final output and domestic real income, respectively, and of trade resistance factors. These include the trade inhibiting influence of average nominal tariffs applied by country j, Z_j, and the trade stimulating influences (expressed as dummy variables) of being members of the same preferential trading group, G_{ij}, of having common borders, B_{ij}, or of having common languages, L_{ij}. This relationship is expressed in equation (5.1). The model may now be shown as:

$$X_{ij} = f(Y_i, Y_j, Z_j, G_{ij}, L_{ij}, B_{ij}, T_{ij}^*) \qquad (5.1)$$

$$T_{ij} = g(T_{ij}^*) \qquad (5.2)$$

$$T_{ij}^* = h(D_{ij}, V_i) \qquad (5.3)$$

In effect, this specification enables the estimation of equation (5.1) using as input the estimates of equation (5.3) via the use of the proxy for the true measures of transportation cost, T_{ij}.

The model was applied to 306 bilateral trade flows among 19 OECD countries during 1970. The results suggested that while both transport costs and tariffs were significant determinants of bilateral exports, transport costs are more important than tariffs in explaining variations in the trade flow data. The results also show explicitly the inter-relationships between distance, transport costs and trade flows: distance was by far the most important determinant of the transport cost factor; while the transport cost factor was in turn, a highly significant determinant of trade flows. Implicitly, their results show that the "cost" of distance may be considered in large part, to be embodied in the transport cost barrier to trade, which is a major subject of the remainder of this, and of the following chapters.

5.2 The Relative Heights of Tariffs and International Transport Costs: The United States' Case

Of the empirical evidence concerning the relative heights of tariffs and transport cost barriers, almost all refers in some way to trade with the United States. This section looks briefly at the results of four studies of tariffs and international transport costs : by Waters (1970); Finger and Yeats (1976); Yeats (1977); and Sampson and Yeats (1977), which are summarised in Table 5.2.[3] The present purpose is to establish that on average, international transport costs, at least in the case of imports from various sources to the United States, "are not trivially small relative to tariffs". (Waters, 1970, p. 1015).

Though the data used in these studies encompass a period of 16 years and use a variety of weights in computing the various means, an examination of the results shows a remarkable consistency. From the table it would appear that, overall, average nominal and *ad valorem* transport costs are roughly 10 per cent compared with an average nominal tariff of about two-thirds of that magnitude. The estimates for Indonesian and Malaysian exports have been made both for these countries' total trade with the United States and

---

3. The nominal tariff and transport costs of Table 5.2 are defined as, respectively, "the ratio of actual duties paid relative to the value of competitive imports . . ." (i.e. imports competing directly with local products) and "actual freight and insurance margins relative to the value of competitive imports" (Waters, 1970, p. 1014). The latter are operationally defined as the ratio of the values of c.i.f. minus f.o.b. imports to f.o.b. imports. The last two studies (Yeats, 1977; Sampson and Yeats, 1977) use free alongside ship (f.a.s.) values rather than f.o.b. values. In practice the difference between the two values is likely to be small. The year appearing in the table refers to the period which the data are derived.

TABLE 5.2

COMPARISON OF AVERAGE NOMINAL TARIFFS AND TRANSPORT COSTS

Year	1958	1964	1974					
Study	Waters (1)	Finger and Yeats (2)	Yeats (3)					Sampson and Yeats (4)
Trade Flow to U.S.	Total World Exports	Total World Exports	Total World Exports	Indonesian Exports		Malaysian Exports		Australian Exports
				Total	Excl Oil	Total	Excl Tin	
Nominal Tariff	6.2 (a)	8 (b)	n.a.	6.4 (c)	6.6 (c)	n.a.	n.a.	5.5 (f)
Nominal Transport	10.0 (a)	9 (b)	8.1 (a)	11.8 (c)	9.7 (c)	6.4 (d)	9.0 (d)	11.8 (f)

Sources: (1) W.G. Waters II, 1970
        (2) J.M. Finger and A.J. Yeats, 1976
        (3) A.J. Yeats, 1977
        (4) G.P. Sampson and A.J. Yeats, 1977

Notes: Weighted by value of:

    (a) U.S. imports
    (b) O.E.C.D. exports to the U.S.
    (c) Indonesian exports to the U.S.
    (d) Malaysian exports to the U.S. computed from data supplied in (3)
    (f) Australia exports to the U.S.
    n.a. Not available

their trade excluding their major export commodities — respectively, crude petroleum and tin. These latter data may provide a more representative picture of the "average" barrier a typical exporter in these countries would face in trading with the United States. At present, the major interest concerns the barriers faced by Australian exporters. Table 5.2 shows that the average transport cost for Australian exports to the U.S. was roughly twice as high as the average tariff barrier and as such, should not be ignored.[4]

Waters (1970) and Finger and Yeats (1976), also throw light on effective rates of transport cost protection in the case of United States' imports.[5] For 57 industries drawn from the 1958 United States input-output table, Waters

---

4. A more detailed discussion of Sampson and Yeats' (1977) study concerning the respective heights of these barriers is provided in Chapter 6.

5. Details of effective transport cost computations may be found in Chapter 7.

found median values for effective tariffs and effective transport costs of approximately 17 and 7 per cent, respectively ; and corresponding weighted[6] means of about 10 and 13 per cent.[7] Finger and Yeats' study used a 1965 U.S. census Bureau - Tariff Commission sample of about 13,000 commodities, and found weighted average effective tariffs of 13 and 14 per cent, respectively, using one set of weights[8] and 15 and 17 per cent, respectively, using an alternative set.[9] While both sets of weights yielded slightly higher transport costs than tariffs, "within the accuracy of the figures it is reasonable to consider the tariff and transport cost averages as equal" (Finger and Yeats, 1976, p. 173).

While these averages are illuminating, another important issue addressed by Waters (1970) and Yeats (1977) is the relative incidence of tariffs and transport costs for categories of products at successively higher stages of fabrication. The issue is one of special importance to developing countries which typically export primary products, or manufactures at relatively low levels of fabrication. Waters and Yeats' evidence showed a consistent decline in the *relative* importance of transport costs vis-a-vis tariffs with increasing product fabrication.[10] The results of both studies suggested that the "escalation in the United States' tariff structure (the higher tariff levels on processed goods) is offset by de-escalation in the freight factors" (Waters, 1970, p. 1020).

In summary, the empirical studies of transport costs suggest two primary conclusions:

(i) in the case of exports to the United States, transport costs appear to be on average a barrier at least as important as tariffs; and

(ii) transport costs tend to fall more heavily on raw and semi-processed commodities than on commodities at higher stages of fabrication.

---

6. Weighted by the value of actual imports. Potential imports which are excluded by the tariff or by transport cost are, of course, excluded from the calculation. Waters recognises that this method of weighting under-estimates the true level of protection available to local producers.

7. Waters computes effective rates on two bases: firstly, assuming a zero elasticity of substitution among all inputs and factors; and secondly, a measure designed to examine the effects before resources move in response to protection, assuming a unitary elasticity of substitution. See Corden (1966) and Anderson and Naya (1969). The data referred to above, use the first base. The difference between the two sets of estimates is, however, small.

8. The data are aggregated into 38 commodity groups and weighted by OECD imports from other OECD countries.

9. The same 38 commodity groups weighted by OECD imports from less developed countries.

10. Yeats however found no consistent relationship between *ad valorem* transport and stage of product fabrication.

From these conclusions it appears possible that:

(i) action (either by governments or by shipper organizations) taken to moderate international transport costs may provide greater potential for increased trade and be more likely to be realised than efforts to achieve bilateral or multilateral tariff reform;[11] and

(ii) for a given country, the greater the proportion of exports (imports) at higher stages of fabrication, the less the transport barrier (protection) faced (afforded) by (to) the domestic industry, and this is likely to result in a relatively greater trade barrier for developing countries.

This chapter began with a discussion of distance and ended with the consideration of transport costs as barriers to trade. The theoretical analysis of Chapter 3 established the analogy between transport costs and tariffs, and the last parts of this chapter examines much of the available evidence concerning the respective heights of these two barriers. The formal links between distance, transport costs and trade flows have been made by Geraci and Prewo. The empirical analysis of Chapter 6 explores the relationships established in their work in a rather less formal way. It looks at the influence of distance as a determinant of liner freight rates for Australian exports, and attempts to evaluate the contribution of the "cost" of Australia's isolation to the shipping costs of Australian exports; and then looks at Bryan's (1974a; 1974b) empirical analysis of transport costs and tariffs as influences inhibiting Canadian exports.

---

11. Moderation of non-tariff barriers may be more important than either, but they are not discussed here. A brief discussion of pricing by liner shipping conferences, which are important to the trade of both countries, may be found in Chapter 6.1. A discussion of some of the policy implications arising from such policies may be found in Chapter 10.4.

6. Trade Barriers to Australian and Canadian Exports

This chapter begins the formal empirical analysis of this study. From the previous Chapter it is apparent that both transport costs and tariffs are important inhibiting influences on trade. Equally, it is apparent that different sectors of the economy are effected by trade barriers in different ways. They are advantage to import-competing producers (neglecting for the moment their effect on input prices), and a disadvantage to exporters. The advantage is dealt with in Chapter 7. A major aim is now to examine one aspect of the disadvantage: that facing Australian exporters as a result of Australia's relative isolation. The previous Chapter established that distance is an important determinant of transport costs, and here an attempt is made to estimate the "cost" of distance in adding to freight rates for Australian exports.

The estimates discussed in Section 6.1 are based on work which the present writer has undertaken with John Zerby,[1] and are derived from the Australian liner shipping trade to Europe, Japan and the Arabian Gulf during 1972/73.[2] The regression analysis of our joint work is used here as a means of estimating the contribution of distance to the determination of liner freight rates for Australian exports. The method is then used to estimate transport costs of exports to the United States, and these are

---

1. The aim of our joint work was concerned almost exclusively with analysing the pricing policies of liner shipping conferences (this term is explained later in this Chapter) and estimating the implicit taxes and subsidies on Australian exports which are a consequence of those policies. Our studies (1977, 1976b, 1982a, 1982b, 1983) are all based on a Report commissioned by the Australian Bureau of Transport Economics (1977). The second reference (1978b) is a brief summary of the 1977 results published in the Proceedings of the Australian Transport Research Forum. The third reference (1982a) is a discussion paper published by the Centre for Applied Economic Research, a shorter version of which appears in the *Journal of Industrial Economics* (1983), while the reference (1982b) is an abridged version of the original (1977) report published on behalf of the Bureau of Transport Economics by the University of New South Wales. In this chapter, subsequent references will in the main, be to the 1978 summary paper.

2. It is submitted that such estimates are representative of the transport costs for all Australian manufacturers. There are two primary reasons for this belief: first, though data concerning the exact proportion of Australian manufactures carried by liner are not available, it is nevertheless certain that few manufactured exports are carried by other means; and second, the available empirical evidence strongly suggests that there is a marked similarity in liner pricing policies throughout the world (Heaver, 1973; Bryan, 1974a, 1974b; Lipsey and Weiss, 1974; Zerby and Conlon, 1982a).

compared with the heights of corresponding U.S. tariffs. Estimates of transport costs for the 85 manufacturing industries which are the subject of the comparative studies of Chapters 7, 8 and 9 are also derived. Unfortunately data which would enable a similar estimation of the influence of distance and of transport costs for Canadian industries are not available. However, a limited assessment of the relative heights of transport cost tariff barriers faced by Canadian exporters has been made by Raynes (1977), while Bryan's (1974b) regression analysis has looked directly at the relative importance of transport costs and tariffs as influences inhibiting Canadian commodity exports. Both studies are briefly examined in Section 6.2. Thus, in an approach not unlike that of the previous chapter, the following analysis moves from a consideration of distance and its contribution to the cost of transportation; to a comparison of the heights of the transport cost and tariff barriers to trade; and finally, to the relative importance of the two barriers as determinants of trade flows.

6.1 The Contribution of Distance to Transport Costs for Australian Exports

The "Cost" of Distance as a Barrier to Total Exports

In determining the charge for transporting a commodity from one point to another the firm providing the transport service may be influenced by many considerations. These include the costs it incurs in providing the service, the unit value of the cargo, whether the cargo is shipped regularly and in large amounts, and so on. In examining the determinants of ocean liner freight rates (covering ships providing regular, scheduled services), a number of studies have used distance as a proxy variable for operating costs at sea and have shown that the general relationship between freight rates and distance is linear in logarithms (e.g.: Heaver, 1973; Lipsey and Weiss, 1974; Zerby and Conlon, 1978b). The underlying assumptions are that for a given commodity the further it must be carried, the higher will be the cost of its transportation, but as distance becomes longer, its relative influence on freight costs declines.[3]

In order to gauge the contribution of distance to the determination of ocean freight rates, Zerby and present author (1978b) fitted a regression equation to a random sample of 100 Australian commodity exports to each

---

3. In effect, the specification averages "ordinary" (constant) handling costs into the distance measure. Any "extraordinary" handling costs (e.g. heavy lifts) are considered separately in equation (6.1).

of the European and Arabian Gulf trade areas, and to Japan during 1972/73.[4] The equation was of the following form:

(6.1)   Freight rate $= aD^b x_1^c x_2^d \ldots x_{11}^m$

where D denotes the distance variable and the other explanatory variables included in the regression are denoted as $x_1, x_2 \ldots x_{11}$. These variables were chosen to reflect influences considered most likely to affect the freight charges imposed.

If for example, a commodity requires refrigeration (e.g. meat), is in some way dangerous (e.g. explosives), or requires special handling (e.g. large items of capital equipment may require special cranes for loading and unloading), the shipping company could be expected to pass on the costs of providing these special services, thus increasing freight rates for such cargoes. Other variables were chosen to reflect the competitive environment in which freight rates are determined. For example, in the case of Australian exports to Japan and Europe, aside from the bulk cargoes such as iron ore (which are not considered here) much of the trade is carried by shipping cartels known as "conferences". A shipping conference is usually made up of a number of shipping companies which between them charge a common set of freight rates. For the most important export commodities (e.g. meat, wool, dairy produce, fruit, etc.) rates are set in consultation with the Australian Shipping Council, an organization of Australian exporters and producers. Rates for some commodities are likely to result from the process of bargaining between these two groups. The larger is the quantity of a particular cargo shipped, the greater is likely to be the bargaining power of the shipper and the greater his influence in seeking the moderation of freight charges. Other cargoes may have the potential for shipment in vessels especially chartered for the purpose (e.g. mineral sands shipped containers, grain in bags, etc). The rates for such commodities may be kept relatively low in an attempt to reduce the attractiveness of chartered vessels as an alternative means of shipment. Finally, *ceteris paribus*, conferences tend to charge a higher rate, the higher the unit-value of the commodity to be shipped, because they believe that shippers of valuable cargoes (e.g. scien-

---

4. These were selected from freight rates for a total of 5,484 Australian Export Commodity Classification (AECC) commodities from the following rate schedules:

   Australia-to-Europe Conference : 3611 A.E.C.C. Commodities

   Arabian Gulf Rate Agreement : 1126 A.E.C.C. Commodities

   Northbound Conference (Japan) : 747 A.E.C.C. Commodities

   Obviously the number of commodities shipped to Europe dominates the set, and thus it was considered that a more reliable estimate of the distance coefficient would be obtained by using a sample of data containing equal numbers of observations from the Europe, Japan and Arabian Gulf trades.

tific instruments) are less responsive to changes in freight charges than are shippers of low value cargoes.[5]

The results of the Zerby and Conlon study suggest that all these influences are important determinants of ocean liner freight rates. At present interest centres on the influences of distance upon the determination of freight charges. The coefficient estimated from the equation is was $D^{.276}$ and was different from zero at greater than the one per cent level of significance.[6] This compared with Lipsey and Weiss' estimate of $D^{.30}$ in the case of foreign exports to the United States (1974, p. 166).[7]

The contribution of distance to the determination of linear freight rates for Australian total exports is illustrated in Table 6.1. Underlying the computations is the assumption that the estimated distance coefficient is valid for exports to all destinations. In the light of Lipsey and Weiss' results, this assumption appears to be not unreasonable. The Table lists the approximate distances in nautical miles from Sydney to some important destinations of Australia's exports, together with the application of the estimated coefficient to those distances.

---

5. Full description of the dependent and independent variables of equation (6.1) and of the method of their estimation may be found in Zerby and Conlon (1978b, pp. 308-218; 1982a; 1982b).

   The very high levels of significance of value-per-tonne, the importance of its contribution to the determination of freight rates, and the similar importance of other "non-cost" influences as determinants found by Zerby and Conlon and by other researchers (Sturmey, 1962; Deakin, 1973; Heaver, 1973; Jansson, 1974; Laing, 1975; Shneerson, 1976; Evans, 1977), raise the likelihood of cross-subsidies between commodities shipped, as a result of conference pricing policies. It seems generally agreed that the shippers of some commodities pay less than what could reasonably be considered to be long run marginal cost, while others pay substantially more. To the extent that some are charged more than LRMC, on the import side, this constitutes an element of "man made" protection to import competing industries; if less, this constitutes an implicit subsidy to imports and thus, "negative" protection. On the export side, "excess" transport costs may be considered a barrier which, like foreign tariffs, must be surmounted; while "deficient" transport costs may be considered as an export subsidy. As well, the very natures of shipping conferences as cartels suggest that average rates charged are likely to be in excess of average rates that could be charged in competitive markets.

   While it may be that the implicit taxes/subsidies work in the direction desired by governments, of course this need not be so. Thus, through liner pricing policies comes the possibility of both "undesirable" cross subsidies, and an overall "excess" average transportation cost, which may legitimately be considered to be artificial barriers and/or stimulants to trade. The points raised here are further discussed in Chapter 10.4. See Zerby and Conlon (1983) for an explicit, and detailed consideration of cross subsidisation arising from liner shipping pricing policies.

6. The R^2 of the equation was 0.864.

7. Zerby and Conlon included more independent variables, and therefore it is not surprising that a slightly lower distance coefficient was obtained.

TABLE 6.1

ESTIMATED CONTRIBUTION OF DISTANCE TO THE DETERMINATION OF LINER SHIPPING FREIGHT RATES
FOR AUSTRALIA'S EXPORTS 1972/73

Port of Discharge	Distance from Sydney Naut. Miles	Index of Distance (Sydney-Wellington = 100)	$D^{.276}$ ($)	Index of Distance Cost (Sydney — Wellington = 100)
Wellington	1200	100	7.07	100
Kobe	4400	367	10.13	143
Vancouver	6800	566	11.42	162
London	11400	950	13.17	186
Hamburg	11800	983	13.30	188
Baltimore	13400	1117	13.77	195

Sources: *Reeds New Maritime Distance Tables*; and calculations from regression results of Zerby and Conlon (1978b).

From Table 6.1 it may be observed that while distances increase by a factor of eleven, the "cost" of distance increases by a factor of only two. To put these costs into perspective, during 1972/73 the estimated average liner freight rates per tonne for commodities shipped to Europe and Japan were about $A88 and $A75 respectively (Zerby and Conlon, 1977, pp. 112-113). The estimated contribution of distance to these destinations (roughly $13.30 and $10.13) therefore represented on average about 15 and 13 per cent, respectively of the average total freight charge. There appears little doubt that Australian exporters are disadvantaged by Australia's relative isolation, and this is at least partly captured by the distance term as defined and interpreted here.

The "Cost" of Distance and Barriers to Exports of Individual Commodities

It is now possible to use the distance coefficient just described to estimate the "cost" of distance facing Australian exporters. For individual commodities, the estimated cost of distance has been deducted from the appropriate Conference freight rate, yielding an estimated distance-free freight rate. With this as a base, the *additional* effect of distance on the distance-free rate has then been computed. Underlying these computations is the assumption that the influence of distance is the same for each commodity. In view of the efforts which were made to take account of the remaining influences on the determination of freight rates, this appears to be a reasonable assumption.

The procedure used may be summarised in the following way. The estimated coefficient of distance ($D^{.276}$) was multiplied by the log of the distance in nautical miles and the antilog of the result subtracted from the actual freight rate. This result then constitutes an element in the set of converted (net of distance) freight rates. For example, the Australia-to-Europe freight rate for frozen, boneless beef was $113 per tonne. From this was deducted the antilog of .276 times the log of the weighted average distance to Europe for this commodity, 12,965 nautical miles.[8]

(Actual Freight Rate)	–	(Influences of Distance)	=	(Freight rate net of Distance)
$113.00	–	$13.65 ($=12965^{.276}$)	=	$99.35

The average value of exports in this category during 1972/73 was approximately $1,000 per tonne, so that the total *ad valorem* freight rate was about 11.3 per cent, of which nearly 1.4 per cent was due to the influence of

---

8. For every commodity, the proportions of total exports by State during 1972/73 were used as weights and an average distance of Europe calculated.

distance. Viewed another way, in this case distance adds 13.7 per cent ($113.00/99.35 = 1.137$) to the freight rate net of distance in determining the cost of exporting frozen, boneless beef to Europe.

In order to gauge the reliability of this method of estimating the relative cost of distance for individual commodities, the Australian export data was reconciled with the commodity categories of Gruber and Vernon's (1970) study which was discussed in Chapter 5. The absolute values of the distance coefficients of Gruber and Vernon's equations were ranked and compared with the rankings of the *ad valorem* cost of distance for the commodities derived in the manner just described.[9] As all the commodities are manufactures, the distance chosen for this exercise was the mean of the distance to Europe from New South Wales and Victoria, the major manufacturing states (12,630 nautical miles). The "cost" of this distance added $13.55 per tonne to the freight rate net of distance for each commodity. The ranking of the *ad valorem* equivalents of this cost and the ranking of the absolute values of Gruber and Vernon's distance coefficients were found to be remarkably similar, the Spearman rank correlation coefficient being different from zero at greater than the 1 per cent level of significance. Not only does the comparison provide some comfort concerning the reliability of the method used here, it also provides support for Gruber and Vernon's findings that high technology goods are less disadvantaged by distance than other commodities. However it was suggested in Chapter 5 that "technology intensive" commodities are likely to have relatively high unit values, and clearly the addition of a specific distance charge will have relatively less effect on the total freight rate as unit value increases.

The Case of Australian Exports to the United States

As research has shown that there are similarities in liner shipping pricing policies throughout the world (Heaver, 1973 ; Bryan, 1974a ; Lipsey and Weiss, 1974 ; Zerby and Conlon, 1978b), it is instructive to compare results derived by the methods of this study with those of Sampson and Yeats (1977) who analysed the relative heights of transport costs of Australian exports to the United States, and the corresponding U.S. tariff barriers. Their study is particularly valuable in that it enables a direct comparison of the magnitudes of the "natural" barrier of transport costs with the "man-made" barrier of tariffs.

Table 6.2 summarises Sampson's and Yeats' results, which compare United States' most-favoured nation (MFN) nominal *ad valorem* tariffs

---

9. Office machinery and Petroleum and coal were omitted from the comparison as there were no recorded Australian exports of these commodities to Europe during 1972/73.

TABLE 6.2

A COMPARISON OF TRANSPORT COSTS AND TARIFFS FOR AUSTRALIAN EXPORTS TO THE UNITED STATES

Stat. Group (Sched. 'A') (AECC)	Description	1974 Value of Australian Exports to U.S. (US$m) (a)	U.S. Tariffs (a)	Nominal Transport Costs (a)	Total (a)	Total Estimated Transport Cost (D = 10,000 naut. miles) (b)
00	Live animals	1.1	3.7	13.0	16.7	—
01	Meat and meat prep.	365.6	5.4	12.9	18.3	14.6
02	Dairy products, eggs	15.9	10.7	15.1	25.8	18.7
03	Fish and fish prep.	54.3	1.9	3.7	5.6	5.3
05	Fruits, vegetables	6.0	8.6	38.4	47.0	25.4
06	Sugar prep. and honey	154.4	6.0	8.2	14.2	8.0
11	Beverages	1.1	5.4	29.2	34.6	35.1
26	Textile fibres	17.1	7.7	7.2	14.9	5.5
28	Metalliferous ores & scrap	74.7	2.1	18.6	20.7	18.0
29	Animal and vegetable materials n.e.s.	2.9	2.3	8.0	10.3	9.2
321	Coke, coal and briquettes	2.9	0.0	88.1	88.1	—
51	Chemical elements and compounds	160.9	6.8	15.2	22.0	2.3
59	Chemical products, n.e.s.	16.0	6.8	7.6	14.4	15.7
62	Rubber manufactures	1.7	7.4	51.8	59.2	10.3
64	Paper, paper board	1.1	4.7	46.9	51.6	11.3
66	Non-metallic mineral prods.	6.0	8.6	5.2	13.8	16.5
67	Iron and Steel	11.1	5.9	14.0	19.9	27.0
68	Nonferrous metals	58.1	5.7	3.0	8.7	12.9
69	Manufactures of metal	4.9	9.0	6.7	15.7	6.5
71	Non-electrical machinery	17.0	5.3	6.1	11.4	4.1
72	Electrical machinery	5.7	7.5	4.9	12.4	3.9
73	Transport equipment	9.5	6.5	6.2	12.7	12.4
86	Professional instruments	2.2	12.5	8.8	21.6	2.3
89	Misc. manufactured goods	8.0	9.4	7.6	17.0	9.0

Average World Trade Weights	6.5	22.3	28.8	n.a.
Australian trade weights-all commodities	5.5	11.8	19.2	n.a.
Australian trade weights-omitting 00 and 321	5.5	11.7	19.2	10.9

Sources: (a) Sampson and yeats (1977, pp. 146-147).
(b) Calculated from regression results Zerby and Conlon (1978).

Note: n.a. not available.

and transport costs for Australian exports of 24 commodity groups.[10] The nominal transport costs are defined as the ratio of the c.i.f. (cost, insurance and freight) values to f.a.s. (free alongside ship) values of the commodities, while the nominal tariffs are based on the f.o.b. (free on board) values. An examination of the Table reveals that for the commodities comprising the food and live animals group (Group O), transport costs are all higher than the corresponding tariffs, and in the case of semi-processed commodities, scrap, chemicals, and basic manufactures (Groups 11-67) the clear tendency is for transport costs to exceed tariffs. For the manufactured products and machinery groups (Groups 69-89) however, *ad valorem* transport costs tend to be lower than MFN tariffs.

The average *ad valorem* transport cost using respectively, the values of Australian and world exports to the United States as weights, is 11.8 per cent, and 22.3 per cent compared with 5.5 per cent and 6.5 per cent for the corresponding *ad valorem* tariff averages. World trade weights yield higher averages as world trade comprises a higher proportion of raw materials and semi-finished products, both of which are characterised by high transport costs in relation to their value. Whichever system of weighting is used, however, one thing is clear : transport costs provide an average barrier to Australian exports to the United States roughly two to three times as high as United States' tariffs.

A comparison (and further test of the reliability) of freight rates derived by the method described earlier in this Chapter, and Sampson and Yeats' estimates of transport costs are also shown in Table 6.2. To the estimated distance-free costs for the 2-digit commodity groups in the Table are added the influence of the estimated distance coefficient, assuming that the destinations of Australian exports to the United States are evenly divided between the West and East coasts, an average distance of about 10,000 nautical miles. Also underlying the computations is the important assumption that the average values of Australian exports to Europe are representative of Australian export values to the United States.[11]

An examination of Table 6.2 shows a marked similarity between Sampson's and Yeats' nominal transport costs and the estimated Australia-to-United States freight rates ($D = 10,000^{.276}$ nautical miles) for most of the 22 commodity groups. For all but two of the freight rate estimates (those for 62

10. These are defined by the U.S. Schedule 'A' statistical classification for which at the 2 digit level, the commodity descriptions are virtually identical to those of the Australian Export Commodity Classification.

11. Two commodity groups (00 - live animals, and 321 - coke, coal and briquettes) were omitted from the comparison as there were no recorded Australian exports to Europe during 1972/73.

- rubber, and 64 - paper) are within 1 standard deviation of Sampson and Yeats' nominal transport costs.[12] Of these, all but six[13] are within 0.5 standard deviations. The coefficient of rank correlation between the two sets of estimates is significant at the 5 per cent level, while the use of Australia-U.S. trade weights for the 22 commodity groups yields an estimated average freight rate of 10.9 per cent compared with Sampson's and Yeats' average nominal transport rate of 11.7 per cent. It should be remembered too, that the latter included not only transport costs but also insurance charges, and also are based on the f.a.s. value of U.S. imports. Both of these influences will create an upward bias in comparison with this study's estimates.

Transport Costs of Australian Exports of Manufactures

There is no published data which would enable a direct estimation of the transport barrier facing Australian exporters. Thus, given the apparent success of this study's method of estimation, the method has been used to estimate transport costs for exports of the 85 Australian industries which are the subjects of the comparative studies in succeeding Chapters.[14] The costs of distance have been estimated assuming that a representative distance for the exports of Australian manufacturers is the average distance to Europe from New South Wales and Victoria, the major manufacturing

---

12. In the cases of both 62 (rubber . . .) and 64 (paper. . .), the values of Australian exports to both Europe and the United States are relatively low (a total of less than $A1 million to Europe, and $A3 million to the United States) and as a result either or both estimates may not be representative. The commodity mix within a group may also affect the relative values of the transport costs estimates, as well its mode of transportation. The relative transport costs of chemical elements and compounds (51) may well be affected in these respects. The total value of these exports to Europe was $A2.5 million during 1972/73, and $160.9 million to the U.S. during 1974. The commodity group includes alumina (AECC 513.65.09) and in 1972/73 the total value of Australian exports was $A154.9 million and total gross weight shipped was 3.0 million tonnes. Unfortunately, the Australian Bureau of Statistics keeps confidential the countries of destination for this commodity but it seems likely that a significant proportion was shipped to the United States. Alumina is a relatively low unit-value commodity, (its average value was $A51 per tonne in 1972/73, compared with an average value of nearly $150 per tonne for the remaining exports classified to AECC 513), and one which is suitable for transportation in bulkships. It appears likely therefore, that Sampson's and Yeats' nominal transport costs for chemical elements and compounds is a reflection of a bulk-ship rate for alumina.

13. Commodities 05, 51, 66, 67 and 68.

14. For this purpose, data concerning 5485 7-digit AECC commodities were aggregated to the 4-digit level (369 commodity groups), and these were reconciled with the Australia-Canada Industry Classification (ACIC) used in the analyses of Chapters 7, 8 and 9 and which is described in Chapter 7.1.

states (12,630 nautical miles), and are simply the percentage increases when the contribution of distance is added to the freight rates net of distance.[15] The estimated distance-free liner freight rates, and the "cost" of distance for the 85 manufacturing industries appear in Table 6.3.

The data of Table 6.3 provide broad confirmation of the tendencies observed in Chapter 5 for high technology and for high unit value commodities to be less disadvantaged by distance and by transport costs. Foodstuffs and beverages (ACIC 1-15) and non-metalic mineral products (ACIC 45-48) tend to suffer relative disadvantages (i.e. : having *ad valorem* transport costs above the median) as a result of low unit values. Despite the very high specific rates for yarns, textiles, clothing and footwear (ACIC 18-28), as a result of their high unit values, these commodities generally suffer comparatively little disadvantage as a result of transport costs and isolation. The same is true of industries producing relatively high technology and/or highly fabricated products (ACIC 68-76), with aircraft building and repair (ACIC 68) having the lowest *ad valorem* transport costs after jewellery (ACIC 82). Basic iron and steel (ACIC 49) a major Australian exporter is, after other non-netalic mineral products (ACIC 47), more disadvantaged than any other industry by the relative increase in transport costs as a result of the distance effect; the industry suffering least in this respect is knitted goods (ACIC 27).

6.2 Trade Barriers to Canadian Exports

Unfortunately, it was not possible to gather Canadian data similar to the Australian data just analysed. Nevertheless, there are two studies available which shed light on the relative importance and effects of foreign tariffs and international transport costs to Canadian exports : those by Bryan (1974b), and Raynes (1977). The former is a regression study which concentrates on the importance of foreign tariffs and transport costs in determining Cana-

15. ACIC industries 16, 22, 57 and 82 all recorded exports with a total weight of less than 1 tonne. However, despite the obvious paucity of observations, it is considered that the rates per tonne used in this study are reasonably accurate as the rates for the commodities classified to these industries were taken directly from the Conference freight tariff. The *ad valorem* rates however in these cases rely on the value-per-tonne of the commodities actually exported, and with so few shipments these values should consequently be viewed with caution. There are 3 industries (ACIC 45, 46, 48) for which there were no recorded exports to Europe during the study period: again, the rate per tonne is that quoted in the Conference tariff. For the purpose of estimating the *ad valorem* rate however, it was necessary to obtain representative values of the commodities classified within these industries directly from industry sources. The estimates for ACIC 65 and 66-ship and boat building-should also be viewed with caution. Most exports classified to these industries travel under their own power and the rates appearing in Table 6.3 refer to exports shipped on liner vessels and are not representative of all such exports.

TABLE 6.3

ESTIMATED FREIGHT RATES: AUSTRALIA TO EUROPE 1972/73
EIGHTY-FIVE MANUFACTURING INDUSTRIES

ACIC	Industry Description	(1)	(2)	(3)	(4)
1	Meat products	91.26	18.22	20.92	14.8
2	Poultry products	70.13	11.06	13.19	19.3
3	Milk products	79.04	15.67	18.35	17.10
4	Fruit, vegetable products	25.10	10.43	11.23	17.14
5	Flour, starch, cereals	28.15	13.73	20.33	48.06
6	Margarine, oil, fats	31.64	40.92	58.44	42.82
7	Bread, cake, pastry	41.12	5.92	7.87	33.95
8	Biscuits	41.12	5.92	7.87	33.95
9	Confectionery, cocoa	75.74	9.52	17.39	11.22
10	Fish products	49.14	2.75	3.50	27.57
11	Animal foods	33.58	12.80	17.96	40.35
12	Sugar, malt, other foods	20.19	8.25	13.78	67.00
13	Soft drinks, cordials	71.69	10.03	11.92	18.90
14	Beer	43.44	21.38	28.04	31.19
15	Wine, alcoholic beverages	65.63	23.44	28.27	20.64
16	Tobacco	39.70	.54	.72	34.13
17	Wool: scoured, carbonised, tops	67.79	4.58	5.49	19.98
18	Manmade fibre yarn and fabrics	131.04	2.75	3.03	10.34
19	Cotton yarn and fabric	247.37	.90	.94	5.47
20	Wool yarn and fabric	192.50	4.63	4.96	7.03
21	Household and other textiles	175.15	4.60	4.96	7.73
22	Textile floor covers	242.04	4.75	5.02	5.59
23	Felt and products	236.10	10.16	10.74	5.73
24	Canvas and products	146.52	4.44	4.85	9.24
25	Rope, cord, twine	169.00	15.63	6.08	8.01
26	Hosiery	303.00	1.87	1.95	4.47
27	Knitted goods	590.00	3.68	3.76	2.29
28	Clothing, footwear	276.94	9.04	9.48	4.89

Code	Industry			
29	Sawmill, wood products	22.74	19.93	31.80	59.58
30	Ply, veneers and wood boards	53.60	5.53	6.92	25.27
31	Furniture	124.10	7.28	8.07	10.91
32	Pulp, paper and paper board	66.68	32.00	38.50	20.32
33	Paper bags, containers	84.48	5.81	6.74	16.03
34	Paper products, printing and publishing	60.10	9.72	11.91	22.54
35	Basic chemicals	56.72	7.43	9.20	23.88
36	Chemical products excl. agricultural	44.33	11.30	14.75	30.56
37	Paints	56.83	2.85	3.53	23.84
38	Pharmaceuticals incl. veterinary products	48.47	3.13	4.00	27.95
39	Soap, detergents	46.74	3.66	4.72	28.99
40	Cosmetics, toiletries	185.00	3.34	3.58	7.32
41	Petroleum refining	62.71	13.17	16.01	21.60
42	Petroleum and coal products	237.09	10.18	10.76	5.71
43	Glass and products	132.51	16.35	18.02	10.22
44	Clay products	38.04	4.20	5.69	35.62
45	Cement (a)	34.11	128.09a	178.97	39.72
46	Concrete products (a)	34.11	211.47a	295.47	39.72
47	Other nonmetallic mineral products	14.66	41.62	80.08	92.42
48	Stone products (a)	35.56	5.80	8.01	38.10
49	Basic iron and steel	17.94	17.22	29.53	71.50
50	Iron, steel castings and forgings	27.36	5.05	7.55	49.52
51	Steel pipes and tubes	27.14	1.85	2.77	49.92
52	Smelting nonferrous metals	25.95	7.97	12.13	52.21
53	Aluminum rolling, drawing, extruding	55.00	4.53	5.64	24.63
54	Nonferrous metals rolling, drawing, extruding	24.98	3.43	5.29	54.24
55	Fabricated structural steel	51.96	6.03	7.60	26.07
56	Architectural metal products	90.20	5.22	6.00	15.02
57	Boilers and plates	69.16	.59	.71	19.59
58	Metal products n.e.c.	122.26	18.74	20.81	11.08
59	Cutting and hand tools	76.58	1.75	2.06	17.19
60	Wire products, nuts and bolts	51.02	6.44	8.15	26.55
61	Other fabricated metal products	44.12	2.89	3.77	30.71
62	Motor vehicles	189.88	9.95	10.66	7.13
63	Truck, bus bodies	45.65	1.86	2.41	29.68

		(1)	(2)	(3)	(4)
64	Motor vehicle electrical parts	67.45	2.06	2.47	20.08
65	Ship building and repair (b)	736.50	116.48	118.62	1.02
66	Boats, other transport equipment (b)	736.48	116.43	118.62	1.02
67	Loco stock and repair	111.50	1.90	2.13	12.15
68	Aircraft building and repair	179.64	.47	.51	7.54
69	Photo, optical, scientific equipment	125.48	2.15	2.58	10.79
70	TV, radio, electrical equipment	161.45	2.69	2.91	8.39
71	Household appliances	162.49	5.94	6.43	8.33
72	Electrical and telephone wire	36.18	2.14	2.94	37.45
73	Batteries	171.48	4.71	5.08	7.90
74	Other electrical equipment	55.12	2.96	3.68	24.58
75	Agricultural machinery and equipment	83.10	4.25	4.94	16.30
76	Other industrial machinery	127.48	3.22	3.56	10.62
77	Leather tanning	79.70	2.03	2.37	17.00
78	Leather and substitute products	84.07	2.04	2.37	16.11
79	Rubber tyres, tubes etc.	177.88	20.78	22.36	7.61
80	Other rubber products	79.46	3.38	3.96	17.05
81	Plastic and related products	83.74	11.43	13.28	16.18
82	Jewellery, silver	61.43	.26	.32	22.05
83	Brooms, brushes	492.09	26.99	27.73	2.75
84	Signs and advertising displays	50.44	1.46	1.85	26.86
85	Other manufacturing	155.99	4.54	4.93	8.68
	All industries — unweighted mean	117.20	14.40	16.20	12.50
	weighted mean	59.86(c)	9.76(d)	11.96(d)	22.54

(1) Freight Rate (Net of Distance) ($/tonne)
(2) Freight Rate (Net of Distance) (%)
(3) Total Freight Rate (D = 12630) (%)
(4) Relative Increase in Freight Rate (Net of Distance) (%)
(i.e. (((3) ÷ (2)) − 1) x 100)

Notes: (a) Estimates of *ad valorem* freight rates based on values provided by industry sources.
(b) Rates based on estimates of gross weights and values of exports by liner vessels provided by Australian Bureau of Customs.
(c) Weighted by gross weights of Australian exports to Europe, 1972/73.
(d) Weighted values of Australian Exports to Europe, 1972/73.
Source: Calculated from regression results of Zerby and Conlon (1978b).

dian exports of individual commodities. The latter is based on Raynes' work in contributing to Wonnacott's (1975) study of Canada's trade options, and is valuable in providing an indication of the relative magnitudes of the tariff and transport cost barriers to Canadian trade.

Raynes' study attempted to assess the effects of international transport costs on Ontario and Quebec as part of a study of potential Canada-Europe, and Canada-United States free trade areas. For a relatively small selection of Canadian exports of materials and partially processed goods, she found that trans-Atlantic transport costs were at least of the same magnitude as United States' tariffs. Her evidence suggested that Canadian transport costs to the United States, while lower than trans-Atlantic charges, were also of comparable height to U.S. tariffs. An examination of shipments of 15 commodity groups provides the results shown in Table 6.4, but it should be stressed that they are based on a narrow range of goods and thus should be viewed with caution.[16]

TABLE 6.4

TARIFFS AND TRANSPORT BARRIERS TO CANADIAN EXPORTS

	Mean*	Range
U.S. Tariff (%)	5.9	free - 16.7
Transport cost to EEC ex Montreal	˙ 11.9	1.3 - 3.42
Transport cost to U.S. ex Montreal	8.1	.4 - 38.0

Sources: Calculated from Raynes (1977, p. 11) and Wonnacott (1975, p. 214).
*Simple unweighted arithmetic mean of rates quoted.

While the range of products covered by Raynes' study is admittedly narrow, her results are consistent with the studies examined earlier in this Chapter and in Chapter 5. It would appear that, on average, the transport barrier faced by a Canadian exporter both to the E.E.C. and to the United States is likely to be as high as the corresponding U.S. tariff barrier.[17]

These simple averages, while providing some idea of the relative heights of the two barriers, provide little information about whether they are in fact

16. It appears likely that her estimated transport costs to the U.S. are not strictly comparable with those to the E.E.C. By far the majority of the quoted U.S. rates are for road transport. In such cases it is likely that many goods are shipped directly from the place of manufacture to importers' warehouses in the U.S. In the case of trans-Atlantic (mainly sea) cargoes the goods must first be delivered to the port of shipment and from the port of destination. Based on Australian experience this may add about 1 to 2 per cent to Raynes' estimates of transport costs to the E.E.C.

17. It should be realised that for Canada - U.S. trade, internal transport costs may be higher than international transport costs. This will tend to provide a stimulus to international trade.

important in inhibiting Canadian exports. Bryan's (1974b) regression analysis looked specifically at this question. For 17 commodities characterised as "primary manufactures and some of the cruder secondary manufactures", her results showed that foreign tariffs were generally not statistically significant determinants of Canadian exports,[18] and that transport costs were. However, for 5 comparatively technologically advanced products[19] her results suggested that neither tariffs nor transport costs were important barriers to Canadian exports.

In summarising her results, Bryan suggested that for 10 of the 22 commodities for which regression results were provided,[20] "the structure of exports . . . is affected by transport costs" (p. 652), and that they tend to be more important for primary than manufactured commodities.[21] For relatively homogenous products such as these, relative prices could be expected to play a much larger part in determining trade advantage than for the more differentiated "secondary manufactured" commodities. To the extent to which freight costs contribute to the determination of relative landed prices, this result is in line with *à priori* reasoning and also with the findings of the studies discussed earlier. In the case of the relatively technologically advanced products, which Bryan found to be not affected by transport costs, she argues that for such commodities "design, quality, speed of delivery and guarantees may be more important than delivered price . . ." (p. 652). In finding that overall, "variations in transport costs have a larger effect on the structure of exports than variations in tariffs . . . (p. 652), she concluded that the most likely reason is that transport costs have a larger effect on relative prices than tariffs. If transport costs are as important as her results indicate, she argued that it would be desirable to amend trade theory to take more explicit account of them. Moreover,

> "Given that transport costs are significant in determining the structure of trade for some commodities, it would seem that it would be very important for an exporting country to keep a close watch on freight rates, both freight rates on its own exports and on those of its main competitors." (p. 653).

With the importance of the conference system to Australia's exports and imports, particularly on manufactured goods, virtually all of which are

---

18. In 12 of the 17 equations, the transport cost variable was different from zero at, or better than 10 per cent level of significance. The same was true of the tariff variable in only 3 equations.

19. Insulated wire and cable, telephone apparatus, aircraft engines, agricultural machinery, and construction machinery.

20. Whiskey, flour, tobacco, hemlock, plywood, newsprint, sheet and strip steel, copper, nickel, and passenger automobiles.

21. Eight of the 10 commodities for which the freight variable is statistically significant are classified by Bryan as "primary manufacturing".

transported on conference vessels, this conclusion has perhaps even more relevance for Australia than it does for Canada, which exports mainly to the United States.

6.3 Summary and Conclusions

From the discussion in this, and the preceding Chapter, it is apparent that distance itself is an important barrier to trade. Not only is it likely to limit businessmen's horizons along the lines of the "psychic distance" hypothesis (Gruber and Vernon, 1970), it is also directly associated with the cost of transportation. In this Chapter an attempt has been made to measure the cost of distance using a method which it is believed has not been used before. Consistent with Linneman (1966), Gruber and Vernon (1970) and Geraci and Prewo (1978), the results show that distance is important; it is likely to add about 13 to 15 per cent to the cost of transporting Australian exports to Japan and Europe. Information which would enable similar estimates of the costs of distance for Canadian exports were not available to this study; but can any assessment be made of the *extra* cost which must be borne by exporters in Australia as a result of that country's comparative isolation? If the estimated distance coefficient is applied to Australian exports to its most important trade areas (New Zealand, North America, Africa, Arabian Gulf and EEC), and the resulting costs of distance, are weighted by the values of exports to these areas, the resulting *ad valorem* equivalent of the "weighted average cost of distance" is just under 14 per cent (assuming an average value of exports of A\$85 per tonne). If, assuming the estimated distance coefficient can be applied to Canada, and that the average values of Australian and Canadian exports are the same, the corresponding weighted average to Canada's major trade areas is approximately 9 per cent. Thus, under the strong assumption that all else is equal, Australia's isolation on average adds about 4 or 5 per cent to the cost of transporting exports, when compared with the cost in Canada.

For individual commodities, both the cost of distance (as defined) and distance-free liner freight rates to Europe fall less heavily on high unit-value commodities, and consistent with this, on goods which are relatively highly fabricated. Studies for Australia by Sampson and Yeats, and for Canada by Raynes suggest that if U.S. evidence is representative, on average transport costs are likely to be higher than the corresponding foreign tariffs for the two countries' exports. From the data in Table 6.3, the estimated weighted average *ad valorem* liner freight rate to Europe during 1972/73, including the cost of distance of nearly 12 per cent, compares with the 1975 weighted average tariff rate on manufactures imposed by the countries comprising the European Economic Community of 7.5 per cent (Industries Assistance Commission, 1978, p. 78). Bryan's work suggest that while both tariffs and transport costs are both probably important determinants of trade flows, transport costs may well be the greater inhibiting influence, particularly on primary manufactures and the "cruder" secondary manufactures which are major export commodities of the two countries. It seems apparent that despite Canada's favourable trade location, transport costs are still an important barrier to Canadian exports; one which should not be ignored.

The remainder of this study deals almost exclusively with *ad valorem* transport costs as a barrier to trade rather than the estimates of the "costs of distance" in fulfilling that role. It should be remembered that there is strong evidence that distance is at least partially embodied in the transport costs which are subsequently to be considered. Geraci and Prewo in establishing that distance is an important determinant of transport costs, and in turn, that transport costs are an important determinant of trade flows, have provided the necessary link between the study of distance as a barrier to trade as Linneman (1966) conceived it, and the studies of *ad valorem*, transport costs of such researchers as Yeats and Waters.

This Chapter has been concerned with trade barriers as a disadvantage facing exporters. Having established that the influence of distance may be considered to be embodied in transport costs, Chapter 7 which follows, estimates *ad valorem* transport cost barriers which may provide an *advantage* to manufacturing industries in Australia and Canada. It uses the general approach of Yeats and Waters and compares these costs with the corresponding tariff barriers protecting the Australian and Canadian manufacturing sectors. Thus, the respective aims of Chapters 6 and 7 are to provide an assessment of the foreign and domestic barriers to trade. From the analysis of Chapters 3 and 4, such barriers are important determinants of trade patterns and, in turn, influence the structures and performances of industries. It is these influences which are the prime subjects of Chapters 8 and 9.

7.   Trade Barriers to Australian and Canadian Imports

The previous chapter examined some estimates of transport costs associated with Australia's isolation from its major export markets, and the
consequent disadvantage faced by Australian exporters. In Linnemann's
(1966) study discussed in Chapter 5, it was suggested that Australia's
foreign trade location was among the worst of the 80 countries examined.
The works of Bryan (1974b), and Raynes (1977) which were discussed in the
previous chapter show that international transport costs are also an important barrier to Canadian exports. From the point of view of import-
competing producers in both countries however, international transport
costs are likely to provide a corresponding advantage as they add to the
price of imports. It is the possible advantage accruing to import-competing
manufacturing industries as a result of protection which is the subject of this
chapter.

7.1 Description of Tariff and Transport Cost Data in this Study

The estimates of Australian and Canadian tariffs and transport costs have
been derived from data provided by the Australian Industries Assistance
Commission (based on Australian Bureau of Statistics data) and Statistics
Canada, respectively. The former were provided for 171 four-digit industries classified by the Australian Standard Industrial Classification, and the
latter for 122 manufacturing industries comprising the L level of aggregation of the Canadian input-output table for 1974 (input-output industries
16-137). Thus an essential part of this study entailed the reconciliation of
the industry classification used in each country, and the construction of an
Australia-Canada Industrial Classification (ACIC), such that a given
ACIC industry consists of a group of operating units engaged in the same
activities. The final concordance produced 85 ACIC industries.[1]

Australia

The nominal tariff rates in this study are defined as the *ad valorem* equivalents of duties collected expressed as a percentage of the free-on-board

---

1. The Concordance may be found in Appendix 8.1.

(f.o.b.) value of imports.[2] Nominal transport costs are defined as the ratio of the difference between the c.i.f. and the f.o.b. values of imports, to the f.o.b. value of imports:

$$[(c.i.f./f.o.b. \text{ value of imports}) - 1] . 100$$

The insurance and other charges which are included in the c.i.f. value of imports are considered to be unavoidable elements in the total cost of international transportation and as such are treated as transport charges.[3]

Effective rates of protection in the following analysis have been calculated in a manner consistent with the basic Australian Industries Assistance Commission formula.[4] To assess the magnitudes of tariffs and transport cost separately requires the estimation of f.o.b. values of all protection variables to enable the addition (and comparison) of the components of protection to be made on a common base.

Thus, the components of total effective protection are the f.o.b. - based effective rate of tariff protection:

(7.1) $ERT = (t_q - Mt_m) / (1-M)$

and the f.o.b. - based effective rate of transport cost protection:

(7.2) $ERF = (f_q - Mf_m) / (1-M)$

where ERP = the (total) effective rate of protection = $ERT + ERF$;
    t_q = duty on the finished product as a proportion of its f.o.b. price;
    f_q = transport cost of the finished product as a proportion of its f.o.b. price (i.e., (c.i.f./f.o.b. value of imports) - 1);

<hr/>

2. The Australian nominal rates of protection which are examined in this study, and which have been used to calculate corresponding effective rates, include not only the effect of assistance provided by tariffs, but also by some forms of non-tariff barriers, such as manufacturing subsidies and import prohibitions. Where necessary, estimates of the effect of excise taxes have been deducted from the tariff rates of relevant items (mainly in the cases of alcoholic beverages and tobacco products) (Industries Assistance Commission, 1976b, p. 47). The rates do not take into account other important forms of assistance such as support value duties, government purchasing policies, local content plans, or quantitative import restrictions (Industries Assistance Commission, 1976b, p. 79). However, the time period chosen for this study, 1973/74, avoids the effect of most of the direct quantitative restrictions which in the main, have been imposed since July, 1974.

3. It should be kept in mind that the import-weighted tariffs and transport costs estimated in this study understate the real level of protection, not only because of the exclusion of some forms of protection mentioned, but also because only imports which *actually* enter the country are included in the computation. Goods which are completely shut out by high tariffs and/or transport costs are, of course, excluded.

4. The formula and its derivation have been outlined by the Australian Tariff Board (1967, pp. 32-36), the predecessor of the Commission.

M   = f.o.b. value of materials incorporated in the protected output expressed as a proportion of the f.o.b. value of the imported, finished product;

t_m = duty on importable materials expressed as a proportion of their f.o.b. prices; and

f_m = transport cost on importable materials expressed as a proportion of their f.o.b. prices.

Canada

The Canadian tariff rates appearing here are based on data derived especially for this study by the Structural Analysis Division of Statistics Canada and are the *ad valorem* equivalents of duties collected as a proportion of the value of imports at the factory gate.[5] To the extent that there are charges incurred in loading the goods onto the mode of transportation, free-on-board, these rates will be higher than f.o.b.-based tariffs. However, as nearly 70 percent of Canadian imports were from the United States,[6] there is the consequent likelihood that the greater proportion of imports were transported by either road or rail, and it would therefore appear likely that in aggregate, the difference between factory gate and f.o.b. tariffs is small. Consequently for the purpose of this exercise, these rates are considered to be equivalent to f.o.b. values. Like the Australian tariff data, the Canadian rates are net of the influence of subsidies and excise taxes.

The estimates of transport costs cover costs from the foreign factory door to the Canadian border[7] and like the Canadian tariff data are expressed as a proportion of their value at the foreign factory gate. For the reasons outlined above, these will again be considered as equivalent to f.o.b. values. The effective rates of tariff and transport costs protection using the nominal rates of protection just described have been calculated according to the formulae of (7.1) and (7.2) respectively.

---

5. Import duties are those appearing in the input-output table row 596 (commodity indirect taxes) under the column "imports" in final demand.

6. During 1973, of total Canadian imports of U.S. $21.3 billion, U.S. $14.8 billion were from the United States (Economic Council of Canada, 1975, p. 98).

7. These have been derived from estimates for imported goods which have been valued either f.o.b. from plant, or from exit port. These respectively comprised 86.4 percent and 6.7 percent of the total value of Canadian imports in 1971. The remainder was valued c.i.f. No transport cost estimates were made for these goods. However, the overall coverage of the data from which the estimates have been made is large and may be reasonably considered to be representative. There is an additional caveat; the proportion of the total value of imports valued f.o.b. is larger for the United States than from overseas sources (95.4 and 87.5 percent, respectively). Thus the measured proportion of imports from the U.S. contributing to the estimates will be greater than the true proportion, and this will almost certainly entail some underestimation of the transport cost barriers to Canadian imports.

7.2 Characteristics of Transport Cost and Tariff Protection of Australian Manufacturing[8]

The results of the computations just described for 85 ACIC groups comprising the Australian manufacturing sector appear in Table 7.1. Of the 85 manufacturing industries, 25 shelter behind nominal transport costs which are higher than the corresponding nominal tariff.[9] In terms of employment, 320,000 persons, or approximately 24 percent of the total workforce of these industries in Australia during 1973/74, were primarily protected by transport costs rather than the tariff.[10] The main activities protected in this manner are within the food and beverage group (ACIC 1-15) where 11 of 15 industries are mainly protected by transport costs, while the same is true of all industries in the non-metallic mineral products group (ACIC 43-47). Both groups of industries produce commodities which tend to be characterised by low unit values. In effective rate terms, 13 industries accounting for over 16 percent of the workforce, are mainly protected by transport costs.[11] Again, these industries concentrated in the generally low unit-value food and beverage, and non-metallic mineral products groups. Comparatively low rates of transport cost protection (ie. below the median) tend to be concentrated in transport equipment (ACIC 32-68) and machinery and equipment (ACIC 69-76). These results conform with observations discussed in earlier chapters of inverse relationships between transport costs and high unit value, and/or high technology commodities.

High nominal and effective tariffs are characteristics of beverages (ACIC 13-15), which are usually subject to high, mainly revenue-raising duties, and of industries producing relatively highly fabricated products, such as knitted goods, clothing and footwear, and cosmetics comprising ACIC 55-58 (see Table 7.1). Within ACIC 55-58, 23 of the 31 industries have nominal rates above the median, while 21 have effective rates above it. Industries producing goods at relatively low levels of fabrication, which rely mainly on inputs which are relatively abundant in Australia (e.g. food (ACIC 1-12), or which have high levels of natural protection, (e.g. cement (ACIC 45) and concrete products (ACIC 46)), tend to be characterised by low levels of nominal and effective tariff protection.

Table 7.5 summarises the data just discussed, and from it may be seen that transport cost protection on average comprises a very significant portion of the total protection available to the Australian manufacturing

---

8. For a more comprehensive analysis of the protection data of both countries see Conlon (1980).

9. ACIC 1,3-6,8,10-14,17,29,30,32,35,41-48,52.

10. See Appendix 8.3 for the distribution of manufacturing employment in both countries.

11. ACIC 1,3,5,6,12,14,29,32,42-46.

TABLE 7.1

NOMINAL AND EFFECTIVE RATES OF PROTECTION (F.O.B.):
EIGHTY-FIVE AUSTRALIAN MANUFACTURING INDUSTRIES

ACIC	Industry Description	Nominal Protection			Effective Protection		
		Transp. (%)	Tariff (%)	Total (%)	Transp. (%)	Tariff (%)	Total (%)
1	Meat products	6.2	0.9	7.2	14.4	0.1	14.5
2	Poultry products	1.4	2.0	3.4	2.7	5.3	8.0
3	Milk products	5.8	4.2	10.1	22.3	13.6	35.9
4	Fruit, vegetable products	20.6	20.2	40.7	19.1	38.2	57.3
5	Flour, starch, cereals	21.2	4.8	26.0	32.1	8.6	40.7
6	Margarine, oil, fats	20.6	15.7	36.3	42.2	20.9	63.2
7	Bread, cake, pastry	0.8	1.0	1.8	-8.9	-2.1	-10.9
8	Biscuits	23.0	16.0	39.0	23.8	23.9	47.7
9	Confectionery, cocoa	18.5	36.7	55.2	7.0	80.6	87.6
10	Fish products	6.2	5.3	11.5	-4.1	-2.4	-6.5
11	Animal foods	12.0	5.6	17.6	2.2	8.9	11.1
12	Sugar, malt, other foods	20.4	4.5	24.9	56.5	18.2	74.7
13	Soft drinks, cordials	55.5	32.7	88.2	88.6	100.9	189.4
14	Beer	56.5	48.5	105.0	93.7	84.8	178.5
15	Wine, alcoholic beverages	24.2	49.1	73.3	44.5	122.2	166.7
16	Tobacco	15.7	35.9	51.6	15.0	27.6	42.5*
17	Wool: scoured, carbonised, tops	3.3	0.0	3.3	-8.6	-1.9	-10.5
18	Manmade fibre yarn and fabrics	10.1	24.0	34.1	7.2	41.8	49.0
19	Cotton yarn and fabric	9.8	26.3	36.1	8.5	54.9	63.3
20	Wool yarn and fabric	11.4	22.8	34.3	9.4	48.1	57.5
21	Household and other textiles	12.6	28.8	41.4	18.1	44.3	62.4
22	Textile floor covers	20.3	20.5	40.8	37.4	40.5	77.8
23	Felt and products	14.7	18.3	33.0	3.6	35.0	38.7
24	Canvas and products	12.9	32.7	45.6	19.4	73.4	92.9
25	Rope, cord, twine	12.9	19.2	32.1	-4.6	24.3	19.7
26	Hosiery	16.8	37.4	54.2	21.7	59.2	80.9

27	Knitted goods	13.5	40.2	53.7	19.7	92.1	111.7
28	Clothing, footwear	14.9	43.0	57.9	19.7	77.4	97.1
29	Sawmill, wood products	28.9	13.8	42.7	25.2	16.1	41.4
30	Ply, veneers and wood boards	36.1	29.9	66.0	43.2	44.4	87.6
31	Furniture	19.0	25.2	44.3	12.4	28.1	40.5
32	Pulp, paper and paper board	24.5	12.5	37.0	20.5	17.8	38.3
33	Paper bags, containers	21.7	41.2	62.9	11.0	115.9	126.9
34	Paper products, printing and publishing	16.7	18.2	35.0	7.6	29.8	37.3
35	Basic chemicals	18.7	10.8	29.6	6.9	13.8	20.7
36	Chemical products excl. agricultural	14.5	22.9*	37.3	10.3*	29.0	39.4
37	Paints	16.3	30.2	46.5	12.5	44.5	57.0
38	Pharmaceuticals incl. veterinary products	5.8	27.5	33.3	3.5	34.7	38.2
39	Soap, detergents	15.6	22.0	37.6	9.3	25.3	34.6
40	Cosmetics, toiletries	13.6	33.0	46.6	9.9	42.2	52.1
41	Petroleum refining	9.9	4.4	14.3	-19.5	3.2	-16.3
42	Petroleum and coal products	50.1	13.5	63.7	86.0	30.4	116.4
43	Glass and products	26.6	12.7	39.2	20.1	12.0	32.0
44	Clay products	38.1	23.2	61.4	43.3	32.0*	75.4
45	Cement	81.2	5.4	86.6	139.2	8.2	147.4
46	Concrete products	43.8	1.4	45.2	38.5	-2.1	36.4
47	Other nonmetallic mineral products	32.3	22.8	55.1	19.5	33.3	52.8
48	Stone products	29.0	21.9	51.0	7.8	25.8	33.6
49	Basic iron and steel	13.0	14.7	27.7	-12.9	20.9	8.0
50	Iron, steel castings and forgings	11.1	20.0	31.1	5.7	24.4	30.0
51	Steel pipes and tubes	15.3	19.6	34.9	-0.6	28.3	27.7
52	Smelting nonferrous metals	5.0	1.7	6.7	-19.0	2.8	-16.2
53	Aluminum rolling, drawing, extruding	12.2	22.4	34.7	25.7	80.9	106.6
54	Nonferrous metals rolling, drawing, extruding	5.8	14.1	19.9	-9.2	47.7	38.5
55	Fabricated structural steel	15.3	31.1	46.5	10.2	49.4	59.5
56	Architectural metal products	12.3	28.7	40.9	11.7	38.3	50.0
57	Boilers and plates	18.9	25.0	43.9	22.2	37.6	59.8
58	Metal products n.e.c.	15.5	32.7	48.2	18.2	58.4	76.6
59	Cutting and hand tools	7.0	15.0	21.9	2.8	14.9	17.7
60	Wire products, nuts and bolts	11.6	26.7	38.3	10.2	40.8	51.0
61	Other fabricated metal products	12.4	35.3	47.8	17.6	62.5	80.1

62	Motor vehicles	7.0	28.9	35.8	2.1	41.9	44.0
63	Truck, bus bodies	17.9	30.7	48.6	28.1	66.2	94.4
64	Motor vehicle electrical parts	5.4	24.3	29.7	-4.0	29.7	25.8
65	Ship building and repair	5.2	34.7	39.9	-10.3	59.1	48.7
66	Boats, other transport equipment	20.0	26.4	46.4	19.1	31.8	50.8
67	Loco stock and repair	9.1	26.2	35.2	-12.8	46.9	34.1
68	Aircraft building and repair	5.8	11.6	17.5	7.2	19.7	26.9
69	Photo, optical, scientific equipment	7.7	13.3	21.1	0.9	10.7	11.6
70	TV, radio, electrical equipment	10.0	29.7	39.7	5.7	31.7	37.4
71	Household appliances	15.5	31.3	46.9	17.2	47.4	64.6
72	Electrical and telephone wire	10.4	17.7	28.0	9.3	35.0	44.2
73	Batteries	10.0	31.9	41.9	5.8	43.8	49.6
74	Other electrical equipment	9.6	23.0	32.7	7.4	23.8	31.3
75	Agricultural machinery and equipment	12.6	21.4	34.0	6.1	22.2	28.3
76	Other industrial machinery	8.6	24.9	33.5	3.1	28.9	32.0
77	Leather tanning	9.5	13.1	22.7	12.3	26.8	39.1
78	Leather and substitute products	19.5	29.9	49.3	28.5	46.6	75.1
79	Rubber tyres, tubes etc.	11.1	22.2	33.3	3.1	29.2	32.3
80	Other rubber products	15.3	32.3	47.6	15.3	50.0	65.4
81	Plastic and related products	15.2	23.0	38.1*	14.2	18.7	32.8
82	Jewellery, silver	3.1	20.6	23.7	-2.0	37.8	35.8
83	Brooms, brushes	14.4*	29.7	44.2	1.1	40.8	41.9
84	Signs and advertising displays	20.8	31.4	52.2	21.8	47.2	69.0
85	Other manufacturing	9.4	26.9	36.3	-1.0	36.4	35.5

Notes: *Median.
Data have been rounded.

Sources: See text.

TABLE 7.2

NOMINAL AND EFFECTIVE RATES OF PROTECTION (F.O.B.):
EIGHTY-FIVE CANADIAN MANUFACTURING INDUSTRIES

ACIC	Industry Description	Nominal Protection			Effective Protection		
		Transp. (%)	Tariff (%)	Total (%)	Transp. (%)	Tariff (%)	Total (%)
1	Meat products	6.0	2.6	8.6	24.3	5.8	30.1
2	Poultry products	1.3	11.8	13.1	-46.1	34.5	-11.6
3	Milk products	4.6	12.1	16.7	17.2	8.1	25.3
4	Fruit, vegetable products	5.9	9.3	15.2	5.7	19.7	25.4
5	Flour, starch, cereals	3.3	2.8	6.1	16.3	11.8	28.1
6	Margarine, oil, fats	7.6	3.3	10.9	39.4	20.0	59.4
7	Bread, cake, pastry	5.3	7.6	12.9	8.4	14.7	23.1
8	Biscuits	0.9	4.9	5.8	-6.2	5.2	-1.0
9	Confectionery, cocoa	8.1	10.9	19.0	17.2	28.4	45.6
10	Fish products	10.7	7.7	18.4	32.4	22.1	54.5
11	Animal foods	16.7	6.5	23.2	81.8	36.9	118.7
12	Sugar, malt, other foods	7.9	3.9	11.8	24.9	8.2	33.1
13	Soft drinks, cordials	1.1	4.8	5.9	-5.4	2.4	-3.0
14	Beer	11.6	25.0	36.6	26.5	60.9	87.4
15	Wine, alcoholic beverages	3.7	85.1	88.8	8.6	444.4	453.0
16	Tobacco	0.6	56.3	56.9	0.5	106.9	107.4
17	Wool: scoured, carbonised, tops	6.6	12.3	18.9	13.6	32.3	45.9
18	Manmade fibre yarn and fabrics	5.1	16.2	21.3	9.4	34.4	43.8
19	Cotton yarn and fabric	5.3	18.6	23.9	10.2	42.2	52.4
20	Wool yarn and fabric	3.0	14.0	17.0	3.0	31.3	34.3
21	Household and other textiles	3.5	11.9	15.4	4.1	13.4	17.5
22	Textile floor covers	7.7	25.9	33.6	28.5	107.9	136.4
23	Felt and products	2.8	16.9	19.7	-7.4	43.6	36.2
24	Canvas and products	2.3	11.2	13.5	-0.8	8.9	8.1
25	Rope, cord, twine	8.8	6.8	15.6	15.3	8.5	23.8

26	Hosiery	3.7	22.7	26.4	1.7	44.9	46.6
27	Knitted goods	3.2	25.9	29.1	1.7	61.6	63.3
28	Clothing, footwear	4.6	20.9	25.5	9.2	39.9	49.1
29	Sawmill, wood products	2.8	3.4	6.2	4.2	7.2	11.4
30	Ply, veneers and wood boards	1.8	10.5*	12.3	1.7	25.7	27.4
31	Furniture	4.0	14.8	18.8	6.8	24.7	31.5
32	Pulp, paper and paper board	1.9	6.4	8.3	1.4	12.9	14.3
33	Paper bags, containers	4.0*	14.9	18.9	7.1	27.1	34.2
34	Paper products, printing and publishing	2.2	7.2	9.4	2.7	7.5	10.2
35	Basic chemicals	10.1	4.7	14.8	16.5	9.9	26.4
36	Chemical products excl. agricultural	4.4	10.0	14.4	2.2	20.8	23.4
37	Paints	1.8	19.7	21.5	-6.2	55.6	49.4
38	Pharmaceuticals incl. veterinary products	1.1	7.3	8.4	-0.5	11.7	11.2
39	Soap, detergents	5.3	11.6	16.9	6.6	24.1	30.7
40	Cosmetics, toiletries	1.6	13.0	14.6	0.6	22.8	23.4
41	Petroleum refining	6.9	0.8	7.7	-25.0	4.2	-20.8
42	Petroleum and coal products	6.3	10.8	17.1	6.1	19.2	25.3
43	Glass and products	4.1	11.9	16.0	2.4	17.4	19.8
44	Clay products	5.1	9.4	14.5	3.8	15.3	19.1
45	Cement	9.6	0.5	10.1	15.9	-0.2	15.7
46	Concrete products	3.1	3.5	6.6	-5.7	6.1	0.4
47	Other nonmetallic mineral products	4.1	8.9	13.0	0.2	15.8	16.0
48	Stone products	5.9	10.0	15.9	-6.6	19.4	12.8
49	Basic iron and steel	8.9	7.9	16.8	10.0	21.2	31.2
50	Iron, steel castings and forgings	2.8	8.0	10.8	-2.3	15.3	13.0
51	Steel pipes and tubes	8.0	9.7	17.7	12.6	18.6	31.2
52	Smelting nonferrous metals	4.7	1.2	5.9	3.0	4.2	7.2
53	Aluminum rolling, drawing, extruding	2.7	5.5	8.2	0.0	14.4	14.4
54	Nonferrous metals rolling, drawing, extruding	2.6	5.2	7.8	-17.4	20.9	3.5
55	Fabricated structural steel	4.8	11.3	16.1	1.2	16.6	17.8
56	Architectural metal products	4.0	16.8	20.8	5.9	39.0	44.9
57	Boilers and plates	4.2	10.0	14.2	2.5	15.0	17.5
58	Metal products n.e.c.	2.9	12.0	14.9*	0.2	20.1	20.3
59	Cutting and hand tools	5.0	11.1	16.1	5.5	17.3	22.8

No.	Category						
60	Wire products, nuts and bolts	5.6	9.7	15.3	-0.6	15.1	14.5
61	Other fabricated metal products	4.1	8.6	12.7	1.7	13.0	14.7
62	Motor vehicles	1.8	1.8	3.6	0.1	-0.9	-0.8
63	Truck, bus bodies	1.4	12.4	13.8	-3.5	23.9	20.4
64	Motor vehicle electrical parts	2.8	1.5	4.3	1.7	-2.7	-1.0
65	Ship building and repair	6.3	18.8	25.1	9.6	44.2	53.8
66	Boats, other transport equipment	2.8	8.8	11.6	4.5	19.2	23.7*
67	Loco stock and repair	3.2	10.5	13.7	0.2	15.3	15.5
68	Aircraft building and repair	2.7	0.5	3.2	3.3*	-0.9	2.4
69	Photo, optical, scientific equipment	5.1	7.2	12.3	9.2	11.7	20.9
70	TV, radio, electrical equipment	2.5	12.5	15.0	3.2	17.2	20.4
71	Household appliances	6.8	12.9	19.7	17.2	29.8	47.0
72	Electrical and telephone wire	3.2	14.0	17.2	8.1	48.1	56.2
73	Batteries	1.0	7.9	8.9	-5.7	9.8	4.1
74	Other electrical equipment	1.6	11.8	13.4	0.4	19.5*	19.9
75	Agricultural machinery and equipment	3.8	1.2	5.0	2.1	-4.3	-2.2
76	Other industrial machinery	3.9	7.6	11.5	5.2	10.0	15.2
77	Leather tanning	0.5	7.0	7.5	-4.0	21.3	17.3
78	Leather and substitute products	6.5	15.9	22.4	16.8	29.4	46.2
79	Rubber tyres, tubes etc.	2.8	12.7	15.5	1.6	25.4	27.0
80	Other rubber products	1.8	12.5	14.3	-0.9	20.5	19.6
81	Plastic and related products	3.6	13.2	16.8	4.7	27.0	31.7
82	Jewellery, silver	2.3	7.4	9.7	5.2	27.4	32.6
83	Brooms, brushes	4.5	19.2	23.7	7.4	39.3	46.7
84	Signs and advertising displays	0.1	43.1	43.2	-1.7	88.0	86.3
85	Other manufacturing	4.5	13.3	17.8	7.6	23.6	31.2

Notes: *Median.
Data have been rounded.
Sources: See text.

90

sector. Of the average nominal protection available to manufacturing, over two-thirds may be attributed to transport costs, while of average effective protection, approximately one-quarter may be attributed to protection afforded by transport cost. All the measures of central tendency (median, unweighted mean and weighted mean) show the effective transport cost protection as being less than the corresponding nominal rate, suggesting that the transport cost burden on inputs is greater than the protection provided by transport costs to the final products of import-competing industries.[12] Nevertheless, that rates of effective transport cost protection are generally positive (as average materials/output ratios are less than unity) suggests the structure of transport cost protection tends to provide a stimulus to Australian manufacturing: it enables the domestic value of factors used in manufacturing activities to exceed their value at world market prices.

The matrices of rank (Spearman) correlation (r_s) and Pearson correlation (R) coefficients of the respective protection variables are shown in Table 7.3. Perhaps the most striking feature of the table is the high rank and simple correlation between nominal and the corresponding effective rates of transport, tariff and total protection. Following Waters, from this ". . . it appears that the much more easily obtained nominal rates might do a satisfactory job of indicating the pattern of protection among industries" (1970, p. 1915).

It may be thought that part of the process of determining levels of tariff protection through Australian Tariff Board/Industries Assistance procedures may be an attempt to offset low transport cost protection by high tariff protection. Thus, over a period it is possible that if an industry has little natural protection it may be given man-made protection instead. The data provide no statistical support for this hypothesis, or more generally for the existence of an inverse relationship between transport cost and tariff

_____

12. This is borne out when the structure of tariffs and transport costs on inputs of the Australian manufacturing sector is analysed. The unweighted and weighted means of transport costs of materials (19.4 and 16.5 percent, respectively) are higher than for final products, though the differences are not great. The opposite is true of tariffs on materials, where the corresponding means are 12.1 and 11.0 percent, respectively. Further Australian evidence concerning the incidence of tariffs and transport costs, with respect to the stage of commodity fabrication may be found in Conlon (1979). Briefly, the relative importance of transport costs tend to decline as the stage of product fabrication increases. The proportion of transport costs in total protection (ie. transport cost plus tariff) declines from 89 percent for raw materials, to 49 percent for materials at higher levels of fabrication, and to 27 percent of total protection for consumer goods. The tendency is reversed for investment goods where transport costs provide 40 percent of the total protective barrier. These results are similar to those of Waters (1970) in his study of U.S. protection.

TABLE 7.3

MATRIX OF RANK (AND PEARSON) CORRELATION COEFFICIENTS OF PROTECTION CHARACTERISTICS FOR 85 AUSTRALIAN MANUFACTURING INDUSTRIES 1973/74

	(1)	(2)	(3)	(4)	(5)	(6)
(1) Nominal Transport	1.000	.204	.734	.772	.178	.582
		(.095)	(.777)	(.891)	(.162)	(.661)
(2) Nominal Tariff		1.000	.735	.211	.869	.660
			(.700)	(.113)	(.852)	(.625)
(3) Total Nominal Protection			1.000	.637	.640	.813
				(.710)	(.655)	(.869)
(4) Effective Transport				1.000	.251	.743
					(.230)	(.774)
(5) Effective Tariff					1.000	.772
						(.795)
(6) Total Effective Protection						1.000

Significance levels: see Table 7.4

protection as is commonly expected (Yeats, 1977, p. 468). On the contrary, it provides evidence of a positive relationship between them.[13] However the relative dispersion of total protection (both nominal and effective) is less than the transport cost component (and in the case of nominal rates, the tariff components as well), and therefore it would appear that there is some tendency for total protection barrier to be more "uniform" than its components.

7.3 Characteristics of Transport Cost and Tariff Protection of Canadian Manufacturing[14]

Nominal and effective rates of protection of the industries comprising the Canadian manufacturing sector are shown in Table 7.2. Of the 85 industries, 16 are protected by nominal transport costs which are higher than the corresponding tariffs.[15] These industries employ nearly 361,000 persons — just over 20 percent of the Canadian manufacturing industry workforce in 1974.[16] Fourteen industries are protected by effective rates of transport cost protection which are higher than corresponding effective tariff rates.[17] As in Australia, in Canada, the industries primarily protected by transport costs are concentrated in the food group (ACIC 1-12). While within the non-metallic minerals product group (ACIC 43-48), only cement (ACIC 45) is protected by transport costs higher than the corresponding tariff, nominal transport costs for the group do tend to be relatively high (ie. above the median) as they are in Australia.

Also consistent with the Australian results are the lower than median rates for the Canadian transport equipment (ACIC 62-68) and machinery and equipment groups (ACIC 69-76). The results provide further confirmation of the tendency for inverse relationships between high unit-value/technology commodities and transport costs.

The tariff protection of the two countries also displays broad conformity. High levels of tariff protection (after netting out excise taxes) are provided under the Canadian tariff to the revenue-raising beer, wine and tobacco industries (ACIC 14, 15 and 16 respectively) as they are in Australia.

---

13. In the case of tariffs and transport costs on inputs, there is weak evidence of an inverse relationship. Pearson and Spearman correlation coefficients are both negative, but at low levels of significance ($R = -.114$, $r_s = -.0716$).

14. A more comprehensive discussion of Canadian protection may be found in Conlon (1980).

15. ACIC 1,5,6,10-12,25,35,41,45,49,52,62,64,68,75. See Appendix 8.3 for the distribution of employment in Canadian manufacturing.

16. Included in this total are the 99,000 employed in passenger motor vehicles and parts (ACIC 62 and 64) which are additionally protected under the U.S. Canada Auto Agreement. See Footnote 18.

17. ACIC, 1,3,5,6,10-12,25,35,45,62,64,68,75.

Knitted goods (ACIC 27) and clothing and footwear (ACIC 28) are also very highly protected in both countries, as is much of the remainder of the textiles and clothing groups (ACIC 17-28). Higher than median rates are also characteristic of the machinery and equipment group (ACIC 69-74), and other manufacturing (ACIC 77-85). Low nominal rates are characteristic of the food group (ACIC 1-12), but unlike Australia, the Canadian passenger car industry (ACIC 62 and 64) has rates of tariff protection below the median. This is almost certainly the result of the United States-Canada Auto Agreement.[18] The Canadian aircraft industry (ACIC 68) also has low levels of tariff protection, and like its Australian counterpart, this is probably at least the partial result of government purchasing policies of which no account is taken in the present study.

A summary of the data just discussed may be found in Table 7.5. From the table it may be seen that while the average level of total protection (median, unweighed mean) available to Canadian industry is less than half that available to Australian manufacturing, transport costs are still a significant component of the protective structure in Canada, comprising about one-third of the total nominal rate of protection, and about one-fifth of the total effective rate. There is no strong evidence to suggest that the burden of transport costs on Canadian manufacturing inputs outweighs the protection they provide to final products. While both the median and weighted mean effective transport costs are slightly lower than the corresponding nominal rates, the same is not true of the unweighted mean.[19] Also, while the nominal transport cost on materials is slightly below the rate in final products,[20] the difference is well within the standard errors of the

---

18. An evaluation of the agreement may be found in Beigie (1970). Connidis (1983) suggests that the method of calculating *ad valorem* equivalents of duties paid on outputs and material inputs which is used here and elsewhere (e.g. Wilkinson and Norrie, (1975) is inappropriate in the case of Canadian motor vehicle manufacture. She suggests *inter alia*, that the output tariff is underestimated because total imports include duty free imports by assemblers, and that the input tariff is overestimated because imports of parts consist of both dutiable replacement parts and duty-free original equipment parts. The result is an underestimation of the effective tariff.

19. The measures of central tendency of Canadian tariffs which are found in Table 7.5 may be compared with Melvin and Wilkinson's means of nominal tariffs of 16.0 (unweighted), and 13.1 percent (weighted); their means of effective tariffs were 26.4 and 30.6 (unweighted), and 21.0 and 24.4 percent (weighted), the calculated means depending on the tariff rate chosen for unspecified inputs (respectively, 11.3 and 5 percent) (1968, p. 29). Wilkson and Norrie found nominal rates 11.94 (unweighted) and 10.09 percent (weighted); and effective rates, depending on the method of calculation, varying from 17.41 to 20.09 percent (unweighted), and 12.50 to 15.47 percent (weighted) (1975, p. 35). Melvin and Wilkson's study used 1963 data; Wilkson and Norrie's, data drawn mainly from 1966.

20. For inputs, the unweighted means of transport costs, and tariffs are 4.3 and 5.2 percent, respectively. The corresponding weighted means are 4.4 and 4.1 percent.

estimates. Overall, it must be concluded that the average protection which transport costs afford the final products of import-competing Canadian industries is approximately the same as the average transport cost burden on material inputs. That the effective rate of transport cost protection is positive is a result of an average materials/output ratio which is less than unity. Nevertheless, like those in Australia the positive Canadian effective rates imply that on balance, transport costs provides a stimulus to Canadian manufacturing.

For tariff protection, all the measures of central tendency reflect the so-called "cascade" effect (i.e. tariffs which vary directly with the stage of product fabrication) typical of developed country tariff structures. Average effective rates are all substantially higher than the corresponding nominal rates: the unweighted and weighted means of the tariff on inputs are about half of those protecting final products, and the ranges of both nominal and effective tariffs are much greater than those of the corresponding transport cost protection, as are the respective dispersions. This is primarily the result of high (mainly) revenue-raising rates of alcoholic beverages and tobacco (ACIC 14-16). If these industries are omitted from the calculations, the dispersions of tariff and total protection (both nominal and effective) fall significantly.

Table 7.4 contains the matrices of rank (Spearman) and Pearson correlation coefficients of the protection variables. As for Australia, for Canada there is a high rank and simple correlation between the respective nominal and effective rates, a finding also consistent with previous Canadian studies by Melvin and Wilkinson (1968) and Wilkinson and Norrie (1975). There is no significant relationship between nominal transport costs and tariffs or the corresponding effective rates, and therefore, no apparent tendency for tariffs and transport costs to vary inversely.[21] The coefficient of variation of total nominal and effective protection for the 85 Canadian industries is lower than for their respective transport cost and tariff components,[22] and thus on balance it appears that the total protective barrier is more uniform than its components in Canada, as it is in Australia.

7.4 Comparison of the Protective Structures of Australia and Canada

Table 7.5 shows that for all the protection variables there is a significantly lower mean for the 85 industries in Canada than in Australia. If alcoholic

---

21. In the case of tariffs and transport costs on inputs, there is evidence suggesting an inverse relationship. Pearson and Spearman correlation coefficients are both negative at less than the 10 percent level of significance ($R = -.2267$ (.018) $r_s = .1500$ (.086) — significance levels in parentheses).

22. When ACIC 14-16 are omitted however, this is not true of the effective rates of protection.

TABLE 7.4

MATRIX OF RANK (AND PEARSON) CORRELATION COEFFICIENTS OF PROTECTION CHARACTERISTICS
FOR 85 CANADIAN MANUFACTURING INDUSTRIES 1974

	(2)	(3)	(4)	(5)	(6)
(1) Nominal Transport	−.039 (−.124)	.366 (.118)	.747 (.742)	−.058 (−.015)	.387 (.183)
(2) Nominal Tariff		.870 (.971)	.076 (.001)	.845 (.896)	.665 (.847)
(3) Total Nominal Protection			.386 (.180)	.835 (.893)	.835 (.892)
(4) Effective Transport				.175 (.072)	.621 (.333)
(5) Effective Tariff					.807 (.964)
(6) Total Effective Protection					

Significance levels: r_s - 1 percent = .282; R - 1 percent = .275
 - 5 percent = .214   - 5 percent = .211

TABLE 7.5

SUMMARY STATISTICS, COMPARISONS OF AUSTRALIAN (1973-74) AND CANADIAN (1974) PROTECTION FOR 85 COMPARABLE MANUFACTURING INDUSTRIES

Protection	Medians		Means[a,b] (weighted)		Means[a,c] (unweighted)		Standard[c] deviations		Wilcoxon test[c]	Variance ratio[c]
	Aust. %	Can. %	Aust. %	Can. %	Aust. %	Can. %	Aust. %	Can. %	Z	F
Nominal Transport	14.4	4.0	13.6	4.4	16.9 (16.3)	4.4 (4.4)	12.9 (12.3)	2.8 (2.7)	7.69 (7.53)	21.07 (20.70)
Nominal Tariff	22.9	10.5	18.8	8.2	22.1 (21.3)	12.1 (10.5)	11.4 (10.6)	11.6 (6.7)	6.44 (6.94)	1.03 (2.54)
Total Nominal Protection	38.1	15.0	32.4	12.5	39.0 (37.6)	16.5 (14.9)	18.0 (16.2)	11.6 (6.8)	7.55 (7.55)	2.42 (5.66)
Effective Transport	10.3	3.3	9.7	4.2	16.1 (14.8)	5.7 (5.4)	24.4 (23.1)	14.0 (14.1)	4.11 (3.81)	3.02 (2.68)
Effective Tariff	32.1	19.5	29.4	16.9	36.5 (35.6)	28.4 (22.0)	25.5 (23.5)	49.5 (18.0)	4.36 (4.81)	3.84 (1.69)
Total Effective Protection	42.5	23.7	39.1	21.2	52.6 (49.8)	34.1 (27.5)	39.1 (35.0)	52.9 (24.2)	4.76 (5.18)	1.82 (2.08)

[a]May not add owing to rounding
[b]Weighted by industry value added
[c]Data in parenthesis omit ACIC 14-16
Significance levels: difference in means $Z = 2.57$ (1 per cent); $F = 1.63$ (1 per cent)
Sources: See text.

beverages and tobacco (ACIC 14-16) are omitted[23] from the computation, the difference between the nominal and effective tariff variables for the two countries becomes greater. As a consequence the differences between the respective means of the total protection variables also increase. Though there is reason to believe that nominal Canadian transport costs are understated,[24] the difference between the means of the respective nominal rates is nevertheless extremely significant. The difference between transport costs, while also highly statistically significant, is not so great. This is to be expected as any understatement will affect both outputs and materials and so tend to be cancelled out in the effective rate calculation. The dispersions of rates around the respective means also tend to be significantly less in Canada than in Australia.[25]

In summary, the data of Table 7.5 suggest that for a given measure the protective structure is more uniform (i.e. tends to vary less) in Canada than in Australia, and that the average level of protection available to Canadian industries is significantly lower. The latter should come as no surprise. In 1970, Australian tariffs on industrial products were two to three times the world average and, more specifically, were higher than those of Japan or any of the Western European and North American countries with which Australia is usually compared. Only New Zealand tariffs were higher, Despite a 25 percent tariff reduction imposed by the government in July, 1973, Australian manufacturing industry still had higher tariff protection in 1975 than the manufacturing industries of Japan, the European Economic Community, Sweden, Canada and the United States (Industries Assistance Commission, 1978, p.78). Comparing the geographic isolation of Australia with the proximity of the United States and its importance to Canadian trade, it would have been most surprising if international transport costs had not been significantly lower for Canada. Despite differences in means and variances, the relative tariff structures of the two countries display substantial similarities: those industries in Australia which are relatively highly protected also tend to be relatively highly protected in Canada. Table 7.6 which contains the matrix of correlation coefficients of the corresponding protection variables in each country, confirms this observation by

---

23. In Canada, the very high effective tariff on the protection of wine and other alcoholic beverages — in excess of 400 percent — alone contributes over 5 percent to the mean of the 85 industries.

24. See Footnote 7.

25. An exception is the nominal tariff, but if ACIC 14-16 are omitted the variances are significantly different for all variables.

TABLE 7.6

MATRIX OF SPEARMAN RANK (r_s) AND PEARSON (R) CORRELATION COEFFICIENTS OF PROTECTION CHARACTERISTICS FOR EIGHT-FIVE COMPARABLE AUSTRALIAN AND CANADIAN MANUFACTURING INDUSTRIES

		(1)	(2)	(3)	(4)	(5)	(6)
(1) Nominal Transport	— r_s	.077					
	— R	.176					
(2) Nominal Tariff	— r_s		.602				
	— R		.544				
(3) Total Nominal Protection	— r_s			.341			
	— R			.361			
(4) Effective Transport	— r_s				.034		
	— R				.166		
(5) Effective Tariff	— r_s					.419	
	— R					.440	
(6) Total Effective Protection	— r_s						.248
	— R						.358

Significance levels: see Table 7.4

showing highly significant rank and simple correlations between the respective nominal and effective tariffs in each country.[26]

There are no significant relationships between the nominal transport cost variables in the two countries, nor between the two countries' effective transport costs. There is no reason to expect that there should be, except for to the extent that transport costs in both countries may be set noncompetitively, and shippers "charged what the traffic will bear" (see Chapter 6.1). The measured transport costs here depend *inter alia* on the composition of imported commodities classified to a particular industry, and their respective values; and the source of the imports, and their mode of transportation. In the case of Canada, international transportation may involve extremely short distances from the United States factory gate to the Canadian border. Thus for Canada, the international transport costs of a given commodity may be less than the cost of its internal transportation and this fact will tend to provide a stimulus rather than a barrier to international trade.

The evidence of this chapter suggests that the means of the two components of total protection examined here — tariffs and transport costs — differ significantly in both countries. Not only is the mean of each protection variable significantly lower in Canada than in Australia, but the relative contribution of transport costs to the total protective barrier in Canada is also substantially lower. In Australia, nominal transport costs

---

26. The omission of ACIC 14-16 makes little difference to the correlation coefficients of the sets of variables.

contribute over 40 percent of the total nominal (unweighted) trade barrier; in Canada, just over one-quarter. In effective rate terms, transport costs provide over 30 percent of the total (unweighted) barrier in Australia; in Canada, just under 17 percent. Clearly, Australian manufacturing has developed behind higher natural and man-made barriers to trade than has the manufacturing sector in Canada. As well, the balance of evidence suggests that international transport costs, especially in Australia, but also in Canada, despite its proximity to the United States, constitute an advantage to import-competing industries.

This, and the preceding chapter have now examined tariffs and transport costs from two points of view: respectively, as a barrier to be surmounted by exports, and as a protective barrier against imports. An aim of succeeding chapters is to examine the possible links between these barriers, and aspects of industrial structure and performance of the two countries which are implied by the theoretical studies examined in chapters 3, and suggested by the survey of empirical literature conducted in chapter 4.

8. A Comparison of Australian and Canadian Manufacturing Industries: A Bivariate Approach

Chapters 3 and 4 examined some likely implications of the effects of trade barriers on aspects of industrial structure and performance. For example, the work of Haberler (1937) and Dornbusch, Fisher and Samuelson (1977) established how, for a given country, both foreign and domestic barriers to trade may affect the range of commodities produced. The theoretical work of Krugman (1979) and the empirical studies of Eastman and Skykolt (1967), West, (1971) and Parry (1977), among others, suggest, *inter alia*, that trade barriers affect ease of entry; the number and size distribution of firms; their diversity of output and level of capacity utilisation; and may provide a motive for foreign direct investment. Any, or all of these influences may affect firms' abilities to exploit economies of scale.

Given the longstanding importance of high levels of tariff protection to the development of manufacturing in Australia and Canada, and the likelihood of significant transport cost barriers to the trade of the two countries, Chapters 6 and 7 provided estimates of the heights of the tariff and transport cost barriers to their exports and imports. Now, a major aim of this, and of the succeeding chapter is to explore the possible links between the estimated barriers to trade, and characteristics of manufacturing industries which are implied by the evidence presented in Chapters 3 and 4, to see if they hold in the cases of Australian and Canadian industries.

Using simple bivariate techniques, this chapter analyzes relationships between measures of protection, foreign participation, industry structure, labour force and other characteristics, and R & D activities in the Australian and Canadian manufacturing sectors. The analysis is conducted in two parts. Essentially, this Chapter analyses, respectively, differences and similarities between the industries comprising the two manufacturing sectors. Section 8.1 makes bivariate comparisons of means and distributions of similarly defined variables in each country to see if there are significant differences in any aspects of the industry characteristics which are used in this, and the succeeding chapter.[1] Section 8.2 uses simple correlation analy-

---

1. A description of some of the problems encountered in deriving a comparable classification of industries, together with the concordance of Australian and Canadian activities appears in Appendix 8.1. The basic census definitions of terms used in each country, and a full description and the sources of the variables used in the following analyses may be found in Appendix 8.2, while Appendix 8.3 provides an outline of the distributions of activity — in terms of value added and employment — within the respective manufacturing sectors.

sis and has two main objectives: first, to assess whether there are relationships in each country between variables measuring protection, and other
characteristics of industries; and second, to see if the relationships so
discerned are consistent for the manufacturing industries of both countries.

The selection of the characteristics which are compared, and the possible
relationships which are examined in this chapter and in the one which
follows, is in some degree arbitrary. There are two justifications for the
selections. First, and most important, the characteristics examined in these
two chapters are, wherever possible, those which the literature suggests are
important in either affecting or in some way "measuring" the structure and
performance of industries. The second is the more prosaic consideration of
the availability (or lack) of data. From Chapter 4 the types of characteristics
which may be of interest include those likely to be associated with the
exploitation of economies of scale, with the use of production techniques
and technology, and with foreign participation in domestic markets. Of the
characteristics examined in this chapter, it is the differences in the sizes of
firms and establishments which are perhaps most striking. For example,
compared with industries in Canada, the results show that on average, in
Australian manufacturing enterprises and establishments are significantly
smaller, and furthermore, the simple correlation analysis reveals inverse
relationships in both countries between the height of tariff barriers and all
the concepts of scale economies — firm-, plant-, and product- — discussed
in Chapter 4. The industrial organisation literature suggests that results
such as these, and such findings as the greater "openness" of Canadian
industries to international trade, are linked with the efficiency of manufacturing activities. In these respects, the results of this chapter imply that
Australian manufacturing industries compare unfavourably with those in
Canada.

8.1 Bivariate Comparisons of Means and Distributions of Characteristics of Australian and Canadian Manufacturing Industries

There are fewer comparisons in this section than in the following section of
this chapter. Here the question of comparability of data definitions is
paramount. In the simple correlation analyses of Section 8.2, given measures of the same basic phenomenon may differ between the two countries.
However for each country the definitions are consistent and as typically a
number of variables have been used as measures of a given phenomenon, no
great emphasis is put on the relationship between any single pair of
variables.

In this analysis however, every effort has been made to ensure the strict
comparability of the data. As a result there are some important items
omitted, particularly comparisons of the means and distributions of the

measures of foreign control, labour skills and research and development in each country. The first is a particularly important omission. While there is generally a close correspondence between the census definitions in each country (see Appendix 8.2), foreign control in Australia is, in brief, the foreign holding of at least 25 percent of the paid-up shares in an enterprise; the criterion for Canada is 50 percent. Nevertheless, it is interesting to note that despite the higher shareholding requirement in Canada, the means of the foreign control variables are all significantly greater in that country than in Australia. On average, approximately one-third of firms comprising this study are foreign controlled (as defined) in Australia, compared with approximately one-half in Canada, using that country's higher foreign control criterion. Had the definitions been strictly comparable, the differences are almost certain to have been even greater. A likely explanation for the high level of foreign control may lie in the relatively short lines of communication between Canada and the United States, the major source of Canada's foreign direct investment. This should permit not only the easier movement of goods, but also technology and managerial practices compared with Australia.

The attributes to be compared and which have been chosen so as to be independent of exchange rates are grouped under five headings:[2] (i) industry structure; (ii) labour force characteristics; (iii) foreign trade characteristics (iv) the use of natural resources; and (v) other characteristics. The Tables of Section 8.1 contain the means, standard deviations, Wilcoxon matched pairs signed-rank test for differences in central tendency,[3] the Kolmorogorov-Smirnov (K-S) two-sample test of whether two independent samples have been drawn from the same population (or from populations with the same distribution),[4] and the F-test for the equality of variances, for the 170 (i.e., 2 x 85) industries comprising the Australian and Canadian manufacturing sectors.

Industry structures

Table 8.1 compares the means and distributions of variables reflecting

2. The classification of the variables of this study into one or another of these categories tends to be arbitrary.

3. The t-test for equality of means was not reported as it relies on the equality of variances. Nevertheless the results of t-tests were, without exception, consistent with the results of the non-parametric tests.

4. The K-S two-sample test is concerned with the agreement between two sets of sample values: "If the two samples have in fact been drawn from the same population distribution, then the cumulative distributions of both samples may be expected to be fairly close to each other, in as much they both should show only random deviations from the population distribution. If the sample cumulative distributions are "too far apart" at any point, this suggests that the samples come from different populations" (Siegel, 1956, pp. 127-8).

TABLE 8.1

COMPARISONS OF MEANS AND DISTRIBUTIONS:
INDUSTRY STRUCTURE CHARACTERISTICS

Variable Name	Means		St. Dev.		Wilcoxon — signs test (diff. in central tendency) Z	Aust. Vs. Can. (K-S Test) Z	Variance Ratio F
	Aust.	Can.	Aust.	Can.			
CONC8	.64	.67	.23	.73	.06	.69	9.45
DIVRAT	.14	.39	.08	.18	7.37	4.98	4.13
EMP10	42.22	29.43	22.49	20.51	5.77	2.07	1.20
EMP20	56.55	43.62	24.55	26.67	5.41	1.99	1.17
EMP50	71.35	62.12	22.64	31.61	4.92	1.68	2.05
EMPLG	18.45	25.21	19.33	31.74	5.03	1.53	2.69
EMPENT	194.04	271.62	355.30	527.70	4.44	1.45	2.20
EMPEST	115.35	170.14	175.67	309.20	4.83	1.45	3.09
ESTENT	1.30	1.34	.35	.75	1.06	1.15	4.62
INTSPEC	.44	.43	.10	.11	.91	.76	1.28
LABINT	.53	.47	.10	.10	5.94	2.14	1.23
PRODEST	88.22	122.44	138.97	224.15	4.10	1.53	2.60
RMES50	.10	.12	.06	.14	.30	.61	4.94
SMALLE	.89	.88	.12	.17	.46	.53	1.81

aspects of the respective industrial structures of the Australian and Canadian manufacturing sectors. The results of these bivariate comparisons suggest that there are a number of significant differences in aspects of the structures of the Australian and Canadian manufacturing sectors. On average, Australian manufacturing is characterised by firms and establishments employing comparatively small numbers of employees (EMP10, EMP20, EMP50, EMPLG, EMPENT, EMPEST, PRODEST) and which use relatively labour-intensive production processes (LABINT). When compared with Canadian enterprises, those in Australia tend to limit their production to their primary activity, and not to diversify to other industries (DIVRAT). When there are significantly different variances, in each case it is higher in Canada than it is in Australia, implying more uniform industry structure in Australian in terms of the criteria of Table 8.1.

Of particular interest are the findings concerning the average sizes of enterprises and establishments in the two countries. While the development of an Australian manufacturing sector characterised by relatively labour-intensive, small firms is probably the result of a complex of many influences, it seems likely that the protected nature of the Australian market may make an important contribution to the formation of industries with such characteristics. Thus, through its effects on relative prices, tariff and/or transport costs protection may increase the size of the *domestic* market available to local firms[5] encourage entry and permit the profitable operation of larger numbers of small firms than would be possible in the absence of protection in a manner suggested by the standard partial equilibrium analysis of tariff protection which was discussed in Chapter 3.1, and by Krugman's (1979) results which were discussed in Chapter 3.3. Indeed, despite the obvious disparity in the sizes of the economies of the two countries, there are on average in each industry, significantly more enterprises and establishments[6] in Australia than in Canada: in Australia 387 and 429, respectively; in Canada 324 and 359. The comparative fragmentation of markets in Australia implied by these data suggest a typical industry structure which may inhibit participant firms' abilities to fully exploit the economies of scale which may be available to them if fewer firms were in the industry.

Labour forces

Table 8.2 shows that there are significant differences in the central tendencies of the two sets of variables in all but the case of percentage of

5. It may however restrict the size of *total* market available to domestic producers. This point is discussed in Section 8.2.

6. Significant at the 5 percent level.

TABLE 8.2

COMPARISONS OF MEANS AND DISTRIBUTIONS: LABOUR FORCE CHARACTERISTICS

Variable Name	Means		St. Dev.		Wilcoxon — signs test (diff. in central tendency) Z	Aust. Vs. Can. (K-S Test) Z	Variance Ratio F
	Aust.	Can.	Aust.	Can.			
EDI	16.16	19.33	4.98	5.42	5.72	1.42	1.18
ED2	3.17	3.62	2.03	2.56	2.96	1.07	1.58
FEMP	.27	.23	.18	.16	4.84	1.07	1.18
FEPROD	.20	.16	.17	.16	5.65	.84	1.20
FMIGRPC	11.07	8.38	1.20	.91	7.68	3.75	1.74
FPROD	.62	.52	.24	.28	6.34	1.07	1.41
INNOV	.94	.91	.06	.04	3.38	1.61	2.46
MIGRPC	39.28	20.21	9.70	8.12	7.74	3.98	1.42
PEMPPC	73.28	72.18	9.37	11.75	1.11	.61	1.57

production employees to total employment (PEMPPC). The differences suggest that in comparison with Canada manufacturing industries in Australia are characterised by higher levels of female participation, by larger proportions of their workforces born overseas, and by lower proportions of their workforces with education to matriculation level (ED1), or with University of similar tertiary qualifications (ED2). Fully consistent with the last two results, there is evidence of "lower quality" management, and perhaps less innovative activity in Australia than in Canada (INNOV).[7]

The higher proportion of females in the Australian manufacturing industry workforce is, to the writer, at first glance a surprising result as the proportion of women of persons who were "economically active" at the time of the 1971 Census conducted in both countries, was higher in Canada,[8] as was the proportion of women participants in the total workforce.[9] That the proportion of women in Australian manufacturing is relatively high stems from the different distributions of economic activity in the two countries. In 1971, manufacturing employment constituted 22.9 percent of total employment in Australia, but only 19.4 percent in Canada. The largest difference, however, is in the relative importance of community, social, and personal services in Canada. While in both countries approximately one-half of employees in this sector are women, in Canada the sector employs 30.4 percent of the total workforce, in Australia only 18.8 percent (I.L.O., 1976, pp. 67, 156). To a lesser extent, *within* the manufacturing sectors, the relative size of the sectors of manufacturing which could be characterised (perhaps chauvinistically) as most suited to the employment of unskilled women (e.g., packaging, light assembly and machining tasks, particularly in food products, clothing and footwear) tend to be larger in Australia. (See Appendix 8.3). Thus it would appear from the data of Table 8.2 that there are relatively more opportunities for women in the manufacturing industry workforce in Australia, and that they are likely to be more commonly engaged in activities requiring fewer skills and less education.

The higher proportion of the Australian manufacturing industry workforce born overseas which may be observed from Table 8.2 stems in great part from the simple fact that there is a higher proportion of such persons

---

7. Reflected by the lower mean of INNOV in Canada than in Australia. "Non-production employees may represent higher paid echelons of management and research, or may represent "middle management", holding responsibility for supervising routine operators, rather than engaging in innovative activity" (Oksanen and Williams, 1978, p. 97).

8. Women comprised 26.7 percent of those "economically active" in Australia and 28.4 percent in Canada (International Labour Organisation (I.L.O), 1976, pp. 19, 45).

9. Women participants in Canada comprised 34.6 of the total workforce compared with 31.7 percent in Australia (I.L.O. 1976, pp. 67, 156).

resident in Australia.[10] In both countries there is disproportionate number of immigrants in manufacturing and this is likely to be a result of the greater availability of unskilled occupations requiring little formal education and/or language skill in that sector of the economy than in others such as wholesale and retail trade, and community, social and personal services.[11] Additionally, within the respective manufacturing sectors, Australian industries tend to be characterised by the greater relative size (in terms of employment) of industries comprising simple assembly/fabrication tasks,[12] and from the previous section there is evidence that Australian industries on average use more labour-intensive methods than those in Canada.

Taken together, these results suggest a productive area for future research in applying a model within the Heckscher-Ohlin framework which looks at the Australian immigration programme, its effects on the relative stock of (low skill) labour, wage rates and the labour intensity of production techniques. Among the questions which arise are (i), has the Australian migration programme created a relative abundance of low-skill, low wage labour and caused the comparatively labour intensive production techniques observed in Australia?; (ii), over time, have these activities become less able to compete with imports, and have they come to need and then to rely on high levels of protection?; (iii), thus, has Australia's immigration programme since World War II made a significant contribution to the apparent need for wide scale protection of manufacturing?

Foreign trade

Table 8.3 contains data which suggest that on average, Australian industries are less open to foreign trade than are their Canadian counterparts. The means of the ratios of exports to turnover and imports to turnover (EXTO and IMTO, respectively) for the two countries are significantly different and are each higher for Canada than for Australia. Canadian industries are also characterised by greater intra-industry trade (INTRA) suggesting that Canadian firms are, within a given industry, on average more specialised in production than are Australian industries (Grubel and Lloyd, 1975).

The finding of a higher level of intra-industry trade in Canada is consistent with the theoretical work of Helpman (1981), who found that such trade

---

10. In 1971 20.2 percent of Australian residents were immigrants compared with 15.3 percent in Canada (ABS, 1971; Statistics Canada, 1971).
11. Together these comprise 39 percent of the workforce in Australia and 45 percent in Canada (I.L.O. 1976, pp. 65, 156).
12. e.g., In basic metal industries, transportation (particularly in motor vehicles and associated industries) and clothing footwear.

". . . tends to be larger between countries with close factor proportions than between countries with far apart factor proportions" (p. 337). Given the proximity of the United States to Canada, and its dominance of Canada's trade, it could be reasonably expected that the U.S. and Canada will have relatively "close factor proportions". This, *ceteris paribus*, should therefore lead to a higher level of intra-industry trade in Canada, than in isolated Australia, where no one country similarly dominates trade, and where trading partners may be expected to have a comparatively wide range of factor proportions.

It appears reasonable to interpret many of these findings as a reflection of greater opportunities for international trade in Canada owing to its proximity to the United States, its major trading partner; a result consistent with Australia's relatively low ratio of trade to GDP observed in Chapter 1.2 and which will be further discussed in Chapter 9. It is possible that there is further encouragement to international trade provided by the likelihood of relatively high internal transportation costs (of which no explicit account is taken here). Canada is a country in which distance from the major U.S. markets on the East Coast and in the mid-West are less than those from many Canadian markets, particularly those on the West coast.

Neither of the measures of industry trade balance (TRADBAL nor EXIMTO) are significantly different in terms of either their central tendencies nor their distributions in each country. The distributions of the ratio of exports to imports (EXIMP) in the respective countries are characterised by a significantly greater dispersion of Australia, indicating widely differing ratios across industries.[13] The data thus reflect are more "uniform" trade pattern across Canadian industries compared with those of Australia. To the extent that Australia's isolation is reflected, *ceteris paribus*, in higher international transport costs than for Canada, these results suggest that such costs serve not only to protect industries from import competition, but to limit their export potential.

Use of resources

The data of Table 8.4 indicate that there are no significant differences in the use of replenishable, non-replenishable, and total natural resources (NATRES1, NATRES2, and NATRES3, respectively), by Australian and Canadian manufacturing industries. That the proportion of electricity and

---

13. That the average ratio of exports to imports in Australia is approximately 3:1 stems mainly from the high levels of exports (and low imports) of the food group of industries and particularly of meat products. If the food group of industries (ACIC 1-12) is omitted, the means of the ratios are .230 for Australia and 1.225 for Canada.

TABLE 8.3

COMPARISONS OF MEANS AND DISTRIBUTIONS:
FOREIGN TRADE CHARACTERISTICS

Variable Name	Means		St. Dev.		Wilcoxon — signs test (diff. in central tendency) Z	Aust. Vs. Can. (K-S Test) Z	Variance Ratio F
	Aust.	Can.	Aust.	Can.			
EXIMP	3.11	1.30	10.77	2.89	.85	.92	13.83
EXIMPTO	-.14	-.16	.34	.46	1.11	.92	1.87
EXTO	.07	.16	.14	.21	5.01	1.91	2.30
IMPTO	.22	.32	.35	.48	3.88	1.45	1.87
INTRA	40.64	47.94	27.38	27.34	2.04	1.22	1.00
TRADBAL	-.33	-.30	.56	.50	.79	.84	1.26

TABLE 8.4

COMPARISONS OF MEANS AND DISTRIBUTIONS:
RESOURCE USE

Variable Name	Means		St. Dev.		Wilcoxon Z	K-S Test Z	Variance Ratio F
	Aust.	Can.	Aust.	Can.			
FUELINT	.05	.04	.09	.13	3.26	1.61	1.30
NATRES1	.06	.06	.15	.16	1.49	1.05	.99
NATRES2	.04	.03	.10	.12	.72	1.39	.53
NATRES3	.10	.09	.17	.19	1.30	1.21	.92

all other fuels in total material usage (FUELINT) is higher in Australia than in Canada is surprising, in view of the extreme winters in that country. No one group of industries dominates this data set in either country and whether, for example, the result reflects a relative inefficient use of fuels or their lower prices in Australia, or the use of different production techniques (these are not of course, mutually exclusive), cannot be determined from the available information.

Other industry characteristics

Table 8.5 contains the remaining comparably defined data for Australia and Canada. These data were not easily classifiable in terms of the categories of data so far used in this analysis. From the Table it may be seen that the average ratio of stocks to turnover (STKTO) is higher for Australia than for Canada, though the distributions in each country are not significantly different. Higher stock holdings in Australia is the expected result, and reflect the likely necessity of maintaining large stock holdings because of Australia's relative isolation. The higher values of both wages as a proportion of value added (WVA), and wages as a proportion of total wages and salaries (WWSAL) suggest greater "production worker intensity" of Australian industries, while the relative means of PCM reflect higher average ratios of gross operating surplus to turnover for manufacturing industries in Canada.

8.2 Bivariate Correlation Analysis of Characteristics of Australian and Canadian Manufacturing Industries

The analysis to follow is selective. The full correlation matrices produced using all the comparative data of this study (i.e., Pearson and Spearman correlation coefficients for each country) each have nearly 8,000 elements (88 x 88 variables). Consequently this section will look only at representative results[14] bearing directly on broad areas which are of primary interest: first, protection and its relationships with aspects of industry structure and performance, labour force characteristics, foreign participation in domestic markets, technology and the size of markets; and second, the relationships between foreign direct participation in the respective manufacturing sectors and certain industry characteristics. The prime objective is to discern areas of consistency of relationships between industry attributes in both countries.

---

14. The use of slightly different measures of the same basic phenomenon (e.g., foreign control through FCONEMPC, FCONTOPC and FCONVAPC) showed highly consistent results. Not all results have been included owing to space limitations. See also Chapter 9.2.

TABLE 8.5

COMPARISONS OF MEANS AND DISTRIBUTIONS: OTHER INDUSTRY CHARACTERISTICS

Variable Name	Means		St. Dev.		Wilcoxon — signs test (diff. in central tendency) Z	Aust. Vs. Can. (K-S Test) Z	Variance Ratio F
	Aust.	Can.	Aust.	Can.			
STKTO	.16	.15	.09	.08	2.00	.69	1.09
WVA	.38	.31	.10	.10	6.32	2.22	1.05
WWSAL	.70	.66	.09	.11	5.20	1.22	1.55
PCM	.20	.22	.05	.07	4.29	1.30	1.65

Significance levels: Z - 1 per cent = 2.57: F - 1 per cent = 1.63
- 5 per cent = 1.96   - 5 per cent = 1.44

Tables 8.6, 8.7 and 8.8 contain the correlation coefficients of the variables of interest, with, respectively, tariff protection, transport cost protection, and total protection. Coefficients of relatively low levels of significance have generally not been reproduced. An analysis of the Tables suggests that there is an association in both countries between aspects of the structures of industries and the nature and heights of their protective barriers. Whether, in the case of tariffs, protection "causes" the structure or structure "causes" the protection is a moot point. As Caves (1976) has pointed out, there is reason to expect some degree of two-way causation.[15] On the basis of the evidence, extracts of which appear in Table 8.6, it can be said that there is an association between tariffs and certain characteristics of industry structure in both Australia and Canada. Relatively high tariff industries are characterised by intra-establishment diversification (INTSPEC) rather than (especially in Australia) diversification across industries (DIVRAT); by firms of small size, however measured;[16] and by enterprises with few establishments (ESTENT). In effect, the concepts of scale economies discussed in Chapter 4 — firm-, plant- and product- — are all inversely correlated with tariff protection. With one very important exception, the transport cost variables do not yield significant relationships. The exception is the direct relationship of the transport cost measures with the ratio of establishments to enterprises (ESTENT) shown in Table 8.7. High transport costs (both intra- and international) are known to encourage multiplant operations, and this result is consistent with that knowledge. It seems likely that the international transport cost variables used in the present study may, in this case, also capture some of the influence of domestic transport costs.

Foreign participation

Foreign participation (FCONVAPC, FCONEMPC, FPEN) in the Australian and Canadian manufacturing sectors is inversely correlated with both tariffs and transport costs. There is no evidence supporting the hypothesis that protection encourages foreign firms to establish manufacturing facilities behind the protective barrier. Quite the contrary: in the case of tariffs, the necessity for high tariffs may be viewed as an indication of the

---

15. This problem is further discussed in Chapter 9.2.
16. The signs of all the "size" variables (TOENT, TOEST, VAENT, VAEST, EMPENT, EMPEST, EMPLG, RMES50) show consistent inverse relationships with tariff protection. However, often the significance level is relatively low and as a result, the correlation coefficients have not been included in Table 8.6.

TABLE 8.6

PEARSON (P) AND SPEARMAN RANK (S) CORRELATION COEFFICIENTS:
TARIFF PROTECTION AND CHARACTERISTICS OF AUSTRALIAN AND CANADIAN
MANUFACTURING INDUSTRIES

		INTSPEC		DIVRAT		ESTENT		FCONVAPC		FCONEMPC	
		Aust.	Can.	Aust.	Can.	Aust.	Can.	Aust.	Can.	Aust.	Can.
NTARIFF	P	.406	.318	-.194	.103	-.138	.110	-.127	-.222	-.091	-.220
	S	.318	.262	-.157	.063	-.342	-.226	-.113	-.147	-.082	-.164
ETARIFF	P	.134	.208	-.167	.112	-.086	.122	-.089	-.194	-.040	-.176
	S	.111	.029	-.186	.183	-.239	-.119	-.123	-.259	-.092	-.262

		FPEN		SKILL1		ED2		AWAGE		MIGRPC	
		Aust.	Can.	Aust.	Can.	Aust.	Can.	Aust.	Can.	Aust.	Can.
NTARIFF	P	-.300	-.212	-.243	-.233	-.194	-.126	-.215	-.136	.230	-.145
	S	-.186	-.349	-.278	-.271	-.212	-.206	-.340	-.399	.192	.103
ETARIFF	P	-.335	-.134	-.230	-.145	-.213	-.164	-.238	-.007	.141	-.219
	S	-.174	-.387	-.308	-.288	-.261	-.191	-.285	-.388	.206	.017

		FEMP		PEMPPC		RDEXVA		CAPINT		NATRES2	
		Aust.	Can.	Aust.	Can.	Aust.	Can.	Aust.	Can.	Aust.	Can.
NTARIFF	P	.307	.236	.097	-.012	.154	-.195	.321	-.145	-.294	-.178
	S	.306	.383	.170	.179	.111	-.277	.377	-.340	-.430	-.320
ETARIFF	P	.238	-.055	.076	-.085	-.038	-.209	.198	.005	-.143	-.089
	S	.236	.296	.183	.250	.048	-.280	.265	-.188	-.337	-.217

		EXTO		MKTSIZE	
		Aust.	Can.	Aust.	Can.
NTARIFF	P	-.446	-.166	-.155	-.237
	S	-.327	-.407	-.099	-.237
NTARIFF	P	-.366	-.030	-.165	-.175
	S	-.320	-.304	-.143	-.311

Significance levels: 1 per cent R = .256; r_s = .254
5 per cent R = .179; r_s = .179
10 per cent R = .140; r_s = .140

TABLE 8.7

PEARSON (P) AND SPEARMAN RANK (S) CORRELATION COEFFICIENTS
TRANSPORT COST PROTECTION AND CHARACTERISTICS OF AUSTRALIAN AND CANADIAN
MANUFACTURING INDUSTRIES

		ESTENT		FCONVAPC		FCONEMPC		FPEN	
		Aust.	Can.	Aust.	Can.	Aust.	Can.	Aust.	Can.
NTRANS	P	.345	.325	-.198	-.103	-.180	-.085	-.318	-.154
	S	.163	.055	-.240	-.108	-.242	-.078	-.416	-.139
ETRANS	P	.272	.151	-.167	-.119	-.142	-.119	-.298	-.158
	S	.094	.040	-.232	-.145	-.207	-.120	-.372	-.176

		RDEXVA		EXTO		MKTSIZE	
		Aust.	Can.	Aust.	Can.	Aust.	Can.
NTRANS	P	-.246	-.180	-.307	-.061	-.145	.012
	S	-.325	-.086	-.466	.050	-.405	.055
ETRANS	P	-.242	-.119	-.299	-.039	-.109	-.014
	S	-.327	-.200	-.451	.058	-.045	.102

Significance levels: see Table 8.6

115

TABLE 8.8

PEARSON (P) AND SPEARMAN RANK (S) CORRELATION COEFFICIENTS
TOTAL PROTECTION AND CHARACTERISTICS OF AUSTRALIAN AND CANADIAN
MANUFACTURING INDUSTRIES

		FCONVAPC		FCONEMPC		FPEN	
		Aust.	Can.	Aust.	Can.	Aust.	Can.
NPROT	P	-.222	-.247	-.187	-.241	-.417	-.250
	S	-.271	-.227	-.224	-.239	-.411	-.394
EPROT	P	-.162	-.215	-.115	-.196	-.339	-.169
	S	-.146	-.244	-.111	-.240	-.282	-.345

		RDEXVA		EXTO		MKTSIZE	
		Aust.	Can.	Aust.	Can.	Aust.	Can.
NPROT	P	-.079	-.239	-.502	-.181	-.202	-.234
	S	-.097	-.321	-.524	-.324	-.178	-.223
EPROT	P	-.176	-.168	-.425	-.039	-.175	-.169
	S	-.202	-.356	-.430	-.206	-.164	-.192

Significance levels: see Table. 8.6

"unsuitability" of an activity for the potential host country environment (e.g., because of the relative lack of appropriate factor endowments) and this lack of suitability may consequently discourage foreign firms from direct participation. Indeed, typical characteristics of multinationals — high technology, large size, capital intensity — are all inversely associated with tariffs. It therefore appears likely that multinationals have little affinity with activities requiring high levels of protection.

The inverse relationship between foreign participation and transport costs has two aspects. First, to the extent that distance and transport costs are positively correlated, transport costs may reflect the geographic horizon of potential foreign investors. If geographic proximity encourages direct foreign investment (lines of communication for example, are short), geographic remoteness (and high transport costs) may well discourage it. The significance of the transport cost variables for Australia, and their relative lack of significance for Canada (though the coefficients are negatively signed) lends support to this hypothesis. Second, high *ad valorem* transport costs are associated with products of low unit value. Again relying on broad evidence of the relative sophistication and high unit values of products produced by multinational firms engaged in manufacturing, such firms may simply have no interest in participating in markets for low unit-value products. From Table 8.8 the evidence in both countries suggests that the effects of the two barriers to trade are cumulative: that the total barrier to trade (NPROT, EPROT) tends to be more significantly (negatively) associated with foreign participation (as either direct participation (FCONVAPC, FCONEMPC) or as total participation (FPEN) than are its components. In Canada for example, transport costs considered alone are apparently "unimportant", but when they are added to tariffs, there is an increase in the level of significance of the correlation coefficients of the resulting total protection variable and between foreign participation, when compared with the coefficients of either of the components of total protection. In short, high total trade barriers are associated with low foreign participation in both countries' manufacturing sectors.

It should be stressed, however, that a cross-sectional analysis of the type conducted here cannot ascertain if foreign investment in an industry under protection is higher than it would be in its absence. The Studies cited in Chapter 4 based on survey data (e.g., Brash, 1966; Johns and Hogan, 1967) all suggest that this is the case. It may be that firms did move behind the tariff wall initially, but as time passed, may have rationalised their operations internationally, or may have found it to their advantage to work for lower tariffs in order to leave their world operations less hindered.[17] In any

---

17. The author is indebted to Bruce Wilkinson for his point.

event, to fully explore the questions raised in this section needs the specification and test of a model within a formal theoretical framework. While the results here point to likely areas of fruitful research in the future, unfortunately this study must leave these questions unresolved.

Labour forces

While there are no significant correlations between the characteristics of the respective labour forces and transport costs, there are significant associations between those variables and tariff protection. The inferences of Table 8.6 are quite clear: a typical employee of an Australian or Canadian industry sheltering behind relatively high tariff barriers is an unskilled (SKILL1), poorly educated (ED2), poorly paid (AVWAGE), migrant (MIGRPC) female (FEMP) production worker (PEMPPC).

Research and development

For Australia there is a negative relationship between R & D expenditure (RDEXVA) and transport cost protection, and a (weak) positive relationship with tariffs. However, the two components of the total protective barrier, when added (NPROT, EPROT), are characterised by negative signs. In Canada both tariffs and transport costs act in the same (negative) direction. The results are consistent with the hypothesis that insulation from foreign competitive pressures provided by protection may also insulate firms from the need to engage in R & D activities in an effort to forestall such pressures.[18]

Production techniques and resource use

Table 8.6 provides evidence of the expected negative relationship between tariff protection and capital intensity. Activities protected by low tariffs tend to be capital intensive (CAPINT), and to be characterised by relatively intensive use of natural resources, particularly non-replenishable resources (NATRES2). In neither country has it been possible to discern any significant relationship between transport costs and the measures reflecting production techniques and the use of resources.

Foreign trade

The data of Table 8.6 reveal an inverse relationship between tariffs and export "performance" (EXTO) in Australia and Canada. It seems apparent

---

18. High levels of R & D are also likely to be associated with "high quality" capital and labour. Thus it is suggested here that for a "given" quality of capital and labour, R & D expenditures may be less, the lower are competitive pressures.

that the characteristics of protected industries are incompatible with the ability to adequately compete on foreign markets. As no one country dominates as a destination for Australian exports in the way in which the United States does for Canada,[19] it is difficult to obtain a representative measure of foreign trade barriers. There is no significant relationship between Australian exports and U.S. tariffs when they are used as a proxy for such barriers. For Canada, however, there is a strong negative correlation between U.S. tariffs and all measures of the export performances of Canadian industries.[20]

The studies examined in Chapters 5 and 6 suggested that transport costs are an important inhibiting influence on trade flows. The correlation coefficients between NTRANS and ETRANS, and EXTO and FPEN in Table 8.7 show evidence of the expected negative relationships, though especially for Australia. Other variables reflecting the export performance of industries in both countries which have not been included in the tables were also generally inversely correlated with transport costs, but at relatively low levels of significance.

For Australia, the freight charges for exports derived in Chapters 6 and contained in Table 6.3 are also consistently negatively correlated with all aspects export performance, but again the levels of significance are often comparatively low.[21]

Though for any given set of variables this correlation analysis tends to provide only weak evidence of the inhibiting influence of trade barriers on

---

19. As has previously been noted the United States during the study period was the destination of 70 percent of Canada's exports. For Australia, while in 1973/74, New Zealand, Japan and the U.S. were the major destinations of Australian exports, accounting for 48 percent of the total, eight countries received in total 70 percent of Australian exports (Jackson, 1975, Vol. 2, p. 147).

20. The correlations coefficients between the two measures of U.S. tariff protection defined in Appendix 8.2 and the Canadian trade variables are:

		EXIMP	EXTO	TRADBAL	EXIMPTO	INTRA
USTAR 61	P	-.132	-.254	-.284	-.267	-.437
	S	-.433	-.298	-.430	-.335	-.435
USTAR 75	P	-.183	-.225	-.297	-.223	-.305
	S	-.375	-.156	-.372	-.355	-.356

Significance levels: See Table 8.6.

21. The following is an extract from the Correlation matrices:

		EXTO	RTRADBAL	EXIMPTO
Total Export	P	-.036	-.038	-.052
Freight Rate	S	-.130	-.291	-.299
Rel. Increase	P	-.069	-.040	-.080
in F. Rate due	S	-.338	-.257	-.322
to Distance				

Significance levels: See Table 8.6

exports, the consistency of the results tends to provide a clearer picture. Taken together they suggest that high levels of protection (both tariff and transport costs) are associated with poor trade performance and this may be at least a partial function of industry structures built up behind high protective barriers to imports. The results also shed light on the other side of the problem. For Canada they clearly show the inimical effect of foreign (U.S.) tariffs on exports, while for Australia, transport costs for exports apparently also act as an inhibiting influence foreign trade performance.[22]

Size of markets

The work surveyed in Chapters 3 and 4 suggests that both domestic and foreign protection affects the size of the total market available to a domestic producer: domestic protection increases market size and foreign protection reduces it. Here, U.S. tariffs (USTAR75) have been used as a proxy for foreign trade barriers facing both Australia and Canada. Inverse relationships found between market size (MKTSIZE) and USTAR75 for Australia and Canada[23] are consistent with the hypothesis that foreign trade barriers restrict the size of the total market available to domestic producers. However, the inverse relationships between domestic tariff and transport cost protection, and market size shown in Tables 8.6, 8.7 and 8.8 are apparently at odds with Eastman and Stykolt's conclusions (see Chapter 3.3). This simple correlation analysis can in no way be construed as a test of their hypothesis. Rather, a test of the hypothesis should attempt to answer the question, "Is the size of the market with (domestic) protection, larger than it would be in its absence?" Unfortunately, the data available do not enable an answer to be provided. It is suggested that these results reflect in large part the significant inverse relationships between domestic protection and the ratio of exports to turnover found for both countries, which were discussed earlier.

---

22. While this is submitted to be a reasonable interpretation of the results, it should be viewed with some caution. Total export freight charges from Table 6.3 and nominal transport costs protection from Table 7.1 are highly correlated, and consequently is not possible to truely separate the possible influence transport costs for imports in providing an environment encouraging inefficiency and poor trade performance, and transport costs as a barrier which must be surmounted by exporters.

23.

		USTAR75	
		Aust.	Can.
MKTSIZE	P	-.160	-.232
	S	-.283	-.321

Significance levels: See Table 8.6

120

Other Characteristics of Australian and Canadian Manufacturing
Industries
  Size of markets

From Table 8.9 for both countries, but particularly for Australia, there is evidence of an inverse relationship between market size and industrial concentration (CONC8). Barriers to entry in Australian industries characterised by large markets may therefore be relatively low, and as a consequence it may be difficult for a few relatively large firms to obtain positions of market dominance. However the coefficients of the variables measuring the absolute sizes of enterprises and establishments in terms of turnover (TOENT, TOEST), value added (VAENT, VAEST) and employment (EMPENT, EMPEST) are all positive and almost without exception, are highly significant. They imply a clear direct relationship between the size of the available market and the sizes of enterprises and establishments in both countries. For Australia there are no consistently strong relationships between market size and aspects of industry, enterprise, and establishment specialisation. The correlation coefficients suggest at relatively low levels of significance, that firms participating in large markets are characterised by specialisation within establishments (INTSPEC) and high levels of intra-industry trade (INTRA); while there is a positive rank correlation between the size of markets (MKTSIZE) and the tendency for firms to be characterised by multiple establishments (ESTENT).

The results for Canada are much more clear-cut. There are direct relationships between MKTSIZE and all measures of firm and establishments size (TOENT, TOEST, VAEST, EMPENT, EMPEST). Further, they suggest that larger markets are characterised by firms which tend to not diversify into other than their primary activity (DIVRAT), and by high levels of intra-industry trade (INTRA). As in Australia, the rank correlation coefficients suggest that there is a positive relationship between market size and the operation of multi-establishment firms. Put simply, in Canada there is a direct association between market size and enterprise and establishment size, and the degree of industry, enterprise, and establishment specialisation; and for firms to be in a position to exploit economies of scale which may accrue to multi-establishment enterprises.

In summary, these results imply that Australian, and particularly Canadian industries characterised by relatively large markets are typified by large enterprises, and (multiple) establishments, and by specialisation rather than diversification of production. The results are consistent with those of the studies examined in Chapter 4 which suggest that there is a direct association between market size, and the ability of firms to exploit all facets of economies of scale.

TABLE 8.9

PEARSON (P) AND SPEARMAN RANK (S) CORRELATION COEFFICIENTS:
MARKET SIZE AND CHARACTERISTICS OF AUSTRALIAN AND CANADIAN MANUFACTURING INDUSTRIES

		CONC8		TOENT		TOEST		VAENT	
		Aust.	Can.	Aust.	Can.	Aust.	Can.	Aust.	Can.
MKTSIZE	P	-.252	-.063	.189	.597	.213	.605	.131	.491
	S	-.210	-.142	.160	.219	.166	.235	.157	.184

		VAEST		EMPENT		EMPEST		PRODEST	
		Aust.	Can.	Aust.	Can.	Aust.	Can.	Aust.	Can.
MKTSIZE	P	.162	.575	.208	.404	.251	.501	.249	.484
	S	.160	.198	.160	.163	.162	.174	.155	.132

		DIVRAT		INTSPEC		INTRA		ESTENT	
		Aust.	Can.	Aust.	Can.	Aust.	Can.	Aust.	Can.
MKTSIZE	P	.020	-.169	-.173	-.274	.159	.234	.089	-.001
	S	.124	-.218	-.115	-.171	-.107	.224	.182	.226

Significance levels: see Table 8.6

Foreign participation

Not surprisingly the correlation coefficients of Table 8.10 suggest that high levels of direct foreign participation are typical of industries characterised by industrial concentration (CONC8), relatively large enterprises and (multiple) establishments (EMPLG, VAENT, VAEST, ESTENT), and capital intensity (CAPINT, LABINT), than are industries more dominated by locally owned enterprises. Industries with levels of foreign participation are typified by highly skilled (SKILL1), educated (ED2), and well-paid workforces (AVWAGE), and particularly in Canada, the relatively large expenditure of funds on research and development activities (RDEXVA). In both countries they are characterised by a relatively small proportion of production workers in the total workforce (PEMPPC), implying comparatively high levels of administrative "overhead" staff in foreign controlled firms, a result which tends to be at odds with the findings of comparatively high proportions of non-production workers in Canadian industries found in previous studies (West, 1971; Spence, 1977, Oksanen and Williams, 1978) which were discussed in Chapter 4.2. It may, however, simply reflect the greater capital intensity of industries with high levels of foreign penetration, and the consequent need for relatively fewer production workers. The evidence suggests that the relative "openness" of an industry to foreign influence, either indirectly through imports, or through direct foreign investment, the better its export performance (EXTO).[24] There is however, no evidence to suggest that foreign investment in manufacturing is undertaken as a means of obtaining more ready access to fuels or raw materials.

Industry structures

The evidence of Table 8.11 suggests that industries in both countries which are characterised by high levels of concentration (CONC8) and large (EMPLG, RMES50) capital intensive (CAPINT, LABINT) multi-establishment (ESTENT) firms, are typified by low rates of female participation in the workforce (FEMP), and at lower levels of significance, by low migrant (MIGRPC) participation, and low proportions of production workers (PEMPPC). Firms in such industries pay relatively high wages and salaries (AVWAGE) to a workforce characterised by high levels of skills (SKILL1) and education (ED2). As expected, industries characterised by relative capital intensity, concentration, and large (multiple-establishment) firms tend to use large amounts of natural resources (particularly in Australia), fuels (FUELINT) and other non-replenishable resources

---

24. For both countries the correlation coefficients of the shares of imports in the respective markets (ISHARE), and EXTO are positive and significant at the 1 per cent level.

TABLE 8.10

PEARSON (P) AND SPEARMAN RANK (S) CORRELATION COEFFICIENTS: FOREIGN CONTROL AND CHARACTERISTICS OF AUSTRALIAN AND CANADIAN MANUFACTURING INDUSTRIES

		CONC8		EMPLG		VAENT		VAEST		ESTENT	
		Aust.	Can.	Aust.	Can.	Aust.	Can.	Aust.	Can.	Aust.	Can.
FCONVAPC	P	.309	.119	.144	.185	.198	.126	.326	.182	-.017	.016
	S	.274	.254	.206	.219	.302	.367	.325	.361	.173	.211
FCONEMPC	P	.276	.116	.140	.244	.198	.181	.318	.223	-.006	.080
	S	.266	.289	.209	.264	.284	.432	.307	.426	.156	.264

		CAPINT		LABINT		SKILL 1		ED2		AVWAGE	
		Aust.	Can.	Aust.	Can.	Aust.	Can.	Aust.	Can.	Aust.	Can.
FCONVAPC	P	.339	.148	-.411	-.368	.559	.397	.580	.415	.343	.219
	S	.368	.123	-.366	-.412	.479	.463	.508	.347	.264	.174
FCONEMPC	P	.346	.207	-.354	-.390	.539	.437	.550	.422	.369	.279
	S	.340	.151	-.295	-.432	.448	.509	.472	.394	.289	.235

		RDEXVA		PEMPPC		EXTO	
		Aust.	Can.	Aust.	Can.	Aust.	Can.
FCONVAPC	P	.083	.245	-.353	-.432	.181	.034
	S	.082	.419	-.265	-.426	.340	.077
FCONEMPC	P	.096	.275	-.317	-.433	.192	.071
	S	.118	.450	-.259	-.440	.351	.142

Significance levels: see Table 8.6

TABLE 8.11

PEARSON (P) AND SPEARMAN RANK (S) CORRELATION COEFFICIENTS:
AUSTRALIAN AND CANADIAN MANUFACTURING INDUSTRIES CHARACTERISTICS

		FEMP		MIGRPC		PEMPPC		AVWAGE		SKILL 1	
		Aust.	Can.	Aust.	Can.	Aust.	Can.	Aust.	Can.	Aust.	Can.
CAPINT	P	-.354	-.396	-.107	-.373	-.207	-.296	.675	.592	.650	.332
	S	-.300	-.478	-.092	-.517	-.364	-.192	.665	.544	.567	.270
LABINT	P	-.075	.113	.212	.347	.464	.530	-.267	-.445	-.472	-.207
	S	-.023	.074	.269	.384	.512	.525	-.257	-.392	-.406	-.375
CONC8	P	-.123	-.160	.289	-.094	.039	-.021	.524	.140	.224	.105
	S	-.172	-.285	.274	-.233	.003	-.207	.500	.427	.380	.391
EMPLG	P	-.173	-.078	.127	-.155	.185	-.070	.450	.358	.147	.204
	S	-.093	-.119	.240	-.220	.234	-.068	.431	.392	.356	.380
RMES50	P	-.117	-.108	.384	-.068	.013	.025	.463	.138	.167	.113
	S	-.145	-.171	.329	-.212	.013	-.127	.461	.355	.354	.397
ESTENT	P	-.338	-.232	.088	-.334	-.113	-.250	.570	.407	.269	.082
	S	-.339	-.259	.007	-.486	-.154	-.346	.665	.502	.526	.332

		ED2		FUELINT		NATRES2		RDEMP2		RDEXVA	
		Aust.	Can.	Aust.	Can.	Aust.	Can.	Aust.	Can.	Aust.	Can.
CAPINT	P	.603	.420	.416	.485	.562	.540	.137	.434	-.306	-.000
	S	.652	.336	.382	.357	.485	.396	-.607	.304	-.441	.129
LABINT	P	-.540	-.452	-.149	-.182	-.225	-.138	.090	-.074	.443	-.003
	S	-.501	-.533	-.082	.035	-.353	-.144	.354	-.108	.453	-.142
CONC8	P	.308	.081	.241	.167	.289	.076	-.269	.125	-.224	.306
	S	.394	.319	.421	.153	.296	.004	-.460	.182	-.245	.173
EMPLG	P	.220	.122	.360	.221	.121	.180	-.186	.252	-.127	.024
	S	.274	.197	.398	.101	.178	-.020	-.469	.226	-.194	.101
RMES50	P	.238	.065	.155	.238	.163	.084	-.238	.182	-.134	.029
	S	.362	.314	.367	.138	.231	.050	-.395	.219	-.153	.252
ESTENT	P	.326	.182	.221	.320	.191	.126	-.171	.105	-.166	.036
	S	.498	.332	.363	.155	.350	.275	-.600	.174	-.298	.241

Significance levels: see Table 8.6

(NATRES2). There are no statistically significant correlations between these industry characteristics and the various measures of export performance used in this study.

The evidence regarding relationships between industry structure and research and development expenditures (RDEMP2, RDEXVA) suggests that there may be a fundamental difference between the two countries in this respect. While adequate data are not available to the present writer to fully explore the apparent difference, and while there may be differences in precise definitions of research and development expenditures, the data of Tables 8.10 and 8.11 are consistent with the hypothesis that in Australia, relatively high research activity may be undertaken in small firms with few establishments. Large firms which are characterised by relatively skilled workforces and high levels of foreign control, to the extent that they engage in R & D, may engage primarily in the adaptation of foreign products to local conditions. Such a result is not apparent for Canada, the data for which are consistent with the common expectation that R & D activity is higher in large firms participating in relatively concentrated markets. Because of Canada's proximity to the United States, it is therefore possible that there is not the same need for adaptation in Canada as there is in Australia. Clearly the hypothesis suggested is speculative. The issue is an important one centering on the degree of technological "spin-off" to host economies which is often associated with foreign investment. If, in Australia's case, R & D effort in foreign controlled firms is mainly for the purpose of adaptation, there may be little real technological benefit flowing to the host country. The issue is one deserving further research.

Comparison of industry characteristics

Table 8.12 contains the matrix of Pearson and Spearman rank correlation coefficients for variables reflecting aspects of the structures of the manufacturing sectors of Australia and Canada. An examination of the matrix reveals marked similarities in the relationships between the variables in the two countries. The measures of relative capital intensity (CAPINT and KINDEX) are inversely correlated with the percentage of establishments employing 50 persons (EMP50) and intra-establishment diversification (INTSPEC); and positively correlated with industrial concentration (CONC8), with "large" establishments (EMPLG) and firms (RMES50) tending to have multiple establishments (ESTENT). The opposite is true of labour intensity (LABINT). Simply, capital intensive firms tend to be large, to operate a number of establishments, to participate in industries characterised by industrial concentration, and by intra-industry specialisation.

There are few apparent relationships between diversification across industries (DIVRAT) and the other industry structure variables. Those

TABLE 8.12

PEARSON (P) AND SPEARMAN RANK (S) CORRELATION COEFFICIENTS
COMPARISON OF INDUSTRY STRUCTURES IN AUSTRALIA AND CANADA

		1 KINDEX Aust.	1 KINDEX Can.	2 LABINT Aust.	2 LABINT Can.	3 DIVRAT Aust.	3 DIVRAT Can.	4 CONC8 Aust.	4 CONC8 Can.	5 EMP50 Aust.	5 EMP50 Can.	6 EMPLG Aust.	6 EMPLG Can.	7 SMALLE Aust.	7 SMALLE Can.	8 RMES50 Aust.	8 RMES50 Can.	9 INTSPEC Aust.	9 INTSPEC Can.	10 ESTENT Aust.	10 ESTENT Can.
1. CAPINT	P	.563	.518	-.527	-.596	.041	.008	.445	.145	-.589	-.336	.414	.306	-.393	-.291	.219	.126	-.170	-.230	.434	.450
	S	.544	.470	-.550	-.567	.269	.021	.549	.399	-.499	-.337	.408	.303	-.085	-.126	.473	.415	-.381	-.281	.689	.528
2. KINDEX	P			-.191	-.217	.071	.061	.127	-.012	-.317	-.259	.291	.335	-.118	.006	.100	-.020	-.178	-.071	.386	.246
	S				-.211	.124	-.138	.038	-.013	-.253	-.181	.237	.235	.148	.200	-.017	.027	-.147	-.099	.376	.446
3. LABINT	P					.048	-.036	-.181	-.155	.110	.250	-.010	-.233	.206	.234	-.141	-.149	.272	.191	-.162	-.359
	S					-.003	-.041	-.213	-.410	.087	.257	.018	-.247	.132	.031	-.190	-.385	.313	.157	-.248	-.524
4. DIVRAT	P							.227	-.021	-.126	.051	.061	-.074	.085	.039	.201	.017	-.331	.059	.143	-.051
	S							.188	.048	-.245	-.032	.259	.045	.037	.022	.186	.090	-.228	.040	.318	-.022
5. CONC8	P									-.709	-.161	.639	.126	-.267	-.028	.884	.653	-.146	.048	.565	.105
	S									-.727	-.519	.678	.467	-.223	-.086	.592	.814	-.158	-.101	.688	.445
6. EMP50	P											-.904	-.972	.480	.434	-.592	-.139	.052	.125	-.664	-.357
	S											-.914	-.971	.383	.439	-.631	-.445	.140	.165	-.728	-.581
7. EMPLG	P													-.471	-.404	.539	.125	-.015	-.098	.657	.334
	S													-.285	-.385	.607	.430	.107	-.138	.670	.601
8. SMALLE	P															-.099	.137	-.024	.050	-.563	-.603
	S															-.015	.142	.011	.074	-.245	-.084
9. RMES50	P																	-.106	-.061	.476	.034
	S																	-.141	-.079	.614	.443
10. INTSPEC	P																			-.153	.126
	S																			-.317	-.345

Significance levels: see Table 8.6

discernable are only for Australia, and are an inverse relationship with INTSPEC, indicating a high degree of intra industry specialisation; and a positive relationship with ESTENT. Firms diversified across industry classifications tend to be characterised by multiple establishments, but *within* their respective industry classifications, tend to be relatively highly specialised. These results are consistent with firms attempting in this way to exploit firm level economies of scale though their multiple establishments, and plant- (and perhaps product-) level economies through their intra-industry specialisation. Industrial concentration is positively and significantly correlated with size in both countries. The coefficients of the size variables EMP50 and SMALLE (measuring "small size") and EMPLG and RMES50 (measuring "large size") are all correctly signed and in the main, are highly significant.

8.3 Bivariate Comparisons of the Australian and Canadian Manufacturing Sectors: A Summary

Section 8.1 has shown that there are significant differences in the means and distributions of many pairs of variables reflecting given attributes of the manufacturing sectors of both countries. The simple correlation analysis of Section 8.2, however, showed that there are strong similarities in the directions of apparent relationships between attributes of manufacturing industries in Australia and Canada. In general, the signs of the correlation coefficients and their levels of significance showed a marked consistency.

Comparisons of Means and Distributions

Only the most tentative conclusions can be drawn from the bivariate comparisons which have been so far conducted. Nevertheless, the results of Section 8.1 suggest that there may well be relationships between protection and the industry labour, and foreign trade characteristics of the Australian and Canadian manufacturing sectors. While it is difficult to establish directions of causation, the data are consistent with the hypothesis that the relatively higher average levels of protection in Australia may act to encourage entry, and permit the profitable operation of a larger number of small firms and establishments than would be possible under lower protection. Whatever the cause, the finding that despite the obviously larger size of the Canadian economy, there are on average in Australian industries significantly more enterprises and establishments than in Canadian industries is an important result. All else being equal, it implies a fragmentation of Australian markets which may act as a significant restriction on the ability of participant firms to exploit economies of scale which may be available to them in its absence. While the evidence is circumstantial, protection may well provide an environment which encourages "excess" entry and causes the apparent fragmentation characteristic of Australian markets. From all this, the picture which emerges is highly consistent with the findings of Daly, Keys and Spence (1968), West (1971), and Spence (1977) in their studies of Canada and the U.S. Taken together they found that in Canada tariffs contributed to ease of entry; that the size of plant which could profitably be used in small, protected economies is smaller than in a larger, more competitive one; and that the result is likely to be lower output per unit of input than in a less protected environment. With respect to Canada, the same is apparently true of more highly protected Australian manufacturing. The industries which have developed in Australia on average use relatively labour intensive production techniques, tend to be less specialised and provide greater scope for the employment of women, immigrants and the unskilled than does manufacturing in Canada.

While protection against imports, whether by means of tariffs (or other artificial trade barriers) or by transport costs, may well increase the size of the *domestic* market available to local firms, the results of Section 8.1 suggest that Canada's proximity to the U.S. may provide it with greater opportunities for international trade than isolated Australia.[25] Thus, the international transport costs discussed in Chapters 6 and 7 must be observed from two viewpoints: respectively, as a disadvantage which must be surmounted by export and potential export industries; and as a protective advantage to import-competing industries. The data are consistent with the hypothesis that Australia's isolation and higher artificial protection may on balance, act to reduce the *total* size of markets (i.e., domestic sales + exports - imports) available to Australian firms. The existence, singly or in combination of comparatively large numbers of enterprises and establishments, a market of restricted (total) size, and less intra-industry specialisation and trade, suggest an inability to exploit economies of sale which, in the absence of these factors, may otherwise be available.

Simple Correlation Analysis

The simple bivariate correlation analysis of Section 8.2 suggests a high degree of similarity in the relationships between protective barriers and variables reflecting many of the characteristics of the Australian and Canadian manufacturing sectors. Again it is difficult to validly infer causal relationships on the basis of these simple tests, though the results are highly suggestive. They provide a case for suggesting that protection does affect aspects of industry structure and as a result, affects production techniques,

25. See also Chapter 1, Table 1.3.

the characteristics of industry workforces and ultimately, industry performance. In particular, tariff protection appears to be inversely related to measures reflecting firm-, plant- and product-level economies of scale in both countries. High levels of protection are associated with industries characterised by relatively small markets, enterprises and establishments, and by a high level diversification within establishments. These results are consistent with the broad findings of the studies discussed in Chapter 4, and with the implications of the bivariate comparisons conducted in Section 8.1.

One other feature of Section 8.2 is especially noteworthy: the relative "failure" of effective rates of protection to "explain" the industry characteristics examined in this chapter. Almost without exception, nominal rates, whether for transport costs, tariffs or total protection, are more strongly related to the variables appearing Tables 8.6 to 8.8, than their effective rate counterparts. Whether this stems from problems in measuring "true" effective rates cannot be determined here, and attention is drawn to the discussion of Chapter 3.1, which outlines some of the problems involved in the computation of effective rates of protection.

9. An Analysis of Australian and Canadian Manufacturing Industries: A Multivariate Approach

Like Chapter 8, this chapter is concerned with the analysis of both differences and similarities between the manufacturing sectors of Australia and Canada. To these ends it uses two multivariate techniques: respectively, discriminant analysis and regression analysis.

The discriminant analysis of Section 9.1 essentially looks at possible differences between the manufacturing sectors of the two countries. It attempts to assess which attributes of the respective sectors make the greatest contributions to the statistical "separation" of Australian and Canadian manufacturing industries. The regression analysis of Section 9.2 looks at possible determinants of some important attributes of the industries comprising the two sectors, and gives particular emphasis to the possible roles of tariffs and international transport costs as influences on industrial structure and performance.

The variables which appear in the two sets of analyses here are substantially the same as those which appeared in Chapter 8, and the justifications for their inclusion are the same as those used in the previous chapter. Subject to the limitation of the availability of appropriate data, the attributes examined are those which the industrial organisation literature suggests are characteristics which are likely either to affect, or be used to measure industry performance. Thus, the analysis of this chapter looks at such attributes of industries as the absolute and relative sizes of the enterprises and establishments of which they are comprised, the diversity of their outputs, the composition of their work forces, their use of resources, their foreign trade performance, and the trade barriers which either shelter them from imports, or which impede their exports to foreign markets.

In this chapter stress is again given to the analysis of attributes which are likely to affect the ability of firms to exploit economies of scale. In this respect the discriminant analysis finds significant differences in the sizes of firms and establishments in the two countries and in the diversity of their outputs. The implications of these results are not clear-cut. For example, while it would appear that industries in Canada are characterised by a greater ability of participants to exploit firm-level economies of scale, Australian firms may have some advantages at the plant-, and product-levels. However these advantages may well be eroded by the greater tendency of Australian firms to divide production among a greater number of establishments than firms in Canada. Among the findings of the regression analysis are that in both countries foreign-controlled firms are likely to be more specialised in all respects, and may therefore be better able to exploit plant-and product-level economies of scale than firms which are locally controlled.

9.1 Multivariate Discriminant Analysis
Discriminant Analysis of Four Aspects of Australian and Canadian Manufacturing Industries

Chapter 8.1 made bivariate comparisons of means and distributions of variables in each country reflecting: (i) industry structure; (ii) labour force characteristics; (iii) foreign trade characteristics; (iv) the use of resources; and (v) other industry characteristics.

This section uses multivariate discriminant analysis in considering possible differences in the variables comprising a given set of attributes, (i) to (iv) when they are considered jointly. It then combines variables chosen from these four sets of attributes in an effort to construct a composite discriminant function which may enable the accurate classification of industries as either Australian or Canadian. Finally, two further composite discriminant functions are computed. To the original composite discriminant function are added the components of the two countries' protective structures of interest to this study: tariff protection and the protection afforded by international transport costs. Separate functions are computed: the first adding nominal tariffs and nominal transport costs to the composite function; and the second, adding effective tariffs and effective transport costs. The aim is to assess, when taken with the other industry characteristics, the relative contributions of these elements of the respective protective structures, to the statistical separation of Australian and Canadian industries.

In each case the multivariate discriminant analysis to follow is used as a means of predicting with a given set of attributes, the correct group membership (i.e. Australia or Canada) of the 170 industries (i.e. 2 x 85) considered in this study. In this process the individual industries are assigned to the group of industries which have characteristics most like its own. Since the true memberships of the groups are known, a table (sometimes called the "confusion matrix" or the "hits and misses" table) may be prepared incorporating the correct and incorrect classifications. Essentially, the fewer the misclassifications of individual industries, the more distinct or dissimilar are the groups in respect of that set of attributes. Thus, this section has two aims: to ascertain if there are differences in certain attributes of Australian and Canadian manufacturing industries considered jointly, and if so, which variables contribute most to the statistical separation of the two groups; and to see if it is possible to accurately determine the national origins of industries from these attributes.

The tables of this section contain standardised discriminant functions using variables reflecting various aspects of the industry structure and industry characteristics of both countries. The functions have been computed first using the data for all (170) industries, and second using data for 86 (i.e. 2 x 43) randomly selected industries from the full data sets. The experiment using randomly selected industries was repeated five times. The reason for the estimation of the second set of functions stems from the upward bias arising from the use of all *n* observations to calculate the discriminant function, and then classifying the *same n* individuals with the function. A method of avoiding this bias, which was adopted here, is to fit a discriminant function to part of the data (86 items) and to use the resulting function to classify the remaining 84 (i.e. 2 x 42) items (Frank, Massy and Morrison, 1965). The former is called the "grouped data"; the latter the "ungrouped data." (See Appendix 9.1 for a more detailed discussion of the discriminant analysis used in this study.)

Industry structures

For the six experiments conducted on the data, Table 9.1 contains the standardised discriminant function coefficients derived in the manner just described for the variables listed in Table 8.1 together with extracts from the hits and misses table described earlier. The standardised discriminant function coefficients of the table suggest that of the industry structure variables considered, interindustry diversification (DIVRAT), and the percentage of establishments employing fewer than 10 persons (EMP10) provide the greatest relative contributions to the prediction of the group memberships. DIVRAT is prominent in each function, and in the case of the function derived in the fifth sample experiment, is the only variable entering the analysis.[1] EMP10 has the highest (absolute) value in four of the five functions in which it appears. For all experiments, the value of Chi-square indicates that the respective functions discriminate between real differences in the population at very high levels of significance.

---

1. Variables are entered or removed from the analysis on the basis of the overall multivariate F ratio. Variables are step-wise entered if their multivariate F ratio is greater than one, and removed if the ratio is less than one. Variables may also be omitted if they have low tolerance levels. In these cases the computer programme would have difficulty in inverting a covariance matrix including such a variable. A low tolerance is also likely to cause large rounding errors in computing the discriminant function coefficients.

TABLE 9.1

STANDARDISED DISCRIMINANT FUNCTION COEFFICIENTS :
INDUSTRY STRUCTURE VARIABLES — AUSTRALIA AND CANADA

Variable Name	All Industries	Sample 1	Sample 2	Sample 3	Sample 4	Sample 5
CONC8		-.185	-.244		-.204	
DIVRAT	-.889	.891	.872	.751	.895	1.000
EMP10	.939	-.922	-1.266	-.660	-1.448	
EMP20	-.640		.932		1.073	
EMP50		.919				
EMPLG		.502				
EMPENT						
EMPEST						
ESTENT	.156	-.345		-.590		
INTSPEC	-.160	.194				
LABINT	.339	-.543	-.183	-.488	-.167	
PRODEST						
RMES50						
SMALLE		-.384		.201		
Chi-square	112.13[a]	66.09[a]	54.52[a]	60.24[a]	60.88[a]	61.89[a]
d.f.	6	9	5	5	5	1
GROUP CENTROIDS						
Australia	.980	-1.125	-.964	-1.033	-1.041	-1.035
Canada	-.980	1.125	.964	1.033	1.041	1.035

'HITS AND MISSES' TABLE

Industries Correctly Classified	All Industries			Sample				
				1	2	3	4	5
Australia	(n = 85)	76[a]	(n = 42)	36[a]	36[a]	36[a]	32[b]	36[a]
Canada	(n = 85)	68[a]	(n = 42)	33[b]	32[b]	31[b]	34[a]	35[a]
Total (%)	(n = 170)	84.7	(n = 84)	82.1	81.0	79.8	78.6	84.5

Notes : (a) Chi-square significant at 1 per cent level.
(b) Chi-square significant at 5 per cent level.

The signs of the standardised coefficients should be compared with the signs of the respective group centroids. For example, the group centroids for the discriminant function fitted to the data derived from all industries are +.980 for Australian industries, and -.980 for Canadian industries.[2] Thus the negative sign of DIVRAT for that function indicates that a relatively high value of that variable for a given industry will lead to an industry being classified as Canadian. In summary, the signs indicate that "high" values of concentration (CONC8), establishments employing fewer

---

2. The signs of the group centroids and of the coefficients of the variables may vary from experiment to experiment depending on which variables enter the function, and the order in which they are entered.

than 10 persons (EMP10), establishments per enterprise (ESTENT), and labour intensity (LABINT) lead to an industry being classified as Australian, while "high" values of both interindustry and intra-industry diversification (DIVRAT, INTSPEC) and larger sized establishments (EMP20, EMP50, EMPLG) lead to an industry being classified as Canadian. The signs for "small" enterprises (SMALLE) for random sample experiments 1 and 3 are ambiguous.

The extracts from the hits and misses table show a generally high and statistically significant degree of accuracy in the discriminant functions' abilities to predict correct group memberships, with an overall success rate of about 80 per cent. The percentage of correct classifications in discriminant analysis may be interpreted in a manner analogous to R^2 in regression analysis (Morrison 1969). Just as a high R^2 tells how much variance has been explained by an equation, the results of these tests show how well the functions classify the individuals.

The discriminant analyses of Table 9.1 show that an industry will be classified as Australian if it is characterised by industrial concentration and by small, relatively labour intensive firms which tend to confine themselves to their principal activity, rather than diversifying across industries, but which, nevertheless, are characterised by multiple establishments. Though it enters only two functions, high values of intra-industry diversification (INTSPEC) in classifying industries as Canadian comes as some surprise. A high ratio of value added to shipments implies the purchase of comparatively few intermediate products, suggesting comparatively little within-industry specialisation, and a high degree of vertical integration. In all, these results imply that Canadian industries are more characterised by firms which are more highly integrated, both horizontally and vertically, than those in Australia, and by fewer (and larger) establishments. The net effect of these influences on comparative costs of production is far from clear.

That Australian manufacturing is characterised by *both* industrial concentration and small establishments is also an interesting result. Indeed, there is no inconsistency between the juxtaposition of high concentration and the small (average) size of establishments. Here the image created is one in which Australian manufacturing industries are dominated by few large firms coexisting with a fringe of many smaller ones; it suggests that an application of dominant firm models (e.g. models of price leadership) may be often most appropriate in Australia and points to the need for a more competitive Australian environment. These results are further discussed later in this section.

Labour forces

Table 9.2 contains the standardised discriminant function coefficients for

TABLE 9.2

STANDARDISED DISCRIMINANT FUNCTION COEFFICIENTS : LABOUR FORCE VARIABLES — AUSTRALIA AND CANADA

Variable Name	All Industries	Sample 1	Sample 2	Sample 3	Sample 4	Sample 5
ED2						
FEMP						
FEPROD					.399	
FMIGRPC	-.455	-.568	-.603	-.464		-.494
FPROD				-.388		
INNOV	-.535	-.628	-.517	-.616	.728	-.496
MIGRPC	-.664	-.574	-.569	-.511	.885	-.648
PEMPPC	.439	.569	.480	.766	-.573	.394
Chi-square	100.07[a]	52.40[a]	58.54[a]	56.24[a]	50.24[a]	47.09[a]
d.f.	4	4	4	5	4	4
GROUP CENTROIDS						
Australia	-.904	-.934	-1.008	-.985	.908	-.870
Canada	.904	.934	1.008	.985	-.908	.870

'HITS AND MISSES' TABLE

Industries Correctly Classified	All Industries		Sample				
				1	2	3	4	5
Australia	(n = 85)	67[a]	(n = 42)	34[a]	33[b]	26	30[c]	36[a]
Canada	(n = 85)	73[a]	(n = 42)	34[a]	34[a]	38[a]	34[a]	32[b]
Total (%)	(n = 170)	82.3	(n = 84)	81.0	79.8	76.2	76.2	81.0

Notes: (a) Chi-square significant at 1 percent level.
(b) Chi-square significant at 5 percent level.
(c) Chi-square significant at 10 percent level.

the variables of Table 8.2, and extracts from the associated hits and misses table. When compared with the group centroids, the signs of coefficients of the variables entering some, or all of the functions indicate that the joint attributes of "high" values of INNOV,[3] "high" proportions of female production workers (FEPROD, FPROD) and migrants (FMIGRPC, MIGRPC) lead to an industry being classified as Australian; a "high" value of the proportion of production employees (PEMPPC) leads to an industry being classified as Canadian. The extracts from the hits and misses table for the ungrouped data show that overall, the functions are successful in predicting Canadian membership correctly in 82 per cent of cases (172 of 210), and Australian membership in 76 per cent (159 of 210). Nearly all of the results are of high levels of significance indicating again, that within the

---

3. i.e., low innovative activity; see Oksanen and Williams (1978, p. 97).

population, significant differences exist between the two groups of industries.

In summary, these analyses suggest that the workforces of Australian manufacturing industries are distinguished by their high proportions of migrant employees and by relatively low innovative activity. There is evidence that the proportion of females in the workforces may make a relatively small contribution to group separation and that high proportions of females will classify an industry as Australian. In contrast to the bivariate comparison of Table 8.2, in this analysis a relatively high proportion of production workers in total employment will tend to classify industries as Canadian.[4] On this evidence, Canadian industries are characterised by fewer "overhead" staff than Australian industries.

Foreign trade and the use of resources

The discriminant functions using the foreign trade variables of Table 8.3 do not predict group membership with accuracy. In the case of each experiment the distance between the group centroids in relatively small, while the predicted group memberships of the ungrouped data differ widely with each experiment. Indeed, in the case of Canadian industries, on average the functions derived from these data predict the incorrect group more often than not. The attempt to discriminate between Australian and Canadian industries of the resource use variables of Table 8.4 was also unsuccessful. The conclusions here are simple: it is not possible to accurately distinguish between group memberships on the basis of the industries' foreign trade characteristics, or use of resources.[5]

Discriminant Analyses of Selected Attributes of Australian and Canadian Manufacturing Industries

It has been shown that it is possible to distinguish between Australian and Canadian manufacturing industries with a high degree of accuracy on the basis of the characteristics of the respective industry structures, and of their labour forces, when each group of characteristics is considered separately. Neither the variables reflecting foreign trade characteristics, nor those reflecting the use of resources enable an accurate distinction to be

---

4. The means of PEMPPC, while higher for Australia than Canada, were not significantly different.
5. These functions may be found in Conlon (1981b). From them, EXTO, TRADBAL, and FUELINT, which made the greatest relative contributions to group separation in the respective functions were selected for inclusion in the composite discriminant functions of the following sections.

made. This section combines the foregoing results by choosing from the four sets of attributes examined — industry structure, labour force, foreign trade and the use of resources — variables which, within each set, on average made relatively large contributions to the separation of the two groups of industries, and which illustrate a variety of aspects of industries. Thus, the functions of Table 9.3 include variables reflecting aspects of the respective industry structures (DIVRAT, EMP10, and LABINT), labour forces (FEMP, MIGRPC and PEMPPC), foreign trade (EXTO, INTRA and TRADBAL), and resource use (FUELINT). The functions appearing in Table 9.4 add to these variables nominal tariff, and transport cost protection (NTARIFF and NTRANS); while results of functions which add effective rates of protection (ETARIFF and ETRANS), to the composite function are also reported. These two sets of functions were estimated order to assess (when taken with the other industry characteristics) the relative contributions of the protective structures to the statistical separation of Australian and Canadian industries. It is possible that the addition of these variables may add nothing (or even detract) from the discriminating power of the functions, and this would provide evidence that protection is not an important element of the characteristics of the two manufacturing sectors.

Selected industry characteristics

The discriminant functions of Table 9.3 show that, of the industry characteristics considered, MIGRPC and DIVRAT make the greatest relative contributions to the respective functions. Other variables making relatively large contributions are TRADBAL, and EMP10. The remaining variables, in general, make relatively little contribution to discrimination between the groups. Taken together, the signs of the standardised coefficients (including those which did not enter all functions and/or made relatively little contribution) indicate that *ceteris paribus*, an industry will be classified as Australian if it is characterised by a high proportion of the workforce born overseas (MIGRPC), relative labour intensity (LABINT), a favourable balance of trade (TRADBAL), a large proportion of establishments employing fewer than 10 persons (EMP10), and the use of a relatively large proportion of fuels and electricity in total materials inputs (FUELINT). An industry will be classified as Canadian if it is characterised by a relatively high degree of intra-industry trade (INTRA), a high proportion of exports to turnover (EXTO), enterprises with a relatively high proportion of their output classified to other than their primary activity (DIVRAT), and a relatively high proportion of production employees in total employment (PEMPPC). All of these results are consistent with the previous findings.

TABLE 9.3

STANDARDISED DISCRIMINANT FUNCTION COEFFICIENTS :
SELECTED INDUSTRY CHARACTERISTICS — AUSTRALIA AND
CANADA

Variable Name	All Industries	Sample 1	Sample 2	Sample 3	Sample 4	Sample 5
LABINT	.196	.551			.207	
INTRA	−.259		−.222	−.235	−.454	−.271
EXTO	−.185	−.186		−.212	−.225	−.345
TRADBAL	.492	.475	.507	.658	.482	.446
FEMP					.360	
DIVRAT	−.680	−.682	−.612	−.541	− .812	−.739
EMP10	.259	.407	.518	.551	.318	
FUELINT	.153	.190			.202	
PEMPPC	−.221	−.419	−.398	−.310	−.345	
MIGRPC	.758	.685	.963	.993	.573	.649
Chi-square	168.56[a]	88.14[a]	94.78[a]	84.70[a]	85.99[a]	87.66[a]
d.f.	9	8	6	7	10	5
GROUP CENTROIDS						
Australia	1.335	1.400	1.473	1.349	1.386	1.373
Canada	−1.335	−1.400	−1.473	−1.439	−1.386	−1.373

'HITS AND MISSES' TABLE

Industries Correctly Classified	All Industries			Sample				
				1	2	3	4	5
Australia	(n = 35)	78[a]	(n = 42)	38[a]	32[b]	33[b]	37[a]	38[a]
Canada	(n = 35)	78[a]	(n = 42)	35[a]	40[a]	38[a]	35[a]	39[a]
Total (%)	(n = 170)	91.8	(n = 84)	86.9	85.7	84.5	85.7	91.7

Notes: (a) Chi-square significant at 1 per cent level.
(b) Chi-square significant at 5 per cent level.

The functions all display a high degree of discriminatory power. On average, over the five experiments for the ungrouped data, the function correctly predicts Australian group membership in 85 per cent of cases, and Canadian group membership in 89 per cent, both highly significant results.

Selected industry characteristics and protection

Table 9.4 incorporates the variables discussed above, and the two components of the nominal protective structure, NTRANS and NTARIFF. The addition of the nominal protection variables increases the discriminatory power of the function. Both variables enter all functions and after MIGRPC,[6] NTRANS makes the highest relative contribution to the func-

6. When these functions were computed without MIGRPC, the discriminatory power of the functions was reduced by 5 to 6 per cent, but still remained highly significant.

TABLE 9.4

STANDARDISED DISCRIMINANT FUNCTION COEFFICIENTS :
NOMINAL PROTECTION AND SELECTED INDUSTRY
CHARACTERISTICS — AUSTRALIA AND CANADA

Variable Name	All Industries	Sample 1	Sample 2	Sample 3	Sample 4	Sample 5
NTRANS	.576	.568	-.454	.617	.644	-.419
NTARIFF	.257	.209	-.240	.228	.229	.262
INTRA	-.255		.150		-.310	.219
EXTO						
LABINT	.283	.544		.261	.367	
TRADBAL	.420	.406	-.332	.419	.316	-.304
FEMP				.169	.438	
DIVRAT	-.556	-.545	.533	-.460	-.680	.601
EMP10	.207	.320	.459	.299	.257	-.150
FUELINT						
PEMPPC	-.244	-.389	.217	-.339	-.306	
MIGRPC	.705	.732	.858	.712	.495	.682
Chi-square	216.72[a]	112.01[a]	112.00[a]	107.06[a]	113.84[a]	101.22[a]
d.f.	9	8	8	9	10	7

GROUP CENTROIDS

Australia	1.652	1.727	-1.727	1.666	1.774	-1.567
Canada	-1.652	-1.727	-1.727	-1.666	-1.774	1.567

'HITS AND MISSES' TABLE

Industries Correctly Classified	All Industries		Sample				
			1	2	3	4	5
Australia	(n = 85)	83[a]	(n = 42) 41[a]	36[a]	40[a]	36[a]	38[a]
Canada	(n = 85)	81[a]	(n = 42) 39[a]	41[a]	39[a]	38[a]	40[a]
Total (%)	(n = 170)	96.5	(n = 84) 95.2	95.6	94.0	88.1	92.8

Note: (a) Chi-square significant at 1 per cent level.

tion in five of the six experiments. The relative contribution of NTARIFF is generally small. For the ungrouped data, in every case for both countries the percentage of correct classifications is highly significant, the overall success rate being just over 92 per cent (388 of 420 cases), compared with 87 per cent for the function excluding the nominal protection variables.

When the components of total effective protection, ETRANS and ETARIFF are added to the industry characteristics of Table 9.3, their inclusion increases the ability to accurately discriminate between Australian and Canadian manufacturing industries, though the increase is small.[7] In total, the ungrouped data are correctly classified in 88 per cent of

7. These functions may be found in Conlon (1981b).

cases (369/420). The contributions of ETRANS and ETARIFF to the functions are relatively small, and of the two variables, ETRANS makes the greater contribution in each experiment.

Summary of Discriminant Analysis Results

It has been shown that it is possible to discriminate with a high degree of accuracy between Australian and Canadian manufacturing industries on the basis of characteristics of industry structure and labour forces. In essence, there are significant differences in these two facets of the respective manufacturing industries. Analysis of trade characteristics and the use of natural resources, however, did not enable accurate discrimination between the two groups.

The findings of the discriminant analysis suggest that Canadian industries are both more horizontally and vertically integrated than are those in Australia. Horizontal integration suggests an ability to exploit firm-level economies of scale; vertical integration, implying low levels of intra-industry specialisation, on the other hand, suggests at least an inability to exploit some economies at the plant- and product-levels. While Australian industries may have an advantage in the latter respect, any advantage resulting from comparative intra-industry specialisation may well be foregone by the tendency to divide activities among a greater number of establishments in Australia than in Canada. The net effect on comparative costs of production is therefore uncertain. Further, that industries tend to be classified as Australian if they are characterised by high levels of industrial concentration and by high proportions of small enterprises and/or establishments is consistent with the existence of markets consisting of many small firms dominated by a few large (multiple establishment) firms.

These findings appear to be at least the partial result of two influences. An explanation of the industrial concentration and the fringe of small firms characteristic of Australian industries may lie in the relative heights of internal transportation costs, and the relative geographic dispersions of populations. *Ceteris paribus*, there will be a tendency for a larger number of enterprises and/or establishments the higher are the former and the greater is the latter. A geographic concentration of a large proportion of the population in few centres, with the remainder widely dispersed may permit, or encourage the development of an industry such that relatively few large enterprises/establishments develop to serve the large markets, leaving small enterprises/establishments to serve small local markets. In Australia there is perhaps the most extreme example of the co-existence of areas of high density with a high average dispersion of population (though most of the population is concentrated around the coastal fringes). For example, 39 per

141

cent of the population dwells in Sydney and Melbourne, the major centres of manufacturing, while the average population density is 1.8 persons per square kilometre (Showers 1979, p. 225). In Canada the populations of Toronto and Montreal, the major manufacturing centres, together comprise 24 per cent of the population, while a further 4 per cent dwell in Vancouver. The overall population density is 2.3 persons per square kilometre, with a large majority dispersed in the area along the strip within 100 km of the Canada-U.S. border (Showers 1979, p. 226). Thus, when compared with Australia, there is the tendency for the Canadian population to be more evenly spread, and thus, all things equal, there should be a tendency for a more even "spread" of enterprises and/or establishments. Tending to act in the opposite direction, the other likely influence is Canada's proximity to the United States. There is the likelihood that many small Canadian population centres may have supplies more readily available from U.S., rather than Canadian sources, and moreover, it is possible that the same commodity may be exported from Eastern Canada and imported by Western Canada, or vice versa — a possibility supported by the higher level of Canadian intra-industry trade (see Table 8.3). *Ceteris paribus*, this will lead to fewer and larger enterprises/establishments in Canada than in Australia. Which influence on average is likely to be the most important in determining the size distribution of firms? The data of Table 8.1 suggests that it is the second. If the "evenness" of population distribution is the dominating influence, then it could be expected that the variation of the size distribution of firms would be lower in Canada. In fact the variances of all the "size variables" but one (EMP10) are higher in Canada, and in most cases the differences are statistically significant, as is the larger proportion of "large" establishments (EMPLG) in that country. Canada's proximity to the United States therefore should provide a greater opportunity for intra-industry trade and specialisation than in isolated Australia, and in the process may partially account for the generally larger sizes of enterprises and establishments in Canada.

The discriminant analysis of labour force characteristics showed high levels of migrant and female participation. There is evidence that Australian firms carry a relatively high proportion of non-production employees, and it is likely that a relatively large proportion of these employees represent "middle management", holding responsibility for supervising routine operations, rather than the higher paid echelons of management or research staff who engage in non-routine activity. Both these findings, and more important, the relatively high proportion of non-production workers characteristic of Australian industries have parallels in findings by West (1971), Spence (1977), and Oksanen and Williams (1978) in their studies of Canadian and U.S. industries. Those studies suggested that industries in Canada were characterised by high proportions of non-production workers; and this may be symptomatic of their inability to exploit managerial and administrative economies of scale available to their United States counterparts. Here, the findings suggest that industries in Australia are even more disadvantaged in this respect than Canadian industries.

The "composite" discriminant functions incorporating variables reflecting a range of industry characteristics, on average are able to predict correct group membership in approximately 87 per cent of cases. When transport cost and tariff protection are added to the composite function, the ability to distinguish between Australian and Canadian industries improves and this shows that differences in the protective structures contribute to (rather than detract from) the statistical spearation of the two manufacturing sectors. The addition of nominal rates of protection to the function enables the prediction of correct group membership (on average) in 92 per cent of cases, compared with 88 per cent when effective rates are added to the function. In adding to the discriminating power of the function this provides evidence that protection is an important element of the characteristics of the two manufacturing sectors. For both sets of experiments international transport costs make a relatively greater contribution than tariffs: circumstantial evidence of a greater influence of geographical proximity of the United States than tariff protection, in determining the differences in industry structure characteristics observed in Australia and Canada.

The composite discriminant functions suggest that of the variables considered, the greater the diversity of the activities of Canadian firms (into other than their primary activity) and the higher proportion of migrants in Australian industry workforces, and Australian industry's nominal transport cost protection contribute most to group separation. The results show that structure, employment and protection characteristics of similar industries differ significantly and systematically between Australia and Canada, and that the national origin of an industry can, with a high degree of accuracy, be determined from them.

9.2 Regression Analysis

This section uses ordinary least-squares regression techniques in analysing some attributes of Australian and Canadian manufacturing industries. Its aims are limited. The attributes analysed are aspects of firm diversification, international trade performance, and the degree of foreign control of Australian and Canadian manufacturing industries. Of most interest in the present study are international transport costs and tariffs as elements of the protective barriers of Australia and Canada, and as determinants of the attributes of the two manufacturing sectors examined. However, there may be problems in using tariffs as an independent variable in a cross-section study of this type.

A cross-section analysis assumes that the entities in the sampled populations are in long-run equilibrium, or are displaced only randomly with respect to the independent structural variables that determine their equilibrium positions. In the present context, this requires that structural determinants have been stable over time, or that tariffs are continually adjusted to changes in structural determinants. Evidence by Mackintosh (1940, pp. 83-84), McDiarmid (1946) and Young (1957, pp. 48-54) suggest a high degree of stability of Canadian tariffs, though a "more continuous mechanism of adjustment may have emerged in the last four decades with the rise of administrative tariff making and negotiated tariff reductions" (Caves, 1976, p. 15). In respect of the hypothesised determinants of tariffs, "Our impression is that most of the independent variables . . . have been quite stable for a long time . . . Thus there has been a considerable stability of some structural determinants and some adaptation of tariff rates to their changes. A [cross-section] analysis is, to choose words carefully, not wildly implausible" (Caves, 1976, p. 15).[8] At least until the 25 per cent tariff cut of July, 1973, the Australian tariff structure has also been characterised by a high degree of stability over time. In the circumstances, it does not seem "wildly implausible" to apply regression techniques to the data for both countries.

The regression results presented in this chapter are representative results, and are not necessarily equations of best fit. For each of the aspects of industry structure and performance examined, equations incorporating different specifications and/or slightly different measures of the same basic phenomenon (e.g., foreign control — through FCONEMPC, FCONTOPC and FCONVAPC) have also been estimated, but owing to space limitations have not been included. The results are highly consistent. In particular, the coefficients of the protection variables which are of most interest are characterised by a marked consistency: as explanatory variables of a given characteristic, their signs and sizes display a high degree of stability.

Tariffs, Transport Costs and Characteristics of Australian and Canadian Manufacturing Industries
  Aspects of diversification

The regression analysis provides evidence that tariff protection discourages

---

8. Research is now directed toward the assembly and analysis of data for a later time period in order to compare the results with those of this Chapter.

diversification of Australian firms across industries (DIVRAT),[9] and (at lower levels of significance) encourages vertical integration (INTSPEC) within the primary activity. By contrast, from Table 9.5 there is no significant relationship between tariff protection and the diversification of firms' activities across industries in Canada, and the Canadian tariff apparently discourages vertical integration (measured by the ratio of value added to the value of shipments). Transport costs also apparently act to discourage vertical integration and in both countries there is a positive association between transport costs and the number of establishments per enterprise (ESTENT). The reasons for the former result are not readily apparent as it could reasonably be expected that high transport costs would encourage the firm to produce at successive stages of manufacture at the one location in order to minimise such costs. To the extent that international transport costs are positively correlated with domestic transport costs, the second result may capture attempts by firms to establish plants in geographic proximity to markets and/or raw materials. Thus it may be that the encouragement to diversification (broadly defined) provided by transport costs is manifested as an encouragement to diversify the geographic location of plants, rather than as encouragement to diversify within the plant.

High levels of vertical integration are associated with enterprises with few establishments (ESTENT), having relatively large numbers of employees (EMPENT), and a tendency not to use relatively capital-intensive techniques (KINDEX). Such firms are also characterised by high levels of gross operating surplus (PCM) and by relatively low levels of foreign control. Enterprises with relatively few establishments are, however, characterised by relatively high levels of foreign control, especially in Canada. This may reflect an attempt by foreign controlled firms to more fully exploit plant-specific economies of scale, than domestically controlled firms. Multi-establishment firms tend not to be characterised by labour-intensive production processes (LABINT), and in Canada, little innovative activity (INNOV),[10] both of which imply the use of production line methods for well-established products. In Canada such firms are also characterised by high levels of gross operating surplus.

Foreign trade performance

In the equations of Table 9.6 nominal and effective transport costs, and

---

9. The results of the equations explaining DIVRAT were (and in common with Caves (1975) results) without exception poor. Consequently these results were not incorporated in Table 9.5. The coefficients of the tariff variables for Australia however, were negative and significant at approximately the 5 per cent level.

10. A high value of INNOV reflects low innovative activity. See Oksanen and Williams (1978).

TABLE 9.5

REGRESSION ANALYSIS OF DETERMINANTS OF FIRM DIVERSITY
DEPENDENT VARIABLE: INTSPEC

CONST	CONC8	EMPENT	ESTENT	KINDEX	PCM	FCON VAPC	N TRANS	N TARIFF	E TRANS	E TARIFF		
						AUSTRALIA						
.3668a	*	.0001b	-.0896b	-.0068	1.1015a	-.0015a	-.0009	.0013c			R^2=.4995	F = 12.9783a
.3778a	-.0199	.0001a	-.0830c	-.0099c	1.1631a	-.0016a			-.0007b	.0002	R^2=.4944	F = 11.2700a
						CANADA						
.2411a	-.0048	*	-.0195c	-.0062	1.4953a	-.0011a	-.0068b	-.0014b			R^2=.7089	F = 30.2254a
.2136a	-.0057	$.34 \times 10^{-5}$	-.0257b	-.0070c	1.5399a	-.0011a			-.0010b	-.0004a	R^2=.7041	F = 28.5570a

DEPENDENT VARIABLE: ESTENT

CONST	CONC8	PRODIFF	MKT SIZE	LABINT	PCM	INNOV	FCON VAPC	N TRANS TARIFF	N TARIFF	E TRANS TARIFF	E TARIFF		
							AUSTRALIA						
1.2232b	.9289a	-.0935	$.23 \times 10^{-6}$a	-.4838	-.6839	.2792	-.0026	.0068a	.0013	-.0001		R^2=.4446	F = 8.4718a
1.0396	.9760a	-.0927	$.23 \times 10^{-6}$a	-.3637	-.2183	-.1722	-.0029c			.0032b	-.0018	R^2=.4341	F = 8.1599a
							CANADA						
-3.3469c	-.0211	-.5006	$.58 \times 10^{-8}$	-1.6585c	3.6221a	4.9146a	-.0006	.0508c	*	.0034		R^2=.2740	F = 4.9630a
-3.1124	-.0166	-.6129	*	-2.3438b	4.0082a	5.3176a	-.0027			.0034		R^2=.2593	F = 4.6761a

*F-level or tolerance level insufficient for inclusion. F-Statistic significance levels: a 1 per cent   b 5 per cent   c 10 per cent

tariffs on imports are included as determinants of industry exports for the following reasons.

(i) Tariffs on competing imports provide some measure of the relative international cost competitiveness of local producers. The necessity for high rates of nominal and/or effective tariff protection may therefore reflect the inability of an industry to adequately compete on world markets.

(ii) Transport costs for competing imports may in some degree capture the influence of transport cost on exports.[11]

United States' tariffs (USTAR75) are used in the equations as a proxy for all foreign trade barriers facing Australian exporters. In 1974 the U.S. was the destination for 70 per cent of Canadian exports, thus USTAR75 is a measure of the trade barrier most commonly facing exporters in Canada. Essentially, these equations examine only supply determinants. An implicit assumption in this analysis is that the same industry in each country faces identical demand conditions.

For the equations with the ratio of exports to turnover (EXTO) as the independant variable, for neither country are the coefficients of USTAR75 significantly different from zero, and for Canada, neither are the coefficients of NTRANS, ETRANS, NTARIFF and ETARIFF. For Australia, however, the coefficients of both nominal and effective transport costs are negative and statistically significant. Indeed, for all the experiments conducted on the data (using slightly different specifications and/or data definitions) of which the equations of Table 9.6 are representative, the coefficients of the effective transport cost variable are in each case of a higher level of significance than their nominal transport cost counterparts. The effective rates take account of the transport cost burden on importable inputs, and it may therefore be suggested that not only do the measures of transport costs capture (at least in part) the transport cost barrier facing Australian exporters, but the disadvantage exporters and potential exporters face in purchasing importable materials which are also affected by high international transport costs. The coefficients of NTARIFF are negative and different from zero at the relatively low 10 per cent level of significance. This result is consistent with the hypothesis proposed earlier in this section that industries protected by high nominal tariffs are those with a relative inability to compete on world markets.

11. For Australia, the four measures of barriers to Australia's exports derived in Chapter 6, Table 6.3, i.e., the freight net of distance ($/tonne), *ad valorem* freight rate net of distance, total *ad valorem* freight rate, and the relative *ad valorem* increase in freight rate (net of distance) were also used in equations of the form appearing in Table 9.6. Without exception, the coefficients for these variables were of low levels of significance.

The nominal transport costs used in these equations, however, are highly correlated with the total *ad valorem* export freight rates of Table 6.3.

TABLE 9.6

REGRESSION ANALYSIS OF DETERMINANTS OF INTERNATIONAL TRADE PERFORMANCE

DEPENDENT VARIABLE: EXTO

CONST	EMP20	KINDEX	INTRA	RDEXVA	NATRES 3	FCON VAPC	USTAR 75	N TRANS TARIFF	N TARIFF	E TRANS TARIFF	E TARIFF		
						AUSTRALIA							
.0745	-.0003	.0075	-9×10^{-4}	2.3008	.3317a	.0004	.0045	-.0025b		-.0015a		$R^2 = .3173$	F = 5.3395a
.0185	-.0004	.0066	-9×10^{-4}	2.1180	.4038a	.0005	.0044		-.0025b		-.0006	$R^2 = .3203$	F = 5.3984a
						CANADA							
.1817	-.0004	.0324a	.0005	2.8907a	-.0896	-.0008	-.0028	-.0033		.0007		$R^2 = .1668$	F = 2.8690a
.1186	-.0007	.0343a	.0005	3.1725a	-.0835	-.0005	-.0028		-.0013		.0001	$R^2 = .1638$	F = 2.8292a

DEPENDENT VARIABLE: TRADBAL

CONST	EMP20	KINDEX	INT SPEC	ED2	NATRES 3	FCON VACP	USTAR 75	N TRANS TARIFF	N TARIFF	E TRANS TARIFF	E TARIFF		
						AUSTRALIA							
-.1129	.0032	.0383	-1.2656b	-.0244	1.5825a	.0012	-.0177c	.0074b		.0039c		$R^2 = .4737$	F = 9.4004a
-.1375	.0032	.0445	-1.1359c	-.0212	1.6025a	.0009	-.0180c		-.0003		.0001	$R^2 = .4750$	F = 9.4463a
						CANADA							
-.0541	-.0012	.0749a	-.2964	-.0271	.4103	-.0009	-.0237b	.0153		.0011		$R^2 = .2001$	F = 3.3357a
.0106	-.0011	.0760a	-.2916	-.0262	.4233	-.0009	-.0220b		.0045		.0011	$R^2 = .1991$	F = 3.3202a

F-statistic significance levels: (a) 1 per cent (b) 5 per cent (c) 10 per cent

The results suggest that in Australia the availability and use of relatively large proportions of natural resources in total material inputs (NATRES3) results in a high ratio of exports to turnover, but there is no similarly significant evidence for Canada. There, and in contrast with Australia, the evidence suggests large, capital (KINDEX) and research and development intensive (RDEXVA) firms characteristically export a high proportion of their turnover (by implication) in an attempt to further exploit economies of scale. For neither country is there a significant relationship between foreign control (FCONVAPC) and the ratio of exports to turnover (EXTO).[12]

The major differences between the export performance equations just discussed, and the trade balance equations of Table 9.6 lie in the possible influences captured by the tariff and transport cost measures. It has been suggested that the tariff variables capture the influence of relative costs on the ratio of exports to turnover, and the transport cost variables capture the influence of transport costs for exports. Here the dependent variable (TRADBAL) is a measure of net trade, and the tariff and transport cost variables may be considered to act directly as barriers to imports, and indirectly on exports in the manner just described.

In both the Australian and Canadian equations, high U.S. tariffs (USTAR75) are associated with low levels of net trade. For neither country are there any significant relationships between tariff protection and TRAD-BAL, but for Australia, the coefficients for the transport cost variables are positive and significant. It would therefore appear that the influence of international transport costs in discouraging Australian imports, which was described in Chapter 8,[13] apparently overwhelms whatever influences of export transport costs are captured by NTRANS and ETRANS. Thus the transport cost variables act to lower the import component in the expression (export-imports) with the resulting positive influence of such costs on the balance of trade.

In summary, for Australia there is evidence that high levels of tariff and transport cost protection are associated with low ratios of exports to industry turnover. It is suggested that levels of tariff protection reflects a local industry's relative cost disadvantage on world markets when com-

---

12. It is often the case that exports of local subsidiaries of foreign firms are restricted in various ways by their overseas parents. In these circumstances the expected signs of the coefficients of FCONVAPC are negative.

13. The Pearson (P) and Spearman (S) correlation coefficients (significant at approximately the 1 per cent level) are:

		IMPTO			IMPTO
NTRANS	P	-.266	ETRANS	P	-.238
	S	-.257		S	-.283

pared with its foreign competitors. To the extent that this is true, such tariffs reflect an industry's relative inability to compete on world markets. The transport cost variable may in part capture the influence of the transport cost barriers facing Australian exporters and the consequent disadvantages they face when competing with overseas firms in foreign markets. When net Australian industry trade (i.e.: exports-imports) is considered, the coefficents of the transport cost variables become positive. Apparently the discouragement of imports by transport costs results in a positive influence of such costs on the balance of Australian industry's trade with the rest of the world.

Foreign control[14]

The equations of Table 9.7 support the hypothesis that manufacturing industries characterised by large size (EMPLG), and relatively capital-intensive production processes (through the negative sign of LABINT), attract direct foreign participation. Product differentiation (PRODIFF) in industries may provide a barrier to entry to local firms, and thus play an important role in encouraging foreign entry. Consistent with Caves (1971), for Australia the results suggest that influences which act as barriers to potential local entrants (especially scale economies — reflected by RMES50 and EMPLG) tend to encourage the direct participation of foreign firms.[15] Not surprisingly, the implication is that direct investment tends to be associated with oligopolistic market structure and is in accord with Maureen Brunt's findings: ". . . almost invariably the foreign firm in Australia operated in a highly oligopolistic market setting" (Brunt, 1966, p. 263).

The possible relationships between protection and foreign investment are likely to be ambiguous. On the other hand, the existence of high transport costs and/or tariffs may encourage foreign firms to produce domestically behind barriers to trade: to substitute production abroad for exports. On the other hand, if the necessity for high tariff barriers reflects relative inefficiencies or the relative lack of appropriate resources, or if high trans-

---

14. It should be remembered that the basic criterion for foreign control differs between the countries, but it seems reasonable to expect that basic relationships between the variables examined should remain unaffected for each country. (In essence, an enterprise in Australia is classified as foreign controlled if 25 per cent of shareholdings is in the hand of foreigners; in Canada, only if 50 per cent is in the hands of foreigners.)

15. It has not been possible to test Eastman and Stykolt's (1967, p. 84) hypothesis that an important incentive to direct foreign investment lies in economies of scale in research and development. Such a relationship is also implied by Horst's (1972b) analysis. Information about research and development expenditure undertaken by foreign firms in their country of origin is needed to test the hypothesis. Such data were not available for this study.

TABLE 9.7

REGRESSION ANALYSIS OF DETERMINANTS OF FOREIGN CONTROL
DEPENDENT VARIABLE: FCONTOPC

CONST	PRODIFF	RMES50	EMPLG	LABINT	NATRES3	NTRANS	NTARIFF	ETRANS	ETARIFF		
AUSTRALIA											
86.9837a	35.4068a		.2535b	-88.4747a	-9.8099	-.5101a	-.2421			R^2 = .3937	F = 10.091a
70.7302a	36.1281a		.2562b	-83.7188a	-7.2949			-.2563a	.0568a	R^2 = .3700	F = 9.223a
76.4802a	36.0832a	95.5673a		-75.6730a		-.4516a	-.1742			R^2 = .4302	F = 13.686a
62.7090a	35.4719a	93.1443a		-75.5684a				-.2085c	.0248	R^2 = .4014	F = 12.269a
CANADA											
141.6103a	6.4376a		.0826	-141.8597a	-37.1035a	-2.9278a	-.7941a			R^2 = .3490	F = 8.5064a
125.9024a	7.1038		.0735	-142.4008a	-37.1117a			-.4973a	-.1572a	R^2 = .3251	F = 7.745a
132.5276a	10.9890	10.6199		-128.8237a		-3.1951a	-.6899a			R^2 = .2823	F = 7.610a
116.2279a	12.5901	7.8669		-126.4662a				-.5000a	-.1430a	R^2 = .2557	F = 6.772a

F-statistic significance levels: (a) 1 per cent
(b) 5 per cent
(c) 10 per cent

151

port costs reflect the necessity for long lines of communication, then such barriers may well discourage foreign direct participation. It should also be remembered, from the discussion of Chapter 5 and the empirical analysis of Chapter 6, that *ad valorem* transport costs decline as stage of commodity fabrication and commodity unit-values increase. Multinational firms in manufacturing typically participate in markets for sophisticated, relatively high-technology products, and by implication, those with high unit-values. Relatively high *ad valorem* transport costs therefore may apply to commodities for which multinational firms investing in manufacturing activities have little affinity.

For Australia there is no significant relationship between tariff protection and the percentage of foreign control of turnover (FCONTOPC). For Canada however, the coefficients for both nominal and effective tariffs are negative and highly significant. This suggests that the Canadian tariff acts to discourage the foreign control of Canadian manufacturing, though this suggestion has little intuitive appeal. This result is in conflict with Eastman and Stykolt's reasoning,[16] but is consistent with the negative sign for effective rates of protection found by Spence in his equation examining the determinants of direct foreign investment in Canada (Spence, 1977, p. 268), and the results of the bivariate analysis of Chapter 8. Rather than tariffs providing an active discouragement to direct foreign participation, it is suggested that the need for high tariff barriers reflects the relative inefficiency of a productive activity in the country in question, or that an activity is relatively unsuited in some way (e.g., through the lack of suitable factor endowments) to that country's industrial environment. Consequently such activities hold no attraction to multinational firms characterised by a large scale, and capital intensive production techniques. As well, tariff protection tends to lower barriers to entry and may encourage the entry of small, locally controlled firms. The likely consequence is a relatively low level of foreign control.

There is, however, a relevant question for which the data of this study cannot provide an insight: "Is foreign investment in an industry under tariff protection higher than it would be in the absence of such protection?" Surveys in Australia by Brash (1966) and Johns and Hogan (1967) have indicated that this is likely to be so. Unfortunately the results of the regression equations of Table 9.7 leave the question unanswered as do the earlier bivariate correlations of Chapter 8.2.

In both countries the coefficients of NTRANS and ETRANS provide

---

16. According to the Eastman and Stykolt, the Canadian tariff, by allowing plant sizes to be smaller than they would be in the absence of a tariff, "promotes foreign ownership of Canadian manufacturing industry" (Eastman and Stykolt, 1967, p. 88).

evidence of a strong inverse relationship between transport cost protection and foreign control,[17] and this provides some support for the "lines of communication" argument: that relatively high transport costs reflect long lines of communication and so act to discourage foreign investment. Based on discussion of Chapter 5, and the findings of Chapters 6 and 7, which suggested that there is an inverse relationship between *ad valorem* transport costs, and stage of fabrication and unit-value, this result is also consistent with the hypothesis that high transport costs apply to low unit-value goods in which multinational firms operating in manufacturing industries have little interest.[18]

Summary of Regression Analysis Results

The regression analysis of this chapter has looked at three aspects of industries in Australia and Canada: their diversity, trade performance, and level of foreign control. While the earlier discriminant analysis was concerned mainly with *differences* between the industries comprising the respective manufacturing sectors, the regression analysis has been concerned in large part with *similarities* of structural relationships within the respective sectors.

The regression analysis of firm and establishment diversity implies that firms and establishments characterised by vertical integration and lack of specialisation are likely to be locally owned, labour intensive enterprises, with few (and probably single) establishments. The inverse relationship found between foreign control, and the degree of intra-enterprise, and establishment specialisation is highly significant in both countries and strongly implies that foreign controlled firms are more likely to be more specialised in production within their primary activity than are firms which

---

17. In the bivariate correlation analysis of Chapter 8.2, the signs of the coefficients of the foreign participation variable with the transport cost variables were negative, but at low levels of significance.

18. The relationship (if any) between home-country protection and direct foreign participation is still far from clear. The results discussed in this study do not rule out an attempt by multinational firms to maximise their global profits by, for example, choosing optimally between exporting and subsidiary production in the way suggested by Horst (1972b). He found that ". . . exporting and direct investment may be substitutes for one another . . .", and that ". . . Canadian tariff policy has a definite impact on the choice between exporting and Canadian subsidiary production — the higher the Canadian tariff, the smaller the share of U.S. exports, and the larger the share of Canadian subsidiary production in total U.S. sales to the Canadian market" (1972, p. 38). However in a comment on Horst's work, Orr (1975) has found that Horst's results depend on the level of aggregation of industries chosen for the analysis, and that while higher tariffs discourage imports, there is no evidence that U.S. controlled production in Canada is substituted for these imports (1975, pp. 233-234). The issue is again one which deserves future research.

are locally controlled. Moreover, there is evidence that foreign controlled firms are likely to have relatively few establishments. While the results of the regression analysis of diversification across industries were disappointing and have not been included here owing to space limitations, it is worth reporting that an inverse relationship was found between inter-industry diversification and foreign control in both countries, but especially significant for Canada. In all, the regression results strongly imply that industries with high levels of foreign control are characterised by firms which are highly specialised in all respects. They are firms, therefore, which, at least within the host economy, tend to be neither vertically nor horizontally integrated, and to have comparatively few establishments. The first implies an attempt to exploit plant-, and product-level economies of scale through specialisation within the plant. While the decision to invest abroad is in itself likely to lead to firm-level economies of scale, the last two results suggest that within the host countries, foreign firms may make little further effort to exploit such economies. More likely however, if the hosts are characterised by comparatively small local markets for the products of these industries, there may simply be comparatively little scope to take further advantage of economies of scale for the firm which may be available in larger markets.

The role of protection in encouraging or discouraging diversity is far from clear. In Australia, tariff protection apparently discourages interindustry diversification, but encourages intra-industry diversification, though the levels of significance of the tariff variables in the equations are not high. The latter is an expected result as, *ceteris paribus*, high tariffs, especially effective tariffs, will tend to increase value added, and to increase the measure of vertical integration/intra-industry diversification used here (the ratio of value added to the value of turnover). The former result may reflect the direct relationship observed earlier between tariff protection and the proportions of small firms in industries. Small firms may simply not have the resources to diversify their activities across industries. In Canada there is no significant relationship between the tariff variables and interindustry diversification, but a significant negative relationship with intraindustry diversification. This is certainly not an expected result, for the reasons just outlined, and there is no obvious explanation for it. High transport cost protection apparently does not encourage vertical integration by firms in an attempt to minimise such costs by producing at successive stages of manufacture at one location, nor is there evidence that it encourages horizontal integration. It does apparently result in a high ratio of establishments to enterprises. It is likely that the international transport costs of Chapter 7 are positively correlated with domestic transport costs and thus, may capture some of their influence. These results then suggest that if transport costs do encourage diversification, it is diversification of plant location, rather than of production within, or across, industries.

The regression analysis of the export performance of industries implies that Australian industries which use inputs consisting of high proportions of natural resources are characterised by "superior" export performance in terms of both the ratio of exports to turnover, and trade balance. There is no similar evidence for Canada. On the other hand, Canadian industries with high levels of research and development expenditure tend to export high proportions of their outputs, while in Australia, no such relationship exists. In these respects there may well be fundamental differences between the manufacturing sectors of the two countries: Australian industries tend to export products embodying natural resources; those in Canada, products embodying technology. There is no evidence for either country of any significant influence on trade performance of foreign control of local industries.

What are the effects of trade barriers on the export performance of industries? First, the barriers to exports considered — U.S. tariffs as a proxy for the foreign tariffs faced by exporters in both Australia and Canada, and the transport costs barriers derived in Chapter 6 used as proxies in a similar manner — generally did not perform well. In neither country was there a statistically significant relationship between U.S. tariffs and export performance. The trade balance equations however did show evidence of the inhibiting influence of foreign (U.S.) tariffs, and the relationship with U.S. tariffs, not surprisingly, was stronger for Canada. The coefficients of the transport cost measures derived in Chapter 6, while generally of relatively low levels of significance, were predominantly of correct (negative) sign. Of the trade barriers to imports derived in Chapter 7, only transport costs were significant influences on exports, and only for Australia. In contrast with most of the results of this study, effective rates were of higher levels of significance than nominal rates, and this may reflect a number of influences. First, it has earlier been noted that the transport costs for exports and those for imports are highly correlated, and thus, these results are likely to capture part of the transport cost barrier facing Australian exporters. Second, the effective rates take account of the transport cost burden on inputs, and thus their comparative "success" as an explanatory variable suggests that the effective rates capture not only the transport burden facing exporters and potential exporters, but the disadvantage they face in having to purchase importable materials at prices adversely affected by high international transport costs. A particularly interesting result is the positive relationship between transport costs and the trade balances of industries in Australia. It suggests that whatever inhibiting influence of transport costs for exports is captured by the transport costs estimated in Chapter 7, it is outweighed by their influence in lowering imports. It provides evidence that on balance, Australian manufacturing is advantaged by international transport costs. Generally, tariffs were not significant influences on either facet of trade performance examined, though the signs of the nominal tariff were usually negative. The need for high tariffs implies an inability of industries so protected to adequately compete on world markets, and the results provide some, albeit weak, evidence of that for Australia.

The final set of regressions suggest that in both countries industries with high levels of foreign control are those characterised by barriers to entry — in terms of scale, relative capital intensity, and product differentiation — though the results hold more strongly for Australia. There is no evidence in either country that foreign manufacturing firms move to the respective host countries in an effort to exploit their natural resources. Indeed, for Canada, the evidence suggests the contrary may be true. Similarly, in neither country is their evidence that foreign firms attempt to surmount local tariffs or high international transport costs by moving behind such barriers; for both countries there is evidence to the contrary. To the extent that there is a direct association between transport costs and distance, the negative relationships between foreign control and transport costs appear to provide some support for the "lines of communication" argument, that geographic proximity encourages direct investment. The association of multinational firms with activities characterised by large scale, capital-, and research and development-intensive production of products of (implicitly) high unit values (See Table 8.10) provides an explanation for these results. It is suggested that foreign manufacturing firms are more likely to participate in markets for goods at relatively high stages of fabrication and technology, rather than those comprising the process of raw materials at early stages. These types of high unit-value commodities are generally subject to comparatively low *ad valorem* transport costs, while domestic industries in most need of protection — those comprising small scale, labour intensive firms — produce products which are of comparatively little interest to large foreign firms. Again, it should be stressed that it is not possible to determine here if levels of foreign control are higher with tariffs than they would be in their absence.

10. Summary and Conclusions

In Australia and Canada tariffs have played an important role as a means of promoting the development of manufacturing industry. Their economic and political importance has led to tariff theory and policy being a favoured area of study for economists in both countries. The roles of distance and the associated costs of transportation as barriers to trade have not been as well researched, and the present study is an attempt to fill at least part of this gap in literature.

The Canadian manufacturing sector has been used here as a benchmark for comparison with Australian experience. While Canada has a history of protectionism which is similar to Australia's, and shares many other characteristics with it, Canada's proximity to, and the importance of its trade with the United States, means that as far as transport costs are concerned, it faces quite different circumstances. An important aim of this study therefore is to compare the Canadian manufacturing sector, which has developed primarily behind tariff protection alone, with the Australian manufacturing sector, which has developed behind not only high tariffs, but because of its relative geographic isolation, high barriers of transport costs.

10.1 Protection of Australian and Canadian Manufacturing: A Review of the Literature

From the analysis of Chapter 2 it is apparent that there are a number of marked similarities between the aims, the development and the apparent effects of protectionism over the last century in both Australia and Canada. Both sets of British colonies as they then were, first introduced tariffs in the early 19th century as a means of raising revenue, while protectionism for the purpose of assisting industrialisation became an increasingly important political force from the mid-1800s. In both countries tariffs are now seen by many as contributing to the maintenance of industrial structures inimical to industrial efficiency and inhibiting needed structural change.

Given the importance of protection in Australia and Canada, Chapter 3 examines some of the theoretical literature concerning protection and its possible effects on industry structure and performance. Only brief space is devoted to tariffs, as the literature is well-known. More stress is given to the analysis of international transport costs as analogues of tariffs, and particularly to their influence on the range of commodities produced. It is shown that *ceteris paribus*, the basket of commodities produced by a given country is likely to contain a wider selection the more isolated (by transport costs and/or tariffs) it is from the rest of the world. In the absence of other influences, the work of Haberler (1936) and Dornbusch, Fischer and Samuelson (1977) suggests that the higher are transport cost and tariff barriers, the less specialised in production a particular country is likely to be. If, as these results imply, economies of scale (at the product-level) may be limited, Krugman's (1979) results suggest that protection will lead to a larger number of smaller establishments. Eastman and Stykolt (1967) suggest that the size of markets is important: if the market is relatively small there is likely to be significant interdependance between producers, leading to either high costs or high profits. In economies like Australia and Canada, characterised by oligopoly and relatively high barriers to trade, high profits may attract entry with the consequence that the market structure "... is one in which the number of plants is large, the scale of plants sub-optimal, and average costs are high" (Eastman and Stykolt, 1967, p. 19). It should be stressed that the empirical analysis of Chapters 8 and 9 is not a direct attempt to test the hypotheses outlined in Chapter 3, which show how, under highly restrictive assumptions, trade barriers, both foreign and domestic, affect the range of commodities produced in the protected economy. The purposes of Chapter 3 are twofold: to establish the analogy between transport cost and tariff protection; and to shed some light on the possible effects of protection on the diversity of production, and the likely consequences for the structure of industry.

In Chapter 4, the survey of the empirical literature concerning trade barriers, and the links between market size and industrial structure and performance relies heavily on Canadian work. Evidence provided by Daly, Keys and Spence (1968) suggests that in Canada, tariffs contributed to ease of entry, and that the size of plant and equipment which can profitably be used in a small, protected market is less than it may be in a larger, more competitive one. Caves (1975) contends that the relative output diversity of locally-owned Canadian plants (when compared with U.S. plants) is directly related to the proportion of non-production employees in total employment, and that when non-production employees are a larger proportion of total employment in Canada than in the U.S., the activities of Canadian-owned plants are more diversified across industries. The comparative studies of West (1971), Spence (1977) and Oksanen and Williams (1978) also note the relatively large proportion of non-production workers typical of Canadian industries, when compared with similar industries in the United States. In particular, West's findings suggest a link between high proportions of non-production workers and low productivity. While Caves (1975) casts doubt on the presumption that tariffs encourage "excess" diversity, the work of Scherer *et al* (1975) suggests that domestic and foreign tariffs affect the size of the market available to domestic firms and thus their ability to realise economies of scale. The inference from the studies examined in Chapter 4 is that protection, whatever its form, plays an important role in the determination of industry structure and performance; and may well be associated with highly significant (and detrimental) effects on consumption, and investment; and ultimately, on productivity and growth.

10.2 Barriers to Australian and Canadian Trade: The Empirical Evidence

From the theoretical analyses examined in Chapter 3, and the survey of empirical evidence made in Chapter 4, *both* foreign and domestic trade barriers affect patterns of production and the structure of industries. Thus, this study has attempted to take account of barriers to the trade of Australian and Canadian manufacturing industries from two points of view: that of exporters and potential exporters; and of import-competing producers. Clearly, all else being equal, foreign tariffs and transport costs for exports are a disadvantage which must be faced by those producing exportable commodities; equally, to import-competing producers, domestic tariffs and international transport costs are an advantage, providing barriers behind which they may shelter. Geographic isolation and the "cost of distance", may be viewed as barriers to trade in exactly the same ways.

Barriers to Exports

The evidence of Chapter 5 suggests that exporters in Oceania, including those in Australia, are more disadvantaged by distance than those in any other trade area. The "good" trade location of Canada is owed to its proximity to the United States, its major trading partner. Geraci and Prewo (1977) have made the valuable contribution of explicitly showing the links between distance, transport costs and trade flows: distance is an important determinant of transport costs; transport costs are an important determinant of trade flows. Thus, they show that distance is at least partially embodied in the cost of transportation and its inhibiting influence on trade flows, and moreover, their evidence suggests that transport costs may well be more important barriers to trade than are tariffs. Indeed, in the case of Australian exports to the United States, transport costs are, on average, approximately two to three times as high as corresponding United States tariffs (Sampson and Yeats, 1977).

The empirical analysis of Chapter 6 indicates that geographic distance adds about 13 to 15 percent to the cost of transporting Australian exports to Japan and Europe, and, *ceteris paribus*, that the *extra* cost of distance stemming from Australia's relative isolation adds about 4 or 5 per cent to the cost of transportation, compared with the cost in Canada. Consistent with the findings of Waters (1970) and Yeats (1977), examined in Chapter 5, the estimates of liner freight rates for Australian exports to Europe derived in Chapter 6, show that such freight rates fall less heavily on high unit-value, and by inference, highly fabricated, commodities. If the results of Chapter 6 are representative, they suggest that international transport costs often may well be higher, and provide a greater barrier to trade than the corresponding foreign tariffs for *both* Australian and Canadian exporters. Indeed, despite the comparatively favourable trade location of Canada, Bryan's results suggest that as determinants of Canadian exports, "variation in transport costs have a larger effect on the structure of exports than variations in [foreign] tariffs". (1974b, p. 652).

Barriers to Imports

Chapter 7 examines the other important aspect of tariff and transport cost barriers to trade: the advantage they provide to import-competing producers in Australia and Canada. Distance as a barrier to imports is not explicitly considered in this Chapter, nor in much of the subsequent analysis of this study. Rather it is implicitly assumed on the basis of empirical evidence considered in Chapters 5 and 6 (e.g.: Heaver, 1973; Lipsey and Weiss, 1974; Geraci and Prewo, 1977), that the influence of distance is embodied in the *ad valorem* transport costs derived in Chapter 7, and which were used in the empirical analyses of Chapters 8 and 9.

The evidence presented in Chapter 7 suggests that for Australia there is a general tendency for tariffs and transport costs to act in opposite directions: tariffs increase with stage of fabrication; transport costs decrease. This result is consistent with the studies examined in Chapter 5 and the evidence concerning Australia's exports in Chapter 6.

Analysis of the nominal and effective transport costs protecting the Australian manufacturing industries included in this study reveals that transport costs are a significant component of the total protective structure. Of the 85 ACIC industries, 25 industries which together employ nearly 25 per cent of the manufacturing industry workforce in Australia, shelter behind nominal transport costs which are higher than the corresponding nominal tariffs. In terms of effective rates of protection, 13 industries, accounting for over 16 per cent of the workforce, were mainly protected by transport costs. On average, transport costs comprise nearly one-half of average (unweighted) total nominal protection, and nearly one-third of the average (unweighted) total effective protection available to the Australian manufacturing sector.[1] Despite the proximity of the United States, the

---

1. From Table 7.5, average total nominal protection (unweighted) is 39 per cent; the corresponding effective rate is 53 per cent.

major source of Canada's imports, transport costs also comprise a significant element of the protection available to Canadian Manufacturing industries. They are the major element for 16 of the 85 industries in terms of nominal rates, and the major element for 9 industries in terms of effective rates of protection. Approximately 20 per cent of the Canadian manufacturing industry workforce is more protected by transport costs than tariffs.

The comparison of protective barriers in Chapter 7 shows that on average, Australian manufacturing industries are protected by significantly higher (nominal and effective) tariff and transport cost barriers compared with those of Canada. Average Canadian nominal transport costs are approximately one-quarter of the Australian average of approximately 17 per cent, while average Canadian nominal tariffs are about one-half of the Australian average of approximately 22 per cent. Average Canadian effective transport costs and tariffs are about one-third and two-thirds of the levels of their Australian counterparts (which are approximately 16 and 36 per cent), respectively. Despite these differences between the heights of the respective barriers, there are substantial similarities between the two countries' tariff structures: industries which in Australia are relatively highly protected tend to be relatively highly protected in Canada as well. The analysis of Chapter 7 is the result of the first attempt to compare tariff and transport cost protection in the cases of Australia and Canada, and it shows that to ignore the transport cost component of the protective structures of the two countries is to ignore a highly significant element of the total barriers to their imports.

10.3 Trade Barriers and their Effects on Australian and Canadian Manufacturing

Given the importance of barriers to trade as influences on trade patterns and through them, on aspects of industry structure; and having provided estimates of the tariff and transport cost barriers to Australian and Canadian trade, Chapters 8 and 9 examined, *inter alia*, the possible links between the estimated trade barriers and characteristics of the industries comprising the Australian and Canadian manufacturing sectors. In essence these Chapters have looked at aspects of possible similarities and differences between Australian and Canadian industries: similarities through the simple correlations of Chapter 8.3 and the regression analysis of Chapter 9.2; and differences through the comparisons of means and distributions of Chapter 8.2, and the discriminant analysis of Chapter 9.1. In particular, this study is concerned with trade barriers, both protecting and facing each country, as possible determinants of attributes of industries *within* the respective manufacturing sectors; and the extent to which differences between the respective barriers contribute to differences *between* the two sets of industries.

Similarities Between Australian and Canadian Industries

In both countries high levels of total protection are associated with industries typified by relatively labour-intensive production methods, by many small enterprises and establishments, and by the employment of comparatively large proportions of those who are unskilled, poorly educated, poorly paid, migrants and females. Consistent with these findings, highly protected industries are additionally characterised by low levels of research and development and/or innovative activity. The inverse relationships between levels of foreign control and the heights of protective barriers suggests foreign firms apparently do not attempt to avoid such barriers by moving behind them. It appears likely that industries which shelter behind high levels of protection are characterised by productive processes and products which may have little appeal to multinational firms. This is not to say that levels of foreign control are not higher with protection than they would be without.

In both countries, while high tariffs apparently act to increase the sizes of domestic markets by shutting out imports, they are associated with poor export performance as a likely effect of their adverse influence on industry structures. Taken together, the apparent net result is that the size of *total* markets is reduced by high domestic tariffs and this is further reinforced if industries face high foreign (U.S.) tariffs. High local tariffs are associated with small, vertically integrated enterprises implying a comparative inability of such firms to exploit plant- and product-level economies of scale. Indeed, virtually all of the characteristics of high-tariff industries — small size; labour intensive processes; low levels of skills, research and development and innovation — are associated with poor export performance.

In both countries industries protected by high transport costs for competing imports are characterised by high proportions of multi-establishment firms. It is likely that these transport costs capture some of the influence of domestic transport costs, high levels of which would encourage the siting of establishments close to local markets and/or sources of raw materials. High transport costs for both imports and exports are associated with poor trade performance, though it is not possible to separate their respective effects on levels of imports and exports, as the transport costs derived in Chapter 6 and those in Chapter 7 are generally highly correlated.

In all, while it is apparent that there are advantages to local industries conferred by barriers to imports in sheltering them from import competition, and all else being equal, increasing the sizes of domestic markets, there is evidence that the advantages may well be overshadowed by the sum of two other broad influences. First, barriers to imports are associated with industry structures which are inimical to efficiency, providing for example, apparent encouragement of "excess" entry of firms, and output diversity within industries, both of which may inhibit the exploitation of scale economies. Second, the foreign trade barriers considered here — transport costs for exports (whether measured by the estimates of Chapter 6, or to the extent that they are captured by the transport costs for imports from Chapter 7), and foreign tariffs (via the proxy of U.S. tariffs) — in inhibiting exports, tend to reinforce these adverse effects.

Differences Between Australian and Canadian Industries

Perhaps the most important differences between the two manufacturing sectors (and in many ways, the most illuminating), are the higher absolute numbers of enterprises and establishments which are characteristic of Australian industries. This is despite the obviously larger sizes of domestic markets in Canada, and the proximity of the United States which, all else equal, provides more ready access to export markets. Indeed, it is in trade patterns that many of the differences between Australian and Canadian industries manifest themselves. For example, Australian manufacturing industries tend to export products embodying high proportions of natural resources, while Canadian manufacturers are more likely to export products embodying technology.

It is in respect of technology that another apparent difference manifests itself. In Australia comparatively high levels of research and development activity are undertaken by small firms with few establishments. The evidence is also consistent with the hypothesis that large Australian firms, characterised as they are by relatively skilled workforces and comparatively high levels of foreign control, may primarily engage in the adaptation of foreign-designed products to local conditions. For Canada however, the results comply with the common expectation that R & D is higher in large firms, participating in relatively concentrated markets. It is therefore possible that because of Canada's proximity to the United States, there is not the same need for adaptation. If R & D activities in foreign controlled firms in Australia are mainly "adaptive", there may be little technological benefit flowing to the host country. The relatively greater research effort apparently made by large Canadian firms may well explain, at least in part, their comparative success in obtaining export markets, and the results described in the preceding paragraph.

The discriminant analyses show that differences in the attributes of the respective manufacturing sectors when they are considered jointly, enable industries' correct country of origin to be predicted with high degrees of accuracy. What are differences that enable the correct prediction of country memberships? If an industry has such characteristics as a high level of concentration, high proportions of small firms and establishments, employing high levels of "overhead" staff and comparatively labour intensive processes, a lack of innovative activity with (from other evidence) the likelihood of an unskilled and poorly educated workforce, low levels of exports and intra-industry trade, it will be classified as Australian. Contrary attributes will classify it as Canadian. Clearly it is a comparison which is less than favourable for the "average" Australian manufacturing industry.

Where does protection fit into this picture? It should be stressed that in discriminant analysis, the addition of variables may detract from the ability of a function to correctly predict group members. The addition of the protection variables does not; it adds to the predictive ability of the functions. Discriminant analysis is an analysis of dependency of fixed populations upon a linear combination of discriminating variables. It involves the analysis of causality (by hypothesis) from the group of interdependent discriminating variables to the determination of the membership of populations. Regression analysis by contrast, involves the analysis of dependency of the dependent variable and the fixed independent (and by hypothesis) causal or determining variables. The two techniques therefore, while both involving the analysis of dependency, do so from rather different sets of assumptions (Kendall, 1957, 1975; Kendall and Stewart, 1968, pp. 314-336). In this context, it is hypothesised that the populations (Australian and Canadian industries) depend on a linear combination of explanatory variables. When protection is added to these explanatory variables, the new linear combination results in an improved ability to predict (or "cause") population memberships. The memberships of populations therefore jointly depend (by hypothesis) on protection and the other variables. It is assumed here that the populations are different. The greater degree of hetrogeneity implied by the discriminant functions and reflected by the group centroids, the more evidence is provided that the populations are distinct, and that the functions optimally discriminate between real differences in populations. Protection, in combination with the other variables, therefore adds to the ability to "cause" or "explain" the distinction, and provides evidence that protection *is* an important element of the attributes of the two manufacturing sectors.

The Likely Role of Trade Barriers

What is the causal mechanism that these results imply? The evidence suggests that trade barriers are successful in inhibiting trade and thus affect the size of markets. The barriers examined in Chapter 7, in increasing

164

import prices and reducing the level of imports, increase access by domestic firms to local markets. This encourages entry of a greater number of smaller firms and establishments than could be sustained in the absence of such barriers, in a manner consistent with the theoretical results of Krugman (1979). The fragmentation of markets leads to an inability to exploit economies of scale, particularly at the plant-, and product-levels, and moreover, enables, or even encourages the use of comparatively labour intensive processes entailing few skills. The "parochial view" of the domestic market enabled by protection (Scherer *et al*, 1975, p. 137) is, as suggested by Daly, Keys and Spence (1968), likely to result in lower output per unit of input by firms in protected markets. Distance, and the associated transport costs derived in Chapter 6, and foreign tariffs (via the proxy of U.S. tariffs), reinforce the parochial view. The results suggest that all three act to inhibit exports, contributing to inward-looking strategies of firms and the accompanying adverse effects on firm efficiencies, like those implied by Scherer.

The "Costs" of Protection

This study suggests that an important consequence of protection is likely to be the fragmentation of markets and a concomitant inability to exploit economies of scale. An estimation of the costs of these and other effects of protection can only truly be made by estimating a sophisticated, large scale general equilibrium model, the specification of which incorporates the effects of economies of scale and intra-industry specialisation. The omission of these factors will almost certainly entail serious underestimates of the costs of protection, as has been recognised by researchers in both Australia (e.g. Evans, 1970; Dixon and Butlin, 1978) and Canada (e.g. Wonnacott, 1975; Williams, 1978).

The estimation of the type of general equilibrium model required is well beyond the scope of this study. However it is worth recalling Wonnacott's attempt to add to the consumption benefits of free trade between Canada and the U.S. estimated by Williams (1978, p. 30), the benefits accruing to Canada resulting from the exploitation of economies of scale (see Chapter 4.3). The product of the real productivity differences between the two countries, and the ratio of Canadian value added in manufacturing to G.N.P. was estimated to be the gain resulting from the elimination of the productivity gap through the exploitation of scale economies and specialisation with free trade. The computation implied increase in Canadian G.N.P. of 5.9 per cent, which, when added to Williams' estimated consumption benefit of 2.3 per cent of G.N.P., implied a *total* gain of 8.2 per cent of Canadian G.N.P. as a result of free trade between Canada and the U.S.

If Wonnacott's method is applied in the case of Australia, and assuming that these are the gains both free trade and no international transport costs,[2] the corresponding calculation for Australia[3] implies an increase of 28 per cent of Australian G.D.P. in 1973. This, when added to the increase in real consumption through the elimination of protection estimated by Dixon and Butlin (3 per cent), which is the equivalent of an increase of just under 2 per cent of G.D.P.,[4] results in a total gain of about 30 per cent of G.D.P. owing to the elimination of the productivity gap between Australia and the U.S. with free trade and no international transport costs. Of course unlike tariffs, transport costs cannot be removed at the stroke of a pen. The penalty of distance must still be paid. On average, transport costs provide about 40 per cent of the total (nominal) barrier to imports, so it is obviously unrealistic to expect all of these potential gains to be realised. If the possible gains can be apportioned in the same ratio as the two components of protection, it means that the partial elimination of the productivity gap via the elimination of tariffs will result in an increase of over 15 per cent of Australian G.D.P., roughly twice the estimated Canadian gain.[5] In this respect, it is interesting to recall that average (nominal) Australian tariffs are roughly twice those of Canada, too. Naturally such an estimate of gains should be viewed with caution. It merely serves to illustrate as Dixon (1978) does that the gains from free trade may well be much more significant than previously thought. With Australia's higher average level of protection and its geographic isolation,[6] it certainly appears reasonable to expect a greater gain from free trade than in Canada.

10.4 Policy Prescriptions?

It may be seen in Chapter 2 that an important objective of Australian and Canadian commercial policies has been the promotion of industrial diversity. That this aim has been achieved seems evident from the analysis conducted in Chapters 8 and 9. It is with the legacies of the "success" of

---

2. Evans' model does however implicitly include a consideration of international transport costs. See Evans (1971, pp. 33-34, 69-71).

3. Sources: I.L.O. (1976, Table 13), World Bank (1976, p. 250).

4. Using Evans' investment specification and a constraint on maximum levels of exports (Dixon and Butlin, 1977, p. 346). See also World Bank (1976, p. 250).

5. The possible gains to Canada estimated by Wonnacott have not been "deflated" as a result of the transport cost protection of Canadian industry.

6. See Chapter 6 for a discussion of the relationship between distance and the cost of transportation. While nothing can be done about Australia's physical isolation, action to lower international transport costs may well bring significant gains. For a very brief discussion of some measures which could be undertaken, See Conlon (1979, p. 4). See also Section 10.4.

these policies with which much of this study has been concerned. In Australia, the evidence points to the creation of diversity (broadly defined) carried to the extreme of fragmentation of already small markets, when Canadian industry is used as the basis for comparison. The likely effects of this on the relative abilities of Australian industries to exploit scale economies are obvious. The evidence of other researchers examined in Chapter 4 suggests that with respect to the United States, the same broad conclusions may be true of Canadian manufacturing industries. Scherer *et al* (1975) in particular point to debilitating effects of both Canadian and U.S. tariffs on Canadian industry. Though they are by no means mutually exclusive, the consequence of the former is likely to be lack of incentive to minimise costs; the consequence of the latter, in providing a barrier which must be surmounted, is likely to be an inability to exploit all facets of economies of scale — firm-specific, plant-specific, and product-specific. In these respects the transport cost barriers examined here apparently work in exactly the same way. The evidence suggests that it is international trade, or rather, the lack of it, as a result of barriers to both imports and exports, which is integral to the mechanism of inefficiency in both countries.

Its obvious that the overwhelming objective of imposing "man-made" protection is to restrict the volume of trade to provide an environment conducive to the development of local industries. In neither Australia nor in Canada — both "small" economies — could it be reasonably contended that the "large" country case applies, and that despite restricting trade, protection of manufacturing may increase real incomes by improving the term of trade. It appears reasonable to consider that both countries face "given" terms of trade and that barriers (both tariffs and transport costs) merely reduce the volume of trade and have little, if any effect on the relative prices of imports and exports.

If this is true, and if protection has the adverse effects on industries implied by this and other studies, what can be done about it? First it is necessary to distinguish between tariff and transport cost protection: transport costs reflect (or should reflect) the costs of providing a real service; tariff payments do not. Thus, there is a fundamental difference in the degree of control which may be exercised by governments over these two barriers to trade. Tariffs may be imposed or removed at the stroke of a pen; transport costs may be considered in large part, an economic fact of life, and thus to be largely outside the influence of policy-makers. It is best to deal with the two propositions in turn.

Tariffs

If something may be done about tariffs (and other man-made barriers) what should be done? The possible measures may be arranged in what may be considered to be their decreasing order of desirability. It is an arrangement which, unfortunately, does not correspond with their likelihood of implementation. The first-best answer to the question is readily apparent: the multilateral elimination of all trade barriers. While this answer involves the maximisation of world welfare, it should be realised that the welfare of individual countries may be adversely affected, and there is no guarantee that Australia and/or Canada may not be so affected. Of course this is not a prospect that should worry those in either country since if past attempts at multilateral tariff reform are anything to go by, the probability that the elimination of all trade barriers will ever occur must be very close to zero.

What then are policies that have *some* (albeit small) likelihood of being implemented? For both Australia and Canada, the negotiation of bilateral agreements with major trading partners to reduce trade barriers is a more realistic alternative, though the prospect of implementation of significant bilateral agreement appears again to be very small in both countries. Given the dominance of Canada's trade by the United States, for Canada, a bilateral agreement with the United States creating a free trade area may well provide a reasonable approximation of the effects of multilateral tariff reform. It would bring gains which, on Wonnacott's (1975), and Williams' (1978) results, are by no means insignificant. A century and a half of debate on the issue of "reciprocity" (see Chapter 2) should give lie to the prospect of such an agreement being implemented in any but the very long term, if ever. In Australia strong resistance by vested interests is already being shown to the full implementation of agreement for Closer Economic Relations with New Zealand, (signed in December, 1982), a decade before its proposed consumation in 1995; and New Zealand, while important, is only a comparatively small trading partner for Australia. To have a comparable impact as that on Canada of a free trade area with the U.S., agreements would need to be negotiated by Australia with a relatively large number of countries and/or trading blocs. The need of successful negotiations with many parties would appear to make the attainment of significant reform that much more difficult.

If it is accepted that the likelihood of *significant* multilateral and bilateral agreements being negotiated is negligible, that leaves only the alternative of taking unilateral action. In the last resort, both countries should look toward the rationalisation of their own protective barriers which at least should be directed at the attainment of more uniform levels of protection in an attempt to minimise the distortion of resource allocation between industries (and indeed, between sectors), in much the way advocated by the Australian Industries Assistance Commission, and by the Economic Council of Canada. In the late 1970s there was some suggestion of reform in Australia. There, a Committee had been established (headed by Sir John

Crawford) to examine problems of the structural adjustment of industries. In its report in March, 1979, the Committee recommended a reference be made to the Industries Assistance Commission to examine the possibility of general reductions in protection to manufacturers. Only in late 1981, and then in response to pressure from South East Asian members during a meeting of the Commonwealth Heads of Government, did the Australian government, embarrassed by the high levels of protection against Asian imports, make such a reference to the Commission, requiring it to report by February 1982. The length of time allowed the Commission for such a major study (about 6 months), the exclusion of the very highly protected, politically sensitive, and economically important textile, clothing and motor vehicle industries from its terms of reference, and the subsequent fate of the Commission's report, provide a fair indication of the sincerity of the Fraser Government's commitment to protection reform. In its reports[7] the Commission outlined a series of options to the government, generally involving phased reductions in assistance over a number of years. In rejecting these options as "inappropriate" the door to significant reform closed until at least the end of the 1980s. Certainly, the election of the Hawke Labor government in March 1983 and its actions since then do not provide much hope for earlier, widespread reform.[8]

Now if to some, the advocation of freer trade seems like an appeal in favour of the virtues of motherhood, it cannot be helped. While there are divergent views (e.g. Britton, 1978), very many economists have been advocating what is to them, this form of motherhood, for 200 years. That an argument is long-standing should not of itself reduce its validity. Debate on protection in both countries, at least among economists in more recent years, has centred not so much on the need for protection reform which is now generally accepted, but on methods to minimise dislocation resulting from the implementation of reforms if they ever come about. Much has

---

7. The Commission presented three integrated reports on manufacturing: on export incentives; on fiscal measures of assistance; and on reductions in protection.

8. An obvious question to ask is: Why has so little been achieved? If the costs of protection are as high as economists make out (e.g. see Chapter 4.3), one would think that societies would be clamouring for tariff reform. That they are not may be at least a partial result of three influences: (i) in the main, economists have tended to be busy convincing each other of the benefits of tariff reform, and have been unsuccessful in convincing a wider audience, or have been unwilling to do so; (ii) xenophobia — "foreign" goods are seen by many as undermining the well-being of the home country; and probably most important (iii) those who have most to lose from tariff reform — pressure groups representing both capital and labour in protected activities — are well organised, vocal, and as a consequence have the ear of politicians. The potential gainers — those engaged in unprotected activities, and consumers — are too dispersed, are not heard, are not well-informed and are unable to transform their discontent into political action.

been written in both countries on the need for gradual change, appropriate exchange rate policies, and what has become known as "structural adjustment assistance", to ease the burdens of adapting to freer trade (e.g. Study Group on Structural Adjustment, 1979; Economic Council of Canada, 1975, Ch. 13). The existence of measures which will ease the pain of adjustments to freer trade, will obviously make the move more likely. A discussion of these policies is beyond the scope of this study, but again, most of these prescriptions are well known, and could be described as "traditional recipes".

The debate in Australia and Canada on the merits (or otherwise) of protectionism has been long standing. While history suggests that it is right to take a pessimistic view of the prospect for significant protection reform in both countries, history may also provide a guide for creating a climate conducive to reform. Change will not come from governments until there is pressure from the electorate. The pressures are unlikely to come from the manufacturing sectors, though those in some industries with low levels of protection may be becoming more aware of the burden imposed on them by their highly protected fellows. The brief history of Australian and Canadian commercial policies provided in Chapter 2 suggests that tariffs in both countries have created a persisting resentment of manufacturing by those in agriculture, as tariffs place them in a position of relative disadvantage.[9] The mining sector is similarly disadvantaged (Gregory, 1976). There is a similar regional disenchantment in Australia in Queensland and Western Australia; and in Canada in the Atlantic Provinces and the West as a result of the protection of the manufacturing regions in each country.

Agriculture and mining in both countries, the governments of the States in Australia, and the Provinces in Canada, are all powerful influences on the Central Governments where the primary powers over commercial policies reside. The more evidence that can be made available to these groups, and, indeed, to those on the other side of the debate concerning the effects of protection, the more likely it is that a climate conducive to change will eventually emerge. It is hoped that, in this respect, the evidence provided in this, and studies like it, will make a positive contribution to an informed and rational debate on an issue which is of crucial importance to both countries.

Transport Costs

The evidence of this study suggests that the effect of international transport costs is to reduce the sizes of the tradable goods sectors in both Australia

---

9. Of course, the farm sectors of both countries are far from immune from criticism in the debate on protectionism.

and Canada with the adverse effects which have previously been described. As the need for transportation is an economic fact of life, and to the extent that transport charges involve the real costs of resources used in providing the transportation service, such costs should not be of undue concern, except, of course, insofar as every attempt should be made to minimise them.[10] It is the extent to which transport charges may *not* reflect that real cost of resources that should be of major concern. It is well known, for example, that all else being equal, liner shipping conferences (and for that matter, those operating other modes of transportation) tend to exploit demand elasticities and charge "what the traffic will bear" (Heaver, 1973; Bryan, 1974a, 1974b; Lipsey and Weiss, 1974; Zerby and Conlon, 1982a; see also Chapter 6). This raises the likelihood of cross-subsidisation between commodities arising from such pricing policies.[11] Rates charged for some high-unit value cargoes may be considerably in excess of long-run marginal costs as the elasticities of demand for liner services for shippers of such cargoes will tend to be relatively low. Rates charged for cargoes of low unit value, and comparatively high elasticities of demand, may be below long-run marginal costs. The shortfall in revenues from the latter cargoes may be partially subsidised from the "high" rated cargoes. If F.A.K. (freight-all-kinds) rates[12] are charged, the direction of any tax/subsidy is simply reversed.

The rates of the liner shipping conferences which carry the bulk of imports and exports of manufactures in Australia, and an important part of the Canadian export and import trade in manufactures to destinations other than the United States, are supported or condoned by government policies. The existing pricing policies of conferences are presumably set to maximise conference profits, or at least to provide them with profits based on higher average rates than could be sustained in competitive markets.[13]

It should be realised that the interests of conferences, supported as they are by governments, may not coincide with interests of the communities which they serve. For exporters, it is quite possible that shipping rates are implicitly taxing activities which are of greater benefit to the Australian and

---

10. See for example Webb (1978), for a discussion of measures to lower costs of providing transportation services.

11. See Chapter 6, footnote 5. The question of implicit taxes/subsidies and identification of broad commodity groups affected is the specific subject of Zerby and Conlon (1983).

12. i.e. the same per-unit rate being levied on all cargoes.

13. Though there are exceptions (e.g. the Broken Hill Proprietary (B.H.P.) Company in Australia — a producer of basic steel and fabricated steel products), shippers of manufactures in Australia and Canada are generally too small to "integrate up" to provide their own transportation services as a result of any ability conferences may have to price monopolistically.

Canadian communities than those being implicitly subsidised. For the import-competing producers, the same principle obtains. Rates higher than those obtainable in competitive markets provide an extra margin of man-made protection; those lower, have a tax effect in much the same way as do tariffs on importable inputs. Clearly, the question of the likelihood of "excess" transport costs and the direction of any implicit subsidies or taxes is important to both importers and exporters.

In respect of transport costs, this study has concerned itself principally with the protective effects of measured transport costs for the products of import-competing manufacturing industries. These charges are likely to reflect not only the cost of providing the service (including the influence of distance) but such non-cost influences as the unit-values of cargoes (see Chapter 6). The extent to which the average of all freight charges have been inflated by the anticompetitive market structures of those providing transportation services may be considered to be an additional man-made barrier to trade, and should rightly be treated in the same way as tariffs and other man-made protection.

While the "excess" costs of transportation, and the possibility of "undesirable" cross-subsidies should provide a serious concern to Australians, given the importance of liner conferences to their trade, it is also a concern which should not be lightly dismissed by Canadians, particularly in view of the evidence of Bryan (1974a, 1974b) which suggests that liner pricing policies are important determinants of Canada's trade. The provision of more information on these policies, and their effects, should be an object of future research. If the practices of conferences and Governments can be directed toward creating a more competitive environment resulting in the charging of lower rates, this may be an avenue of making some, albeit small, reductions in man-made barriers to trade which avoids the political odium attached to tariff reform. It is an avenue that apparently neither Australian nor Canadian governments have seriously explored. The results of Chapter 4.3 imply that the possible gains from a lowering of trade barriers, even small reductions, are likely to be well worth pursuing.

APPENDICES

APPENDIX 8.1

The Concordance of Australian and Canadian Manufacturing Activities

An essential part of this study entailed the reconciliation of the statistical classifications used in each country. The basic statistical classifications in Australia and Canada are to the Australian Standard Industrial Classification (ASIC) and the Canadian Standard Industrial Classification (CSIC), respectively. Both are based on the International Standard Industrial Classification of All Economic Activities (ISIC). The process of reconciliation involved the construction of an Australia-Canada Industrial Classification (ACIC) in a way such that a given ACIC Industry in each country consists of a group of operating units engaged in the same activities. The task entailed matching 171 4-digit ASIC industries with 166 4-digit CSIC industries. The final concordance, which appears in this Appendix, produced 85 industries which, for a given ACIC, comprise the same activities in each country. The only significant differences between the two manufacturing sectors are the lack of cotton ginning in Canada and the inclusion of iron ore pelletising in the mining sector (CSIC 058) in that country. As a result, ASIC 2311 (cotton ginning) and ASIC 2911 (iron ore pelletising) have been omitted from the analysis. As far as can be ascertained the only other difference of note involves the rather interesting classification of baby carriage manufacturing to CSIC 393, sporting goods and toy industries in Canada, while the same activity in Australia is classified to ASIC 3225, transport equipment n.e.c. Unfortunately it was not possible to make suitable adjustments to the data, and this difference should be kept in mind. It is likely however, that its impact on the empirical results will be negligible.

The remaining concordance in the Appendix is that between the Canadian Input-Output Industry Classification (CI-0) (in which the Canadian tariff and transport cost data of Chapter 7 were provided by Statistics Canada) and ACIC. Fortunately, there is a readily available published concordance between this classification and CSIC (Statistics Canada, 1977, pp. (35-36). Once the ASIC/CSIC concordance was constructed, it was then a simple matter to use the published CSIC/CI-0 concordance to provide a turn, an ACIC/CI-0 concordance.

Concordance of Statistical Classifications: Australian and Canadian Manufacturing Industries (ACIC) 1973-74

Australian Standard Industrial Classification (ASIC)
Canadian Standard Industrial Classification (CSIC)
Canadian Input-Output Industry Classification (CI-O)

ACIC	Industry Description	ASIC	CSIC	CI-O
1	Meat products	2111, 2113, 2114	1011	016
2	Poultry products	2112	1012	017
3	Milk products	2120	1040	018
4	Fruit, vegetable products	2131-32	1031, 1032	020
5	Flour, starch, cereals	2151-53	1050	022
6	Margarine, oil, fats	2140	1083	027
7	Bread, cakes, pastry	2161-62	1072	024
8	Biscuits	2163	1071	023
9	Confectionary, cocoa	2181	1081	025
10	Fish products	2182	1020	019
11	Animal foods	2183	1060	021
12	Sugar, malt, other foods	2184, 2193	1082, 1089	026, 028
13	Soft drinks, cordials	2191	1091	029
14	Beer	2192	1093	031
15	Wine, alcoholic beverages	2194-95	1092, 1094	030, 032
16	Tobacco	2210	1510, 1530	033, 034
17	Wool: scoured, carbonised, tops	2312-13	1851	046
18	Manmade fibre yarn and fabrics	2314-15	1831-32	045
19	Cotton yarn and fabric	2316	1810, 1891	043, 047
20	Wool yarn and fabric	2317-18	1820	044
21	Household and other textiles	2319, 2321-22, 2335	1880, 1892-94, 1899	049, 052, 055
22	Textile floor covers	2331	1860	051
23	Felt and products	2332	1852	050
24	Canvas and products	2333	1872	053
25	Rope, cord, twine	2334	1840	048
26	Hosiery	2411	2310	056
27	Knitted goods	2412-13	2391-92	057
28	Clothing, footwear	2421-28, 2431-32	1624, 1740, 1750, 2431, 2441, 2450, 2460, 2480, 2491-92, 2499	035, 040, 041, 058

ACIC	Industry Description	ASIC	CSIC	CI-O
29	Sawmill, wood products	2511-12, 2514-16	2511, 2513, 2541-43, 2560, 2580, 2591-93, 2599	059, 061-064
30	Ply, veneers and wood boards	2513	2520	060
31	Furniture	2521-22, 3122	2544, 2611, 2619, 2640, 2660	065-067
32	Pulp, paper, and paper board	2611	2710	069
33	Paper bags, containers	2612-14	1871, 2731-33	054, 071
34	Paper products, printing and publishing	2615, 2621-23	2740, 2860, 2870, 2880, 2890	072-074
35	Basic chemicals	2711-15	3781-83	123, 129
36	Chemical products excluding agricultural	2721, 2724, 2727-28	3791, 3799	130
37	Paints	2722	3750	126
38	Pharmaceuticals including veterinary products	2723	3740	125
39	Soap, detergents	2725	3760	127
40	Cosmetics, toiletries	2726	3770	128
41	Petroleum refining	2730	3651-52	121
42	Petroleum and coal products	2740	2720, 3690	070, 122
43	Glass and products	2811	3561-62	119
44	Clay products	2821-23	3511-12, 3591	115-16
45	Cement	2831	3520	111
46	Concrete products	2832-34	3541-42, 3549-50	113-14
47	Other nonmetallic mineral products	2835, 2841, 2843	3570, 3580, 3599	112, 118, 120
48	Stone products	2842	3530	117
49	Basic iron and steel	2912	2910	075
50	Iron, steel castings and forgings	2913	2940	077
51	Steel pipes and tubes	2914	2920	076
52	Smelting nonferrous metals	2921-26	2950	078, 079
53	Aluminium rolling, drawing, extruding	2927	2960	080
54	Nonferrous metals rolling, drawing, extruding	2828-29, 2931	2970, 2980	081, 082
55	Fabricated structural steel	3111	3020	084
56	Architectural metal products	3112-13	3031, 3039	085
57	Boilers and plates	3114	3010	083
58	Metal products n.e.c.	3121, 3123, 3134, 3136	3041-42	086
59	Cutting and hand tools	3131	3060	088
60	Wire products, nuts and bolts	3132-33	3050	087
61	Other fabricated metal products	3135, 3137	3080, 3090	090, 091
62	Motor vehicles	3211	3230	097
63	Truck, bus bodies	3212	3241-43	098

ACIC	Industry Description	ASIC	CSIC	CI-O
64	Motor vehicle electrical parts	3213-14	3250	099
65	Ship building and repair	3221	3270	101
66	Boats, other transport equipment	3222, 3225	3280, 3290	102
67	Loco stock and repair	3223	3260	100
68	Aircraft building and repair	3224	3210	096
69	Photo, optical, scientific equipment	3311-12, 3441	3911-14	131
70	TV, radio, electrical equipment	3321	3340, 3350	105-06
71	Household appliances	3322-23	3310, 3320, 3370	089, 103-04
72	Electrical and telephone wire	3324	3380	109
73	Batteries	3325	3391	108
74	Other electrical equipment	3326	2680, 3330, 3360, 3399	107, 110
75	Agricultural machinery and equipment	3331	3110	092
76	Other industrial machinery	3332-39	3150, 3160, 3180	093-95
77	Leather tanning	3411	1720	039
78	Leather and substitute products	3412	1792, 1799	042
79	Rubber tires, tubes, etc.	3421	1623	036
80	Other rubber products	3422	1629	037
81	Plastic and related products	3431-34	1650, 3730, 3993	038, 124 135
82	Jewellery, silver	3442	3920	132
83	Brooms, brushes	3443	3991	133
84	Signs and advertising displays	3444	3970	136
85	Other manufacturing	3445-47	3931-32, 3992, 3994-99	134, 137

Sources: Commonwealth Bureau of Census & Statistics, *Australian Standard Industrial Classification, 1969* (Canberra, reprinted 1975).
Dominion Bureau of Statistics, *Standard Industrial Classification Manual (Revised),* (Ottawa: Information Canada, 1970).

APPENDIX 8.2

The Data Used in This Study

This appendix contains the definitions and sources of the variables used in the comparative studies (though not all the variables appear in the present work), and "transformed", and raw data which have been used in the construction of the comparative variables, together with their sources. For example, for Australia, variable ADEMPPC, which is used in the comparative study is derived from variables ADMIN and EMPL which appear in Raw Data and Sources. The source of both of these variables is "M", which from Australian Data Sources is: Australian Bureau of Statistics, *Manufacturing Establishments, Details of* Operations by Industry Class, 1973-74. The Canadian Data are arranged in the same manner.

In making an international comparison of the type undertaken in this study, it is important that the definitions of the basic data are the same (or at least very similar) in each country. The basic units for which data are collected in Australia and Canada — the establishment and the enterprise — fortunately are defined in a similar manner. The typical establishments are "individual mines, factories and retail stores" in Australia (Australian Bureau of Statistics, 1969, p. 4), while in Canada, "In practice, a manufacturing establishment is usually equivalent to a factory, plant or mill" (Statistics Canada, 1979b, p. 13). The number of establishments refers to manufacturing establishments as such, but data for persons employed and wages and salaries paid on an establishment basis include those working in separately located ancilliary units, which in Australia includes administrative and sales offices. In Canada, sales offices are included but administrative head offices are excluded.

In this study "turnover" in Australia and value of "shipments" in Canada are taken to be identical. Both of these concepts include the value of sales, transfers to other establishments, capital work done for own use, revenues from repairs or servicing, etc. However rental revenue is included in the value of total shipments in Canada but excluded in Australia.

There is one highly significant difference of definition. In Australia, "A manufacturing establishment has been classified to foreign control if a single foreign resident investor, or foreign controlled enterprise held at least 25 per cent of the paid-up value of voting shares in the enterprise operating that establishment, provided that there was no larger holding by an Australian controlled enterprise or Australian resident individual" (Australian Bureau of Statistics, 1976, p. 2). In Canada, ". . . a corporation is considered to be foreign controlled if 50 [percent] or more of its voting rights are known to be held outside Canada or are held by one or more Canadian corporations that are themselves foreign controlled". (Statistics Canada, 1977a, p.xxvi). Consequently, while an analysis of foreign control will be made for both countries separately, such data are omitted from certain of the statistical tests which are conducted in this study. Where necessary, comments are made concerning comparability of data during the empirical analysis. However, as a general rule it can be said that there is an extremely close correspondence between the definitions in each country of the data used in comparative study.

Finally, there are two other characteristics of the data which are of note. For some data, 1973/74 information was not available (e.g. all Australian foreign ownership and control data refer to 1972/73). In such cases the implicit assumption is made that information drawn from other periods is representative of the study period: 1973/74 for Australia; 1974 for Canada. In cases where only 2- or 3-digit information is available (e.g. U.S. tariff rates), each of the ACIC industries which comprise the 2- or 3-digit ASIC or CSIC has been assigned the relevant 2- or 3-digit value.

Australian Data Sources

A. Australian Bureau of Statistics, *Australian National Accounts, Input-Output Tables, 1968-69*, Canberra.
B. Australian Bureau of Statistics, *Enterprise Statistics, 1968-69*, unpublished census data.
C. Australian Bureau of Statistics, *Enterprise Statistics, Details by Industry Class, 1968-69*, Canberra.
D. Australian Bureau of Statistics, *Census of Population and Housing, 1971*, unpublished data.
E. Australian Bureau of Statistics, *F.O.B./C.I.F. values of imports by B.T.N., September quarter, 1974*, unpublished data.
F. Australian Bureau of Statistics, *Foreign Ownership and Control in Manufacturing*, 1972-73, Canberra.
G. Australian Bureau of Statistics, *Industry Concentration Statistics, 1972-73*, Canberra.
H. Australian Bureau of Statistics, *Manufacturing Commodities, Principal* Materials Used, 1972-73, Canberra.
I. Australian Bureau of Statistics, *Manufacturing Establishments by Employment Size, 1972-73*, unpublished data.
J. Australian Bureau of Statistics, *Manufacturing Establishments, Details of Operations by Industry Class, 1968-69*, Canberra.
K. Australian Bureau of Statistics, *Manufacturing Establishments, Details of Operations by Industry Class, 1971-72*, Canberra.
L. Australian Bureau of Statistics, *Manufacturing Establishments, Details of Operations by Industry Class, 1972-73*, Canberra.
M. Australian Bureau of Statistics, *Manufacturing Establishments, Details of Operations by Industry Class, 1973-74*, Canberra.

N. Australian Bureau of Statistics, *Overseas Trade, 1972:73*, Bulletin No. 70, Canberra.

O. Australian Bureau of Statistics, *Value of Fixed Tangible Assets, Details for all Enterprises by Industry Class, 1968-69*, unpublished data.

P. Committee to Advise on Policies for Manufacturing Industry (Jackson Committee), *Policies for the Development of Manufacturing Industry: A Green paper. Volume II: Statistics*, (Canberra: Australian Government Publishing Service, 1976).

Q. Commonwealth Bureau of Census and Statistics, *Details of Operations by Industry Class, 1968-69*, Canberra.

R. Department of Industry and Commerce, *R & D in Manufacturing Industry, 1971-72*, Bulletin No. 11, 1974.

S. Industries Assistance Commission, *Annual Report, 1973-74*, (Canberra: Australian Government Publishing Service, 1974).

T. Industries Assistance Commission, *Annual Report, 1974-75*, Canberra: (Australian Government Publishing Service, 1975).

U. Industries Assistance Commission, *Annual Report, 1975-76*, (Canberra: Australian Government Publishing Service, 1976).

V. Industries Assistance Commission, *Annual Report, 1976-77*, (Canberra: Australian Government Publishing Service, 1977).

W. Industries Assistance Commission, *Annual Report, 1977-78*, (Canberra: Australian Government Publishing Service, 1978).

X. Industries Assistance Commission, *Assistance to Manufacturing Industries in Australia, 1968-69 to 1973-74*, (Canberra: Australian Government Publishing Service, 1976).

Y. Industries Assistance Commission, *F.O.B./C.I.F. Ratios for Materials and Final Products by A.S.I.C.*, September Quarter, 1974, unpublished data.

Z. Industries Assistance Commission, Manufacturing and Trade Data Tape.

ZA. Industries Assistance Commission, *Recent Trends in the Australian Manufacturing Sector*, Canberra: Australian Government Publishing Service, 1975.

ZB. Williams, J.R., *Canadian - United States Manufacturing*, (Ottawa: University of Toronto Press, 1978).

Canadian Data Sources

A. Statistics Canada, *Capital Stocks in Manufacturing Industries, 1955-79*, unpublished.

B. Statistics Canada, *1971 Census of Canada (Industries, Industries by Sex, Showing Age, Marital Status, Level of Schooling and Class of Worker for Canada)*, (Ottawa: Information Canada 1975)

C. Statistics Canada, *1971 Census of Canada, Industries, (Industries by Sex, Showing Occupation by Major Groups for Canada)*, (Ottawa: Information Canada, 1975)

D. Statistics Canada, *1971 Census of Canada (Industries, Industries by Sex, Showing Period of Immigration, Birthplace and Ethnic Group, for Canada and Provinces)*, (Ottawa: Information Canada, 1975)

E.   Statistics Canada, *Corporate Financial Statistics*, (Ottawa: Supply and Services Canada, 1977)

F.   Statistics Canada, *Detailed Consumption of Containers and Other Packaging Supplies, 1974*, (Ottawa: Supply and Services Canada, 1977)

G.   Statistics Canada, *Domestic and Foreign Control of Manufacturing Establishments in Canada, 1972*, (Ottawa: Supply and Services Canada, 1977)

H.   Statistics Canada, *Imports and Exports, 1974, for Canadian Manufacturing, Classified by the Canadian Standard Industrial Classification*, unpublished.

I.   Statistics Canada, *Imports, Merchandise Trade, 1972-1974*, (Ottawa: Information Canada, 1975)

J.   Statistics Canada, *Industrial Organisation and Concentration in the Manufacturing, Mining and Logging Industries, 1974*, (Ottawa: Supply and Services Canada, 1978)

K.   Statistics Canada, *Industrial Research and Development Expenditures in Canada, 1967-1976*, (Ottawa: Supply and Services Canada, 1978)

L.   Statistics Canada, *Input-Output Structure of the Canadian Economy* (Ottawa: Supply and Services Canada, 1977)

M.   Statistics Canada, *Input-Output Tables (Use Matrix), 1974*, unpublished.

N.   Statistics Canada, *Manufacturing Industries of Canada, National and Provincial Areas, 1973*, (Ottawa: Supply and Services Canada 1974)

O.   Statistics Canada, *Manufacturing Industries of Canada: National and Provincial Areas, 1974*, (Ottawa: Supply and Services Canada, 1975)

P.   Statistics Canada, *Manufacturing Industries of Canada: Sub-Provincial Areas, 1974*, (Ottawa: Supply and Services Canada, 1978)

Q.   Statistics Canada, *Manufacturing Industries of Canada, Type of Organisation and Size of Establishments, 1974*, (Ottawa: Supply and Services Canada, 1977)

R.   Statistics Canada, public data tape for Canadian manufacturing industry, 1974.

S.   Statistics Canada, *Research and Development Expenditures in Canada, 1963-73*, (Ottawa: Supply and Services Canada, 1976)

T.   Statistics Canada *Selected Statistics on Technological Innovation in Industry*, (Ottawa: Information Canada, 1975)

U.   Statistics Canada, *Tariffs and Transport Costs to the Canadian Border*, prepared for this study by the Structural Analysis Division, unpublished.

V.   Wilkinson, B.W. and Norrie, K., *Effective Protection and the Return to Capital*, (Ottawa: Economic Council for Canada, 1975)

W.   Williams, J.R. *Canadian - United States Manufacturing*, (Ottawa: University of Toronto Press, 1978)

Australia
Data Used For Direct Comparative Study

Variable	Units	Description
ADEMPPC	%	Percentage of administrative employees of total employment, end June 1974 = (ADMIN/EMPL) × 100
AVSTOCK	$'000	Average value of stocks, 1973-74 = (STOCK73 + STOCK74)/2
AVVA	$'000	Average value added per employee, 1973-74 = VA/AVEMPL
AVWAGE	$'000	Average wage per employee, 1973-74 = WSAL/A-VEMPL
CAPINT	Index	Index of capital intensity. Average = 100. Book value of fixed tangible assets per person employed for industry i divided by fixed tangible assets per person employed in the manufacturing sector, 1968-69 = ((FXDASS69i/EMPL69i)/(Σ FXDASS69 / Σ EMPL69)) × 100
CONC8	Ratio	Estimated 8 firm concentration ratio, 1973-74 = (VA1/4 +VA2/4)/VA
DIVRAT	Ratio	Estimated diversification ratio, 1973-74. The ratio: value added of establishments classified to a different industry than that of the parent enterprise *to* value added of all establishments of enterprises in the industry = DIVERS/VA
ED1	%	Percentage of employees whose highest level of education is final year (years 11-12) high school, 1973-74 = (MATRIC/AVEMPL) × 100
ED2	%	Percentage of tertiary qualified employees, 1973-74 = (DEGREE/AVEMPL) × 100
EMP10	%	Percentage of establishments employing less than 10 persons 1972-73 = (EMPL10/ESTAB73) × 100
EMP20	%	Percentage of establishments employing less than 20 persons, 1972-73 = ((EMPL10 + EMPL1019)/ESTAB73) × 100
EMP50	%	Percentage of establishments employing less than 50 persons, 1972-73 = ((EMPL10 + EMPL1019 + EMPL2049) / ESTAB73) × 100
EMP100	%	Percentage of establishments employing less than 100 persons, 1972-73 = ((EMPL10 + EMPL1019 + EMPL2049 + EMPL5099)/ESTAB73) × 100
EMPLG	%	Percentage of establishments employing 100 persons or more, 1972-73 = ((ESTAB73 - (EMPL10 + EMPL1019 + EMPL2049 + EMPL5099))/ESTAB73) × 100

Variable	Units	Description
EMPENT	No.	Estimated employment per enterprise, 1973-74 = AVEMPL/ENTER
EMPEST	No.	Employment per establishment, 1973-74 = AVEMPL/ESTAB
EPROT	%	Total effective protection f.o.b., 1974 = ETARIFF + ETRANS
ESTENT	No.	Average number of establishments per enterprise, 1972-73 = ESTAB73/ENTER73
ETARIFF	%	Effective tariff, f.o.b. 1974. See chapter 7 for details of computation (Source: X, Y)
ETRANS	%	Effective transport cost, f.o.b., 1974. See chapter 7 for details of computation (Source: Y)
EXIMP	Ratio	Ratio of exports to imports, 1973-74 = EXP/IMP
EXIMPTO	Ratio	Ratio of exports - imports to turnover (shipments) 1973-74 = (EXP-IMP)/TOVER
EXTO	Ratio	Ratio of exports to turnover (shipments) 1973-74 = EXP/TOVER
FCONEMPC	%	Estimated percentage of foreign controlled employment, 1973-74 = (FCONEMP/AVEMPL) × 100
FCONTOPC	%	Percentage of turnover (shipments) attributed to foreign controlled firms, 1973-74 = (FCONTO/TOVER) × 100
FCONVAPC	%	Foreign control, estimated percentage of value added contributed by foreign controlled firms, 1973-74 = (FCONVA/VA) × 100
FDPART	Ratio	Foreign domestic participation. Ratio of foreign controlled domestic turnover (shipments) to imports, 1973-74 = FCONTO/IMP
FEMP	Prop'n	Proportion of females of total employees, 1973-74 = FEMPL/AVEMPL
FEPROD	Prop'n	Proportion of female production workers of total employees, 1973-74 = FEMPROD/AVEMPL
FMIGRPC	%	Percentage of female employees born overseas in total female employment, 1973-74 = (FMIGRAN/FEMPL) × 100
FPEN	Prop'n	Foreign penetration of the Australian market, 1973-74 = (IMP + FCONTO)/MKTSIZE
FPROD	Prop'n	Proportion of female production workers of total female employment, 1973-74 = FEMPROD/(FEMPROD + FEMPAD)
FSHARE	Prop'n	Proportion of total Australian market contributed by turnover of foreign controlled firms, 1973-74 = FCONTO/MKTSIZE

Variable	Units	Description
FUELINT	Prop'n	Fuel intensity, 1973-74 = ELECFUEL/MATERIAL
IMPTO	Ratio	Ratio of imports to turnover, (shipments) 1973-74 = IMP/TOVER
INNOV	Ratio	Innovative activity (see Oksanen and Williams, 1978). Ratio of average wages of production employees to average wages and salaries of all employees, 1973-74 = (WSALPROD/PRODEMP)/(WSAL/AVEMPL)
INTRA	Index	Intra-industry trade, 1973-74 $= (((EXP + IMP) - \lvert EXP\text{-}IMP \rvert)/(EXP + IMP)) \times 100$
INTSPEC	Ratio	Intra-industry specialisation (see Oksanen and Williams, 1978). Ratio of value added to turnover (shipments), 1973-74 = VA/TOVER
ISHARE	Prop'n	Imports share of the Australian market, 1973-74 = IMP/MKTSIZE
KEMP	$'000	Fixed assets per employee, 1968-69 = FXDAS-S69/EMPL69
KINDEX	Index	Capital stock index. Derived from CAPINT. Capital of the industry divided by the sum of capital for all industries, 1968-69. $(FXDASS69i/ \Sigma FXDASS69) \times 100$
LABINT	Prop'n	Labour intensity, 1973-74 = WSAL/VA
MKTSIZE	$'000	Estimated market size, 1973-74 = IMP + TOVER - EXP
MES50	$'000	Minimum efficient size. Estimated average value added of the largest firms together producing 50 percent of the industry's value added, 1972-73 (Source: G)
MIGRPC	%	Percentage of employees from overseas, 1973-74 = (MIGRAN/AVEMPL) × 100
M/Q	Ratio	Materials/output ratio, f.o.b., 1974. See chapter 7 for details of computation (Source: X,Y)
NATDUM	0-1	Natural resource dummy variable. Constructed, subjectively using as a guide the proportion of "natural resource" commodities (01.01 - 01.06, 03.00, 04.00, 11.01- 02, 12.00 14.00) from the Australian input-output able, 1968-69
NATRES1	Prop'n	Replenishable natural resource intensity = REPLEN69/INPUT69
NATRES2	Prop'n	Nonreplenishable natural resource intensity = NREPLEN69/INPUT69
NATRES3	Prop'n	Total resource intensity = (REPLEN69 + NREPLEN69)/INPUT69
NPROT	%	Total nominal protection, f.o.b., 1974 = NTRANS + NTARIFF

Variable	Units	Description
NTARIFF	%	Nominal tariff, f.o.b., 1974. (Source: X,Y)
NTARM	%	Nominal tariff on materials, f.o.b. 1974 (Source: X,Y)
NTRANS	%	Nominal transport cost, f.o.b., 1974. (Source: Y)
NTRANSM	%	Nominal transport cost on materials, f.o.b., 1974 (Source: Y)
PCEMP	$'000	Gross surplus per employee, 1973-74 = (VA - WSAL)/AVEMPL
PCK	Ratio	Ratio of gross surplus to capital stock = (VA - WSAL)/FXDASS69
PCM	Prop'n	Price-cost margin, 1973-74 = (VA-WSAL)/TOVER
PEMPPC	%	Percentage of production employees of total employment, end June 1974 = (PRODEMP/EMPL) × 100
PFUNDS	%	Percentage profit to shareholders funds after tax — 3 digit, 1973-74 (Source: V)
PRODEST	No.	Measure of scale (see Oksanen and Williams, 1978). Production employment per establishment, 1974 = PRODEMP/ESTAB
PRODIFF	0-1	Product differentiation dummy variable. Constructed subjectively using as a guide the value of industry advertising and the proportion of containers and packaging of total materials usage.
PROFUNDS	%	Percentage of profits to funds employed — 3 digit, 1973-74 (Source: V)
PROFSLPC	%	Percentage of other professionals employed in industry employment, end June, 1971 = ((PROFSL71)/EMPL71) × 100
PROXMKT	0-1	Proximity to market dummy. Subjectively constructed to reflect an advantage owing to proximity to the market which is not fully reflected in transport costs (e.g.: newspapers). = 0 if no advantage; = 1, otherwise.
RDEMP1	$'000	Estimated research and development expenditure per employee, 1972 = RDEXP72/EMPL71
RDEMP2	$'000	Estimated research and development expenditure per professional, technicial and other qualified person, 1972 = RDEXP72/(SCIENT71 + ENG71 + TECHNS71)
RDEXPTO	Ratio	Estimated ratio of research and development expenditure to turnover (shipments), 1972-73 = RDEXP-72/TOVER73
RDEXVA	Ratio	Estimated ratio of research and development expenditure to value added, 1972-73 = RDEXP72/VA73

Variable	Units	Description
RMES50	Prop'n	Relative MES50 = MES50/VA
RTRADBAL	Index	Relative trade balance, 1973-74 = $(((EXP_i - IMP_i)/TOVER_i)/((\Sigma EXP - \Sigma IMP)/\Sigma TOVER)) \times -1$
SKILL1	%	Percentage of scientists and engineers of total employees, end June, 1971 = $((SCIENT71 + ENG71)/EMPL71) \times 100$
SKILL2	%	Percentage of scientists, engineers and technicans of total employees, end June, 1971 = $((SCIENT71 + ENG71 + TECHNS71)/EMPL71) \times 100$
SMALLE	Prop'n	Number of small enterprises as a proportion of the total number of enterprises in the industry, 1974-73. Small enterprises are those which produce the lower 50 percent of value added of the industry, when all firms are ranked according to size (Source: G)
STKTO	Ratio	Ratio of average stock to turnover (shipments), 1973-74 = AVSTOCK/TOVER
TECHNSPC	%	Percentage of technicians in industry employment, end June 1971 = $(TECHNS71/EMPL71) \times 100$
TOENT	$'000	Turnover (shipments) per enterprise, 1973-74 = TOVER/ENTER
TOEST	$'000	Turnover (shipments), per establishment, 1973-74 = TOVER/ESTAB
TRADBAL	Ratio	Trade balance, 1973-74 = $(EXP - IMP)/(EXP + IMP)$
USTAR61	%	United States' nominal tariff, 1961 (Source: ZB)
USTAR75	%	United States' tariff for (roughly) 2 digit ASIC, 1975 (Source: W)
VAENT	$'000	Value added per enterprise, 1973-74 = VA/ENTER
VAEST	$'000	Value added per establishment, 1973-74 = VA/ESTAB
VAKSTOCK	Ratio	Ratio of value added to fixed tangible assets, 1968-69 = VA69/FXDASS69
WSADMIN	$'000	Wages and salaries per administrative employee, 1973-74 = WSALADMIN/ADMIN
WSPROD	$'000	Wages and salaries per production worker, 1973-74 = WSALPROD/PRODEMP
WVA	Prop'n	Proportion of wages of value added, 1973-74 = WSALPROD/VA
WWSAL	Prop'n	Proportion of wages of production workers of total wages and salaries, 1973-74 = WSALPROD/WSAL

Australia
Transformed Data Used As Input For Comparative Data

Variable	Units	Description
AVSTOCK	$'000	Average value of stocks, 1973-74 = (STOCK73 × STOCK74)/2
DEGREE	No.	Estimated tertiary qualified employees, 1973-74 = Proportion of tertiary qualified employees, 1971 (Source: J) × AVEMPL
DIVERS	$'000	Estimated value added of diversified firms 1973-74 = DIVERS69 × VA
ENTER	No.	Estimated number of enterprises, 1973-74 = (ENTER73/ESTAB73) × ESTAB
FCONEMP	No.	Estimated employment attributed to foreign controlled firms, 1973-1974 = (FCONEMP73/AVEMPL73) × AVEMPL
FCONTO	$'000	Estimated turnover attributed to foreign controlled firms, 1973-74 = (FCONTOPC73/100) × TOVER
FCONVA	$'000	Estimated value added contributed by foreign controlled firms, 1973-74 = (FCONVAPC73/100) × VA
FMIGRAN	No.	Estimated number of female employees born overseas, 1973-74 = (FMIGRN71/100) × FEMPL
MATRIC	No.	Estimated number of employees whose highest level of education is year 11-12 high school, 1973-74 = Proportions of employees whose highest level of education is final year high school, 1971 (Source: T) × AVEMPL
MIGRAN	No.	Estimated number of employees born overseas, 1973-74 = (MIGRAN71/100) × AVEMP
VA1/4	$'000	Estimated value added — first 4 largest enterprises, 1973-74 = (VA1/473/VA73) × VA
VA2/4	$'000	Estimated value added — second 4 largest enterprises, 1973-74 = (VA2/473/VA73) × VA
VA3/4	$'000	Estimated valued added — third 4 largest enterprise, 1973-74 = (VA3/473/VA73) × VA
VA4/4	$'000	Estimated value added — fourth 4 largest enterprises, 1973-74 = (VA4/473/VA73) × VA
VA5/4	$'000	Estimated value added — fifth 4 largest enterprises, 1973-74 = (VA5/473/VA73) × VA
VA1/8	$'000	Estimated value added of 8 largest firms, 1973-74 = VA1/4 + VA2/4
VAREM	$'000	Estimated value added — remaining enterprises, 1973-74 = (VAREM73/VA73) × VA

Australia
Raw Data and Sources

Variable	Units	Description	Sources
ADMIN71	No.	Administrative, executive and managerial employed, end June, 1971.	D
ADMIN	No.	Total administrative employees, end June, 1974.	M
AVEMPL73	No.	Average total employment, 1972-73.	L
AVEMPL	No.	Average total employment, 1973-74.	Z
CONPKG	$'000	Value of containers and other packaging, 1973-74.	M
DIVERS69	Ratio	Diversification ratio, 1968-69. The ratio: value added of establishments classified to a different industry than that of the parent enterprise to value added of all establishments of enterprises in the industry.	C
ELECFUEL	$'000	Value of electricity and fuels purchased and transferred in, 1973-74.	M
EMPL10	No.	Establishments employing less than 10 persons, 1972-73.	I
EMPL1019	No.	Establishments employing 10-19 persons, 1972-73.	I
EMPL2049	No.	Establishments employing 20-49 persons, 1972-73.	I
EMPL5099	No.	Establishments employing 50-99 persons, 1972-73.	I
EMPL69	No.	Total employees, end June 1969	D
EMPL71	No.	Total employees, end June, 1971 (as classified to 4 digit ASIC, excludes employees not sufficiently classified by population census).	M
EMPL	No.	Total employment, end June, 1974.	M
ENG71	No.	Engineers employed, end June, 1971.	D
ENTER73	No.	Enterprises, 1972-73.	L
ESTAB73	No.	Establishments, 1972-73.	L
ESTAB	No.	Establishments, 1973-74.	M
EXP	$'000	Exports, 1973-74.	Z
FCAPEX73	$'000	Fixed capital expenditure, 1972-73.	L
FCONEMP73	No.	Foreign controlled employment, 1972-73.	F
FCONEST73	No.	Number of foreign controlled establishments, 1972-73.	F

Variable	Units	Description	Sources
FCONTOPC73	%	Percentage of turnover attributed to foreign controlled firms, 1972-73.	F
FCONVAPC73	%	Percentage of value added attributed to foreign controlled firms, 1972-73.	F
FEMP	No.	Total females employed, end June, 1974.	M
FEMPAD	No.	Female administrative employees, end June, 1974.	M
FEMPL	No.	Average female employment, 1973-74.	Z
FEMPROD	No.	Female production employees, end June, 1974.	M
FMIGRN71	%	Percentage of female employees born overseas, end June, 1971	T
FXDASS69	$'000	Book value of fixed tangible assets, 1968-69.	J
IMP	$'000	Imports, 1973-74.	Z
INPUT69	$'000	Value of total inputs, 1968-69.	A
MATERIAL	$'000	Value of materials, components and supplies, purchases transferred in 1973-74.	M
MIGRAN71	%	Percentage of employees born overseas, end June, 1971.	T
NREPLEN69	$'000	Value of nonreplenishable resource inputs, 1968-69 = total value of Australian input-output commodities, 11.02, 12,14 used.	A
PRODEMP71	No.	Total production employees, end June, 1971.	D
PRODEMP	No.	Total production employees, end June, 1974	M
PROFSL71	No.	Other professionals employed, end June, 1971.	D
RDEMP72	$'000	Research and development expenditure per R & D employee — 2 digit, 1971-72.	R
RDEXP72	$'000	Research and development expenditure, 1971-72. Derived from 2 digit data for R & D expenditure per employee × number employees in each 4 digit industry.	K,R
REPLEN69	$'000	Value of replenishable resource inputs, 1968-69 = total value of Australian input-output commodities 01, 03, 04 used.	A
SCIENT71	No.	Scientists employed, end June, 1971	D
STOCK73	$'000	Value of stocks, end June, 1973.	M
STOCK74	$'000	Value of stocks, end June, 1974.	M
TECHNS71	No.	Technicians employed, end June, 1971.	D

Variable	Units	Description	Sources
TOVER73	$'000	Turnover, 1972-73.	L
TOVER	$'000	Turnover, 1973-74.	M
VA69	$'000	Value-added, 1968-69.	J
VA73	$'000	Value-added, 1972-73.	L
VA1/473	$'000	Value added-first four largest enterprises, 1972-73.	G
VA2/473	$'000	Value added-second four largest enterprises, 1972-73.	G
VA3/473	$'000	Value added-third four largest enterprises, 1972-73.	G
VA4/473	$'000	Value added-fourth four largest enterprises, 1972-73.	G
VA5/473	$'000	Value added-fifth four largest enterprises, 1972-73.	G
VAREM73	$'000	Value added-remaining enterprises, 1972-73.	G
VA	$'000	Value added, 1973-74.	Z
WAGES73	$'000	Wages and salaries, 1972-73.	L
WSALADMIN	$'000	Wages and salaries paid to administrative, office, sales and distribution employees, 1973-74.	M
WSAL	$'000	Total wages and salaries, 1973-74.	Z
WSALPROD	$'000	Wages and salaries paid to production and all other workers, 1973-74.	M
WPROP	No.	Total working proprietors, end June, 1974.	M
WPROPF	No.	Female working proprietors, end June, 1974.	M

Canada
Data Used For Direct
Comparative Study

Variable	Units	Description
ADEMPPC	%	Percentage of administrative employees of total employment, 1974 = ((MEMPAD + FEMPAD)/A-VEMPL) × 100.
AVSTOCK	$'000	Average value of stocks, 1974 = (INVRAW1 + INVRAW2 + INVWP1 + INVWP2 + INVFG1 + INVFG2)/2.
AVVA	$'000	Average value added per employee, 1974 = VA/EMPL.
AVWAGE	$'000	Average wage per employee, 1974 = WSAL/EMPL.
CAPINT	Index	Index of capital intensity. Average = 100. Gross capital stock per person employed for industry i divided by gross capital stock per person employed in the manufacturing sector, 1974 = ((GKSTOCK1i/EMPL i)/(ΣGKSTOCK1/ Σ EMPL)) × 100.
CONC8	Ratio	8 firm concentration ratio, 1974 = (VA1/4 + VA2/4)/VA.
DIVRAT	Ratio	Diversification ratio, 1974. The ratio: value added of establishments classified to a different industry than that of the parent enterprise *to* value added of all establishments of enterprises in the industry = DIVERS/VA.
ED1	%	Percentage of employees whose highest level of education is final year (grade 12 or 13) high school, 1971 = ((MATRICF71 + MATRICM71)/(EMPM71 + FEMP71)) × 100.
ED2	%	Percentage of tertiary qualified employees, 1971 = ((DEGREEM71 + DEGREEF71)/(EMPM71 + FEMP71)) × 100.
EMP10	%	Percentage of establishments employing less than 10 persons, 1974 = (EMPL10/ESTAB) × 100.
EMP20	%	Percentage of establishments employing less than 20 persons, 1974 = ((EMPL10 + EMPL1019)/ESTAB) × 100
EMP50	%	Percentage of establishments employing less than 50 persons, 1974 = ((EMPL10 + EMPL1019 + EMPL2049)/ESTAB) × 100
EMP100	%	Percentage of establishments employing less than 100 persons, 1974 = ((EMPL10 + EMPL1019 + EMPL2049 + EMPL5099)/ESTAB) × 100

Variable	Units	Description
EMPLG	%	Percentage of establishments employing 100 persons or more, 1974 = ((ESTAB - (EMPL10 + EMPL1019 + EMPL2049 + EMPL5099))/ESTAB) × 100
EMPENT	No.	Employment per enterprise, 1974 = EMPL/ENTER
EMPEST	No.	Employment per establishment, 1974 = EMPL/ESTAB
EPROT	%	Total effective protection, f.o.b., 1974 = ETARIFF + ETRANS
ESTENT	No.	Average number of establishments per enterprise, 1974 = ESTAB/ENTER
ETARIFF	%	Effective tariff, f.o.b., 1974. See chapter 7 for details of computation (Source: U)
ETRANS	%	Effective transport cost, f.o.b., 1974. See chapter 7 for details of computation (Source: U)
EXIMP	Ratio	Ratio of exports to imports, 1974 = EXP/IMP
EXIMPTO	Ratio	Ratio of exports-imports to shipments (turnover), 1974 = (EXP - IMP)/SHIP
EXTO	Ratio	Ratio of exports to shipments (turnover), 1974 = EXP/SHIP
FCONEMPC	%	Percentage of foreign controlled employment, 1974 = (FCONEMP/EMPL) × 100
FCONTOPC	%	Percentage of shipments (turnover), attributed to foreign controlled firms, 1974 = (FCONSHIP/SHIP) × 100
FCONVAPC	%	Foreign control, percentage of value added contributed by foreign controlled firms, 1974 = (FCONVA/VA) × 100
FDPART	Ratio	Foreign domestic participation. Ratio of foreign controlled domestic shipments (turnover) to imports, 1974 = FCONSHIP/IMP
FEMP	Prop'n	Proportion of females of total employees, 1974 = (FEMPROD + FEMPAD)/EMPL
FEPROD	Prop'n	Proportion of female production workers of total employees, 1974 = FEMPROD/EMPL
FMIGRPC	%	Percentage of female employees born overseas in total female employment — 3 digit, 1971 = (FMIGRAN71/FEMP71) × 100
FPEN	Prop'n	Foreign penetration of the Canadian market, 1974 = (IMP + FCONSHIP)/MKTSIZE
FPROD	Prop'n	Proportion of female production workers of total female employment, 1974 = FEMPROD/(FEMPROD + FEMPAD)

Variable	Units	Description
FSHARE	Prop'n	Proportion of total Canadian market contributed by shipments of foreign controlled firms, 1974 = FCONSHIP/MKTSIZE
FUELINT	Prop'n	Fuel intensity, 1974 = ELECTFUEL/MATERIAL
IMPTO	Ratio	Ratio of imports to shipments (turnover), 1974 = IMP/SHIP
INNOV	Ratio	Innovative activity (see Oksanen and Williams, 1978). Ratio of average wages of production employees to average wages and salaries of all employees, 1974 = (WSALPROD/(MPROD + FEMPROD))/ ((WSALPROD + WSALADM)/AVEMPL)
INTRA	Index	Intra-industry trade, 1974 = $(((EXP + IMP) - \lvert EXP - IMP \rvert)/(EXP + IMP)) \times 100$
INTSPEC	Ratio	Intra-industry specialisation (see Oksanen and Williams, 1978). Ratio of value added to shipments (turnover), 1974 = VA/SHIP
ISHARE	Prop'n	Import share of the Canadian market, 1974 = IMP/MKTSIZE
KEMP	$'000	Gross capital stock per employee, 1974 = GKSTOCK1/EMPL
KINDEX	Index	Capital stock index. Derived from CAPINT. Gross capital stock of the industry divided by the sum of gross capital stock for all industries, 1984 = $(GKSTOCK1i/\Sigma GKSTOCK1) \times 100$
LABINT	Prop'n	Labour intensity, 1974 = WSAL/VA
MKTSIZE	$'000	Estimated market size, 1974 = IMP + SHIP - EXP
MES50	$'000	Minimum efficient size. Estimated average value added of the largest firms together producing 50 percent of the industry's value added, 1974 (Source: J)
MIGRPC	%	Percentage of employees born overseas — 3 digit, 1971 = $((MMIGRAN71 + FMIGRAN71)/(EMPM71 + FEMP71)) \times 100$
M/Q	Ratio	Materials/output ratio f.o.b., 1974. See chapter 7 (Source: U)
NATDUM	0-1	Natural resource dummy variable. Constructed subjectively using as a guide the proportion of "natural resource" commodities (00100 to 05000) from the use matrix of the Canadian input-output table, 1974
NATRES1	Prop'n	Replenishable natural resource intensity = REPLEN/INPUT
NATRES2	Prop'n	Nonreplenishable natural resource intensity = NREPLEN/INPUT

Variable	Units	Description
NATRES3	Prop'n	Total resource intensity = (REPLEN + NREPLEN)/INPUT
NPROT	%	Total nominal protection f.o.b., 1974 = NTRANS + NTARIFF
NTARIFF	%	Nominal tariff f.o.b., 1974. (Source: U)
NTARM	%	Nominal tariff on materials f.o.b., 1974. (Source: U)
NTRANS	%	Nominal transport cost f.o.b., 1974. (Source: U)
NTRANSM	%	Nominal transport cost of materials, f.o.b., 1974 (Source: U).
PCEMP	$'000	Gross surplus per employee, 1974 = (VA - WSAL)/EMPL
PCK	Ratio	Ratio of gross surplus to capital stock = (VA - WSAL)/GKSTOCK1
PCM	Prop'n	Price-cost margin, 1974 = (VA-WSAL)/SHIP
PEMPPC	%	Percentage of production employees of total employment, 1974 = ((MPROD + FEMPROD)/EMPL) × 100
PFUNDS	%	Percentage profit to shareholders funds after tax, 1974 (Source: E)
PRODEST	No.	Measure of scale (see Oksanen and Williams, 1978). Production employment per establishment, 1974 = (MPROD + FEMPROD)/ESTAB
PRODIFF	0-1	Product differentiation dummy variable. Constructed subjectively using as a guide the proportion of containers and packaging of total materials usage.
PROFUNDS	%	Percentage of net profit under protection to capital employed — 2 digit input-output industries, 1966 (Source: V)
PROFSLPC	%	Percentage of other professionals employed in industry employment, 1974 = (PROFSL/EMP) × 100
PROXMKT	0-1	Proximity to market dummy. Subjectively constructed to reflect an advantage owing to proximity to the market which is not fully reflected in transport costs (e.g.: newspapers). = 0 if no advantage; = 1, otherwise.
RDEMP1	$'000	Research and development expenditure per employee, 1974 = RDEXP1/EMP
RDEMP2	$'000	Research and development expenditure per professional, technicial and other qualified person employed, 1974 = RDEXP1/PROTECH
RDEXPTO	Ratio	Ratio of research and development expenditure to shipments (turnover) = RDEXP1/SHIP

Variable	Units	Description
RDEXVA	Ratio	Ratio of research and development expenditure to value added, = RDEXP1/VA
RMES50	Prop'n	Relative MES50 = MES50/VA
RTRADBAL	Index	Relative trade balance, 1974 = $(((EXPi - IMPi)/SHIPi)/((\Sigma EXP - \Sigma IMP)/\Sigma SHIP))) \times -1$
SKILL1	%	Percentage of scientists and engineers of total employees, 1971 = $((EMPNSC71 + EMPSSC71)/EMP71) \times 100$
SKILL2	%	Percentage of professionals and technicans (including scientists and engineers), of total employees, 1974 = $(PROTECH/EMP) \times 100$
SMALLE	Prop'n	Number of small enterprises as a proportion of the total number of enterprises in the industry, 1974. Small enterprises are those which produce the lower 50 percent of value added of the industry, when all firms are ranked according to size (Source: J)
STKTO	Ratio	Ratio of average stock to shipments (turnover), 1974 = AVSTOCK/SHIP
TECHNSPC	%	Percentage of technicians in industry employment, 1974 = $(TECHNS/EMP) \times 100$
TOENT	$'000	Shipments (turnover) per enterprise, 1974 = SHIP/ENTER
TOEST	$'000	Shipments (turnover), per establishments, 1974 = SHIP/ESTAB
TRADBAL	Ratio	Trade balance, 1974 = $(EXP - IMP)/(EXP + IMP)$
USTAR61	%	United States' nominal tariff, 1961 (See Australian data source ZB)
USTAR75	%	United States' tariff for (roughly) 2 digit ASIC, 1975 (See Australian data source W)
VAENT	$'000	Value added per enterprise, 1974 = VA/ENTER
VAEST	$'000	Value added per establishment, 1974 = VA/ESTAB
VAKSTOCK	Ratio	Ratio of value added to gross capital stock, 1974 = VA/GKSTOCK1
WSADMIN	$'000	Wages and salaries per administrative employee, 1974 = WSALADM/(FEMPAD + MEMPAD)
WSPROD	$'000	Wages and salaries per production worker, 1974 = WSALPROD/(MPROD + FEMPROD)
WVA	Prop'n	Proportion of wages of value added, 1974 = WSALPROD/VA
WWSAL	Prop'n	Proportion of wages of production workers of total wages and salaries, 1974 = WSALPROD/(WSALPROD + WSALADM)

Canada
Transformed Data Used As Input For
Comparative Data

Variable	Units	Description
DIVERS	$'000	Value added of diversified firms, 1974 = (1 - SPEC) × VA
FCONEMP	No.	Estimated foreign controlled employment, 1974 = (FCONEMPC72/100) × EMPL
FCONSHIP	$'000	Estimated foreign control of shipments, 1974 = (FCONSHIP72/SHIP72) × SHIP
FCONVA	$'000	Estimated value added attributed to foreign controlled firms, 1974 = (FCONVAPC72/100) × VA
NSCIEN71	%	Percentage of natural scientists employed — 3 digit, 1971 = (EMPNSC71/EMP71) × 100
RDEXP1	$'000	Research and development expenditure, 1974. Derived from 2 digit data for R & D expenditure per employee × number of employees in each 4 digit industry = (RDEX/EMP)EMPL
RDEXP2	$'000	Research and development expenditure per R & D employee — 2 digit, 1974 = RDEX/EMP
VA1/8	$'000	Value added of the 8 largest firms, 1974 = VA1/4 + VA2/4

Canada
Raw Data and Sources

Variable	Units	Description	Sources
ADMIN71	No.	Administrative and managerial employees — 3 digit, 1971.	C
AVEMPL	No.	Average total employment, 1974	R
DEGREEF71	No.	Number of female employees with University degress — 3 digit, 1971	B
DEGREEM71	No.	Number of male employees with University degrees — 3 digit, 1971	B
EDF71	No.	Number of female employees whose final year of education is less than grade 9 — 3 digit, 1971	B
EDM71	No.	Number of male employees whose final year of education is less than grade 9 — 3 digit, 1971	B
EDSUNIF71	No.	Number of female employees with some university education — 3 digit, 1971	B
EDSUNIM71	No.	Number of male employees with some university education — 3 digit, 1971	B
ELECTFUEL	$'000	Cost of fuel and electricity used, 1974	R
EMP71	No.	Employment in all occupations — 3 digit, 1971	C
EMP	No.	Total employment — 2 digit, 1974	K
EMPL10	No.	Establishments employing less than 10 persons, 1974	O
EMPL1019	No.	Establishments employing 10-19 persons, 1974	O
EMPL2049	No.	Establishments employing 20-49 persons, 1974	O
EMPL2049	No.	Establishments employing 20-49 persons, 1974	O
EMPL5099	No.	Establishments employing 50-99 persons, 1974	O
EMPL	No.	Total employees, 1974	R
EMPM71	No.	Employment, males — 3 digit, 1971	D
EMPNSC71	No.	Employment in natural science occupations — 3 digit, 1971	C
EMPSSC71	No.	Employment in social science occupations — 3 digit, 1971	C
ENTER	No.	Enterprises, 1974	J

Variable	Units	Description	Sources
ESTAB	No.	Establishments, 1974	R
EXP	$'000	Exports, 1974	H
FCONEMPL72	No.	Employment attributed to foreign controlled firms, 1972	G
FCONSHIP72	$'000	Shipments attributed to foreign controlled firms, 1972	G
FCONVA72	$'000	Value added attributed to foreign controlled firms, 1972	G
FEMP71	No.	Employment, females — 3 digit, 1971	D
FEMPAD	$'000	Administrative employees — female, 1974	R
FEMPROD	No.	Production workers — female, 1974	R
FMIGRAN71	No.	Number of female employees born overseas — 3 digit, 1971	D
GKSTOCK1	$'000	Gross capital stock (current $) — 3 digit, 1974	A
IMP	$'000	Imports, 1974	H
INPUT	$'000	Value of total inputs, 1974	M
INVFG1	$'000	Inventory of finished goods — opening, 1974	R
INVFG2	$'000	Inventory of finished goods — closing, 1974	R
INVGR1	$'000	Inventory of goods for resale — opening, 1974	R
INVGR2	$'000	Inventory of goods for resale — closing, 1974	R
INVRAW1	$'000	Inventory of raw materials — opening, 1974	R
INVRAW2	$'000	Inventory of raw materials — closing, 1974	R
INVWP1	$'000	Inventory of work-in-progress — opening, 1974	R
INVWP2	$'000	Inventory of work-in-progress — closing, 1974	R
MATERIAL	$'000	Cost of materials, 1974	R
MATGR	$'000	Cost of materials and goods for resale, 1974	R
MATRICF71	No.	Number of female employees whose highest level of education is Grade 12 or 13 — 3 digit, 1971	B
MATRICM71	No.	Number of male employees whose highest level of education is Grade 12 or 13 — 3 digit, 1971	B

Variable	Units	Description	Sources
MEMPAD	No.	Administrative employees — male, 1974	R
MMIGRAN71	No.	Number of male employees born overseas — 3 digit, 1971	D
MPROD	No.	Production workers, male, 1974	R
NREPLEN	$'000	Value of nonreplenishable resource inputs, 1974 = total value of Canadian input-output commodities 031000 to 05000 used	M
PROFSL	No.	Other professionals employed — 2 digit, 1974	K
PROTECH	No.	Professional, technicians, and other qualified persons employed — 2 digit, 1974	K
RDEX	$'000	Total research and development expenditure — 2 digit, 1974	K
REPLEN	$'000	Value of replenishable resource inputs, 1974 = total value of Canadian input-output commodities 00100 to 03000 used	M
SHIP72	$'000	Value of total shipments, 1972	G
SHIP	$'000	Value of total shipments, 1974	R
SPEC	Ratio	Enterprise specialisation ratio, 1974	J
TECHNS	No.	Technicians, employed — 2 digit, 1974	K
VA	$'000	Total value added, 1974	R
VA1/4	$'000	Value added — first four largest enterprises, 1974	J
VA2/4	$'000	Value added — second four largest enterprises, 1974	J
VA3/4	$'000	Value added — third four largest enterprises, 1974	J
VA4/4	$'000	Value added — fourth four largest enterprises, 1974	J
VA5/4	$'000	Value added — fifth four largest enterprises, 1974	J
WPROPF	No.	Working proprietors — female, 1974	R
WPROPM	No.	Working proprietors — male, 1974	R
WSAL	$'000	Total wages and salaries, 1974	R
WSALADM	$'000	Administrative salaries, 1974	R
WSALPROD	$'000	Wages and salaries paid to production workers, 1974	R

Note (1):

The Estimation of Canadian Effective Rates of Protection

In the Canadian system, tariffs and transport costs are available by commodity. In order to arrive at an effective tariff rate on the activities of industries, it is necessary to (1) calculate the tariff rates and transport cost rates on commodities, and (2) to weight the tariff and transport cost rates on commodity outputs and inputs in order to calculate them for industries.

There are a variety of values of inputs and outputs that can be used to calculate the rates and weights.

(1) The value under protection.
(2) The free trade value i.e. the protected value deflated by tariff rates.
(3) The free trade value deflated by the transport cost rate.
(4) The free trade, free international transport cost value, i.e. the protected value deflated by tariff plus transport cost rates.

In this study (4) has been used. The tariff rate has been calculated as the ratio between tariffs and the deflated value, and the transport cost rate as the ratio between transport costs and the deflated value. These values of outputs and inputs have been used as weights for both calculations.

Methodology

The Canadian Input/Output Use and Make matrices were revalued to a free trade basis for which the following formulae were used.

The Use matrix was converted by dividing each of its elements by one plus the corresponding tariff rate.

$$I_{ij} (1+t_i)^{-1} \qquad (i)$$

where I_{ij} = the *value* of the ith commodity or service used by the jth industry under protection.

t_i = tariff rates and transport costs imposed on the ith commodity based on imports, valued f.o.b. foreign establishment.

And similarly for the Make matrix :

$$O_{ij} (1+t_i)^{-1} \qquad (ii)$$

where O_{ij} = the value of the ith commodity or service produced by the jth industry under protection.

If we denote:

F_i = free trade price of the ith commodity or service[1]

P_i = protected price of the ith commodity or service[1]

U_{ij} = quantity of the ith commodity or service used by the jth industry (assumed to be the *same* under free trade as protection)[1]

199

M_{ij} = quantity of the ith commodity or service used by the jth industry (assumed to be the *same* under free trade as protection)[1]

If we assume that domestic protected goods are priced at the free trade price plus the tariff and transport costs then:

$$F_i = P_i (1+t_i)^{-1} \qquad \text{(iii)}$$

$$I_{ij} = P_i U_{ij} \qquad \text{(iv)}$$

from equations (iii) and (iv)

$$F_i U_{ij} = \frac{P_i}{(1+t_i)} U_{ij} = I_{ij} (1+t_i)^{-1} \qquad \text{(v)}$$

similarly

$$F_i M_{ij} = O_{ij} (1+t_i)^{-1} \qquad \text{(vi)}$$

---

1. F,P,U,M, are not available in Canadian Input-Output tables, but are used here to illustrate the underlying assumptions of the calculations.

APPENDIX 8.3

The Distribution of Activity in Australian and Canadian Manufacturing

The following Table shows the distributions of the value added and employment of the 85 industries comprising Australian and Canadian manufacturing. The industries have also been aggregated into 21 industry groups in the Table.

The two main differences in activities lie in the greater concentration (in terms of both value added and employment) in the Food Products Group (I) and particularly in meat products (ACIC 1) in Australia; and the relative Canadian concentration in Pulp, Paper Printing and Publishing (Group VII), particularly in pulp, paper and paperboard (ACIC 32). Both are likely to reflect relative factor endowments in the respective countries. In terms of employment, Transport Equipment (Group XIV), mainly as a result of the relatively large employment in motor vehicles (ACIC 62), is also disproportionately large in Australia compared with Canada. It is interesting to note however, that in terms of the respective proportions of total value added contributed by Group XIV and ACIC 62, the Australian industries' contributions are smaller than their Canadian counterparts. Not as great as the differences just discussed, but worthy of note are the relative concentrations of both value added and employment in Australia in Hosiery, Knits, clothing and footwear (ACIC 28); and Steel and Steel Products (Group XI), particularly in basic iron and steel (ACIC 49).

While there are some obvious differences in areas of specialisation in the two countries, the Kolmorogorov-Smirnov (K-S) two-sample test suggests that there are no significant differences (at the 1 percent level) between the respective distributions of either total value added or total employment.

Distribution of Value Added and Employment for Eighty Five Australian (1973/74) and Canadian Manufacturing Industries (1974)

ACIC	Industry Description	Value Added		Employment	
		Australia	Canada	Australia	Canada
1	Meat products	3.33	1.78	3.94	1.86
2	Poultry products	0.40	0.27	0.46	0.51
3	Milk products	1.75	1.45	1.66	1.55
4	Fruit, vegetable products	1.33	0.99	1.13	1.09
5	Flour, starch, cereals	0.80	0.35	0.63	0.28
6	Margarine, oil, fats	0.38	0.09	0.23	0.04
7	Bread, cake, pastry	1.40	1.05	2.07	1.51
8	Biscuits	0.45	0.32	0.54	0.45
9	Confectionery, cocoa	0.61	0.49	0.68	0.54
10	Fish products	0.04	0.65	0.06	1.06
11	Animal foods	0.53	0.62	0.32	0.52
12	Sugar, malt, other foods	1.77	1.70	1.29	1.27
I	Food Products	12.86	9.81	13.02	10.67
13	Soft drinks, cordials	0.85	0.76	0.78	0.77
14	Beer	1.06	1.12	0.64	0.65
15	Wine, alcoholic beverages	0.49	0.99	0.37	0.43
16	Tobacco	0.92	0.81	0.43	0.54
II	Beverages and Tobacco	3.33	3.71	2.22	2.39
17	Wool: scoured, carbonised, tops	0.12	0.02	0.17	0.04
18	Manmade fibre yarn and fabrics	0.86	0.93	0.88	1.28
19	Cotton yarn and fabric	0.52	0.47	0.65	0.68
20	Wool yarn and fabric	0.50	0.24	0.79	0.36

#		Col 1	Col 2	Col 3	Col 4
21	Household and other textiles	1.29	0.79	0.91	0.71
22	Textile floor covers	0.42	0.41	0.36	0.52
23	Felt and products	0.02	0.09	0.01	0.10
24	Canvas and products	0.13	0.21	0.07	0.16
25	Rope, cord, twine	0.04	0.08	0.03	0.10
III	Fibres, Yarns and Textiles	4.24	4.07	3.09	3.63
26	Hosiery	0.30	0.41	0.13	0.29
27	Knitted goods	1.15	1.00	0.59	0.74
28	Clothing, footwear	5.93	6.80	3.00	4.11
IV	Hosiery, Knits, Clothing, Footwear	7.38	8.21	3.74	5.14
29	Sawmill, wood products	5.06	3.69	3.95	3.45
30	Ply veneers and wood boards	0.75	0.58	0.54	0.59
V	Wood Products	5.81	4.27	4.50	4.05
31) VI)	Furniture	3.04	2.37	1.96	1.88
32	Pulp, Paper and paper board	4.88	0.87	8.13	1.20
33	Paper bags, containers	1.53	1.09	1.36	1.12
34	Paper products, printing, publishing	6.22	6.11	5.45	6.12
VII	Pulp, Paper, Printing, Publishing	12.64	8.06	14.95	8.45
35	Basic chemicals	1.28	1.54	2.43	2.88
36	Chemical products excl. agricultural	0.95	0.85	1.09	0.99
37	Paints	0.48	0.55	0.58	0.67
38	Pharmaceutical incl. veterinary goods	0.85	0.84	1.12	1.23
39	Soap, detergents	0.35	0.44	0.56	0.69
40	Cosmetics, toiletry	0.35	0.40	0.48	0.59
VIII	Chemicals and Chemical Products	4.26	4.61	6.29	7.07

41	Petroleum refining	1.01	2.53	0.31	0.93
42	Petroleum and coal products	0.10	0.20	0.08	0.13
IX	Refining, Petroleum, Coal Products	1.12	2.74	0.40	1.07
43	Glass and products	0.83	0.69	0.66	0.73
44	Clay products	1.38	0.34	1.28	0.38
45	Cement	0.54	0.50	0.30	0.26
46	Concrete products	1.35	1.29	1.09	1.18
47	Other nonmetallic mineral products	0.88	0.70	0.73	0.65
48	Stone products	0.05	0.03	0.07	0.05
X	Nonmetallic Mineral Products	5.05	3.59	4.14	3.26
49	Basic iron and steel	4.79	3.73	3.74	3.07
50	Iron, steel castings and forgings	0.82	0.59	0.93	0.68
51	Steel pipes and tubes	0.71	0.40	0.66	0.33
XI	Steel and Steel Products	6.33	4.72	5.32	4.09
52	Smelting nonferrous metals	2.43	2.11	0.98	2.00
53	Aluminium rolling, drawing, extruding	0.46	0.39	0.30	0.35
54	N.F.M. rolling, drawing, extruding	0.78	0.52	0.61	0.49
55	Fabricated structural steel	1.20	1.37	1.30	1.13
XII	Nonferrous Metals and N.F.M. Products	4.89	4.40	3.18	3.97
56	Architectural metal products	0.67	0.74	1.05	0.82
57	Boilers and plates	0.54	0.45	0.50	0.49
58	Metal products n.e.c.	2.69	1.82	2.80	1.77
59	Cutting and hand tools	0.18	0.91	0.21	1.15
60	Wire products, nuts, bolts	1.05	1.23	1.05	1.11
61	Other fabricated metal products	1.71	1.72	1.97	1.96
XIII	Fabricated Metal Products	6.86	6.89	7.57	7.30

Distribution of Value Added and Employment for Eighty Five Australian (1973/74) and Canadian Manufacturing Industries (1974) *(Continued)*

ACIC	Industry Description	Value Added		Employment	
		Australia	Canada	Australia	Canada
62	Motor vehicles	3.92	5.33	4.28	2.80
63	Truck, bus bodies	0.61	0.77	0.68	1.06
64	Motor vehicle electrical parts	2.21	2.78	2.47	2.81
65	Ship building and repair	0.96	0.64	1.21	0.83
66	Boats, other transport equipment	0.33	0.26	0.40	0.42
67	Loco stock and repair	1.26	0.56	1.91	0.45
68	Aircraft building and repair	0.87	1.04	0.90	1.37
XIV	Transport Equipment	10.18	11.40	11.86	9.74
69) XV)	Photo, Optical and Scientific Equipment	0.78	0.89	0.84	0.97
70	TV, radio, electrical equipment	2.05	2.64	2.50	2.98
71	Household appliances	2.15	1.37	2.41	1.50
72	Electrical and telephone wire	0.50	0.66	0.46	0.60
73	Batteries	0.24	0.15	0.19	0.15
74	Other electrical equipment	2.09	2.18	2.60	2.72
XVI	Electrical Appliances, Equipment	7.05	7.02	8.17	7.94
75	Agricultural machinery, equipment	0.77	0.76	0.89	0.86
76	Other industrial machinery	5.00	3.99	5.08	4.19
XVII	Agricultural, Other Machinery	5.78	4.76	5.97	5.05

77	Leather tanning	0.17	0.10	0.21	0.14
78	Leather, substitute products	0.22	0.18	0.32	0.33
XVIII	Leather and Leather Products	0.40	0.28	0.53	0.48
79	Rubber, tyres, tubes, etc.	0.81	0.72	0.72	0.72
80	Other rubber products	0.44	0.61	0.52	0.66
XIX	Rubber Products	1.26	1.34	1.24	1.38
81) XX)	Plastic and Related Products	2.76	2.10	2.56	1.97
82	Jewellery, silver	0.17	0.30	0.23	0.41
83	Brooms, brushes	0.13	0.09	0.18	0.13
84	Signs and advertising displays	0.26	0.26	0.38	0.35
85	Other manufacturing	0.45	1.06	0.60	1.46
XXI	All Other Manufacturing	1.03	1.72	1.38	2.36
	TOTAL MANUFACTURING	100.0[a]	100.0[a]	100.0[a]	100.0[a]
		13130[b]	37498[c]	1339638[d]	1764935[d]
	Mean (X)	154.5	441.2	15760	20763
	Standard Deviation (σ)	157.0	506.1	17667	22505
	Skewness	2.056	2.688	2.515	2.239

Notes: (a) Many not add owing to rounding
     (b) A $ million
     (c) C $ million
     (d) Number

Sources: See Appendix 8.2.

APPENDIX 9.1

Discriminant Analysis:
Some Theoretical Considerations

Discriminant analysis is a statistical method which is used to assign observations to the appropriate one among two or more populations on the basis of a discriminant function. Such a function is a linear combination of "discriminating" variables, whose weighting coefficients are estimated from sample data. In the discriminant analysis used in this study there are two mutually exclusive populations or "groups"[1] which are provided by the two countries, Australia and Canada, and the observations or "items" are the 170 (i.e., 85 x 2) industries.

The objective is to obtain a linear combination of variables that will optimally classify items (industries) into one group or another. The discriminant function is of the form :

$$D_i = d_{i1}Z_1 + d_{i2}Z_2 + \ldots + d_{ip}Z_p \tag{9.1}$$

where D_i is the score of the discriminant function i, the d's are weighting coefficients, and the Z's are the standardized values of the p discriminating variables used in the analysis. When the overall averages (the grand means) for each of the individual discriminating variables are substituted into equation (9.1), the critical value of D is determined. If an individual item's D_i value is above the critical value it is assigned to one group, and if it is below, it is assigned to the other. Here the groups have an equal number of items (85 industries) and thus the *a priori* probability of an observation belonging to one group is the same as the probability it belongs to the other. The "cost" of misclassifying an industry is considered to be the same for all industries in this analysis, and correct classifications are "costless".

The discriminant score for each industry is computed by multiplying the value of each discriminating variable by its corresponding coefficient and adding the resulting products. The coefficients have been so derived that the discriminant scores produced are in standard form: over all the cases in the analysis, the score from one function will have a mean of zero and a standard deviation of one. Thus for any single case, the score represents the number of standard deviations from the mean for all cases on the given discriminant function. The absolute values of the standardized discriminant function coefficients represent the relative contributions of the asso-

---

1. A short discussion of the theory underlying discriminant analysis where the technique is applied (as in the present case) to two mutually exclusive populations may be found in Johnston (1960, pp. 334-340). See also Conlon (1981a).

ciated variables to that function, and their signs indicate whether the variables are making a positive or a negative contribution. The average of the scores for the items within a particular group is the group mean (also termed the group centroid) for the particular function. The group centroid is the most typical location of an item from that group in the discriminant function space, and a comparison of group centroids indicates by how far the groups are separated. The objective then is to estimate a vector, D, which discriminates between the two groups by as much as possible.

Discriminant analysis procedures are based on two important assumptions : that the variables used to describe or characterise the members of the groups are multivariate normally distributed ; and that the group variance-covariance matrices are equal across all groups. A discussion of the implications of a breakdown of the two assumptions follows.

Multivariate normality

Most available normality tests are for univariate, rather than multivariate normality. For the present study no test of multivariate normality was available. According to Eisenbeis, "the tactic which most researchers have adopted is simply to be satisfied that the more standard discriminant procedures yield reasonable approximations and proceed as if the normality assumption held" (Eisenbeis, 1977, pp. 875-76). That "tactic" is adopted here.[2]

Equality of group variance-covariance matrices

A breakdown in the assumption of equality of variance-covariance matrices across groups affects, *inter alia*, the significance test for the differences in group means and the appropriate forms of the classification rules. In the present study, Box's M significance test was conducted with results that indicated a significant departure from equality of the matrices in all cases. While the inequality of the covariance matrices may be expected to lead to some misclassifications, with an excessive number of observations classified to the more dispersed group, here the empirical tests of the success of

---

2. Gilbert's (1968) work suggested that if the multivariate normality assumption fails to hold, there were only a small loss in predictive accuracy using the linear function of the type used here, and that as the number of variables increased, the results were quite stable. Lauchenbruch, Sneeringer and Revo (1973) suggest that in such cases the data be transformed, if possible, to approximate normality. In this respect, Eisenbeis notes that:
   ". . . the application of a transformation (e.g., to natural logs) may change the interrelationships among the variables and may also affect the relative positions of the observations in the group. In the case of the log transformation there is also [the acceptance of] an implicit assumption . . . [that] . . . the transformed variables give less weight to equal percentage changes in a variable when the values are larger than when they are smaller" (Eisenbeis, 1977, p. 877). As a result of these considerations and Gilbert's (1968) findings, no transformations have been used in the present study.

the discriminant functions in correctly classifying industries was reflected in nearly all cases by the absence of any observable tendency to classify more frequently in one group than another.[3]

Summary

The present application of discriminant analysis has the advantages of prior knowledge of the correct group memberships, the equality of group sizes and the consequent *a priori* probabilities of group membership. These all mitigate problems inherent in some applications of the technique. In this application, given this prior knowledge it will be obvious if the classification is successful. In applications without such knowledge it is of course difficult to gauge how successful the classification has been. As the group membership sizes are equal, the classification rule in the present application is straightforward. The costs of misclassification are equal, and the *a priori* probability of an observation belonging to one group is the same as the probability that it belongs to the other.

---

3. An excellent discussion of the breakdown of this assumption may be found in Eisenbeis (1977, p. 882). See also Oksanen and Williams (1979).

BIBLIOGRAPHY

ALLIN, C.D. (1907), *A History of the Tariff Relations of the Australian Colonies*, Ringston, Ont: British Whig Pub. Co.

ANDERSON, J.E. and NAYA, S. (1969). "Substitution and Two Concepts of Effective Rate of Protection." *American Economic Review*, September, pp. 607-612.

AUSTRALIAN BUREAU OF STATISTICS (1976), *Foreign Ownership and Control in Manufacturing Industry, 1972-73*, Canberra: Australian Government Printer

AUSTRALIAN BUREAU OF STATISTICS (1978), *Australian Standard Commodity Classification, 1975-76*, Canberra: Commonwealth Government Printer

BAIN, J.S. (1966), *International Differences in Industrial Structure: Eight Nations in the 1950s*, New Haven: Yale University Press

BALASSA, B. (1966), "Tariff Reductions and Trade in Manufacturers." *American Economic Review*, June, pp.466-472.

BALASSA, B. (1971), "Effective Protection: A Summary Appraisal." in Grubel, H.G. and Johnson, H.G. (1971)

BARBER, C.L. (1955), "Canadian Tariff Policy." *Canadian Journal of Economics and Political Science*, November, pp. 513-530.

BAUMANN, H.G. (1974), "Structural Characteristics of Canada's Pattern of Trade." *University of Western Ontario, Research Report 4701*.

BECKERMAN, W. (1956), "Distance and the Pattern of Intra-European Trade." *Review of Economics and Statistics*, February, pp. 31-40.

BERRY, C.H. (1971), "Corporate Growth and Diversification." *Journal of Law and Economics*, October, pp. 371-383.

BEIGIE, C.E. (1970), *The Canada-U.S. Automotive Agreement: An Evaluation*, Montreal: Private Planning Association of Canada

BHAGWATI, J.N. and SRINIVASAN, T.N. (1973) "The Theory of Effective Protection and Resource Allocation." *Journal of International Economics*, August, pp. 259-281.

BLAINEY, G. (1966), *The Tyranny of Distance: How Distance Shaped Australia's History*, Melbourne: Sun Books

BOADWAY, R. and TREDDENICK, J. (1978), "A General Equilibrium Computation of the Effects of the Canadian Tariff Structure," *Canadian Journal of Economics*, August, pp. 424-446.

BRASH, D.T. (1966), *American Investment in Australian Industry*, Cambridge: Harvard University Press

BRECHER, I. and REISMAN, S.S. (1957), *Canada - United States Economic Relations*, Ottawa: Royal Commission on Canada's Economics Prospects

BRIGDEN, J.B., *et al* (1929), *The Australian Tariff*, Melbourne: Melbourne University Press

BRITTON, J.N.H. (1978), "Locational Perspectives on Free Trade for Canada", *Canadian Public Policy*, Winter, pp. 4-19.

BRUNT, M. (1971), "Riding on the Back of Canadian Economics: Some Recent Work on Efficiency and Scale in Protected Industries." ANZAAS 43rd Congress, May.

BRYAN, I.A. (1974a), "Regression Analysis of Ocean Liner Freight Rates on Some Canadian Export Routes." *Journal of Transport Economics and Policy*, May, pp. 161-173.

BRYAN, I.A. (1974b), "The Effect of Ocean Transport Costs on the Demand for Some Canadian Exports." *Weltwirtschaftliches Archiv*, pp.642-662.

CARELESS, J.M.S. (1953), *Canada*, Toronto: University of Toronto Press

CAVES, R.E. (1975), *Diversification, Foreign Investment and Scale in North American Manufacturing Industries*, Ottawa: Economic Council of Canada

CAVES, R.E. (1976), "Economic Models of Political Choice: Canada's Tariff Structure." *Canadian Journal of Economics*, May, pp. 278-300.

CLARK, S.D. (1939), *The Canadian Manufacturers' Association*, Toronto: University of Toronto Press

Commonwealth Bureau of Census and Statistics, (1969), *Australian Standard Industrial Classification*, Canberra: Commonwealth Government Printer

CONLON, R.M. (1974), *Determinants of Overseas Capital Inflow into Australian Manufacturing Industry, with Particular Reference to the Role of Tariffs*, Unpublished Masters Manuscript, The University of New South Wales

CONLON, R.M. (1979), *Transport Costs as Barriers to Australian Trade*, Sydney: Centre for Applied Economic Research, CAER Paper No. 8

CONLON, R.M. (1981a), *Comparison of Australian and Canadian Manufacturing Industries: Some Empirical Evidence*, University of Western Ontario: Centre for the Study of International Relations, Working Paper 8102C

CONLON, R.M. (1981b), *The Incidence of Transport Cost and Tariff Protection: Some Australian Evidence*, University of Western Ontario: Centre for the Study of International Relations, Working Paper 8103C

CONLON, R.M. (1981c), "The Structure of the Australian Tariff and the Protection of the Textiles and Clothing Industries." *Australian Economic Papers*, June, pp. 179-182.

CONNIDIS, L. (1983), "Effective Rate of Protection for Motor Vehicle Manufacturing in Canada", *Canadian Journal of Economics*, Vol. 16, pp. 98-103.

CORDEN, W.N. (1966), "The Structure of a Tariff System and the Effective Protective Rate." *Journal of Political Economy*, June, pp. 221-237.

CORDEN, W.M. (1970), "The Efficiency Effects of Trade and Protection." in McDougall, I.A. and Snape, R.H., eds.

CORDEN, W.M. (1971), .*The Theory of Protection*, Oxford: Clarendon Press

DALES, J.H. (1966), *The Protective Tariff in Canada's Development*, Toronto: The University of Toronto Press

DALY, D.J. (1979), *Canada's Comparative Advantage*, Ottawa: Economic Council of Canada, Discussion Paper No. 135

DALY, D.J., and GLOBEMMAN (1976), *Tariff and Science Policies: Applications of a Model of Nationalism*, Toronto: Ontario Economic Council

DALY, D.J., KEYS, B.A., and SPENCE, E.J. (1968), "Scale and Specialisation in Canadian Manufacturing." *Economic Council of Canada Staff Study 21*, Ottawa: Queen's Printer

DEAKIN, B.M. (1973), *Shipping Conferences : A Study of Their Origins, Development and Economic Practices*, Cambridge: Cambridge University Press

DIXON, P.B. (1978), "Economies of Scale, Commodity Disaggregation and the Costs of Protection", *Australian Economic Papers*, June, pp. 63-74.

DIXON, P.B. and BUTLIN, M. (1977), "Notes on the Evans Model of Protection," *Economic Record*, June, pp. 337-349.

Dominion Bureau of Statistics (1970), *Standard Industrial Classification Manual (Revised)*, Ottawa: Information Canada.

DORNBUSCH, R., FISCHER, S., and SAMUELSON, P.A. (1977), "Comparative Advantage, Trade and Payments in a Ricardian Model with a Continuum of Goods." *American Economic Review*, December, pp. 823-829.

EASTMAN, H.C. and STYKOLT, S. (1967), *The Tariff and Competition in Canada*, Toronto: MacMillan

ECONOMIC COUNCIL OF CANADA (1967), *Fourth Annual Review*, Ottawa: Queen's Printer

ECONOMIC COUNCIL OF CANADA (1975), *Looking Outward: A New Trade Strategy for Canada*, Ottawa: Supply and Services Canada

EISENBEIS, R.A. (1977), "Pitfalls in the Application of Discriminant Analysis in Business, Finance, and Economics," *Journal of Finance*, June, pp. 875-900.

ENGLISH, H.E., (1964), *Industrial Structure in Canada's International Competitive Position*. Montreal: Private Planning Association of Canada

EVANS, D.H. (1972), *A General Equilibrium Analysis of Protection*, London: North Holland

EVANS, J.J. (1977), "Liner Freight Rates, Discrimination and Cross-Subsidization", *Maritime Policy and Management*, April, pp. 227-233.

FINGER, J.M. and YEATS, A.J. (1976), "Effective Protection by Transport Costs and Tariffs: A Comparison of Magnitudes." *Quarterly Journal of Economics*, February, pp. 169-176.

FRANK, R.E., MASSY, W.R., and MORRISON, D.G. (1965), "Bias in Multiple Discriminant Analysis," *Journal of Marketing Research*, August, pp. 250-258.

GERACI, V.J. and PREWO, W. (1977), "Bilateral Trade Flows and Transport Costs." *The Review of Economics and Statistics*, February, pp. 64-74.

GILBERT, E.S. (1968), "On Discrimination Using Qualitative Variables," *Journal of the American Statistical Association*, December.

GOODWIN, C.D.W. (1961), *Canadian Economic Thought*, London: Cambridge University Press

GOODWIN, C.D.W. (1966), *Economic Enquiry in Australia*, London: Cambridge University Press

GORECKI, P.K. (1976), *Economies of Scale and Efficient Plant Size in Canadian Manufacturing Industries*, Ottawa: Bureau of Competition Policy, Consumer and Corporate Affairs

GREGORY, R.G. (1976), "Some Implications of the Growth of the Mining Sector," *Australian Journal of Agricultural Economics*, August, pp. 71-91.

GREGORY, R.G. and MARTIN, L.D. (1976), "An Analysis of Relationships Between Import Flows to Australia and Recent Exchange Rate and Tariff Changes," *Economic Record*, March, pp. 1-25.

GRUBEL, H.G. (1967), "Intra-industry Specialization and the Pattern of Trade." *Canadian Journal of Economics and Political Science*, August, pp. 374-388.

GRUBEL, H.G. (1971), "Effective Protection : A Non-Specialist Introduction to the Theory." in Grubel, H.G. and Johnson, H.G. eds.

GRUBEL, H.G. and JOHNSON, H.G. eds. (1971), *Effective Tariff Protection*, Geneva: Graduate Institute for International Studies

GRUBEL, H.G. and LLOYD, P.J. (1975), *Intra-Industry Trade: The Theory and Measurement of International Trade in Differential Products*, New York: Halstead Press.

GRUBER, W.H. and VERNON, R. (1970), "The Technology Factor in a World Trade Matrix." in Vernon, R. ed. (1970)

GRUEN, F. (1975) "The 25 Percent Tariff Cut; Was it a Mistake?" *Australian Quarterly*, June, pp. 7-20.

HABERLER, G. (1936), *The Theory of International Trade*, London: William Hodge & Co

HEAVER, T. (1973), "The Structure of Liner Conference Rates." *Journal of Industrial Economics*, July, pp. 257-264.

HELPMAN, E. (1981), "International Trade in the Presence of Product Differentiation, Economies of Scale and Monopolistic Competition", *Journal of International Economics*, 11, pp. 305-340.

HIRSHLEIFER, J. (1980), *Price Theory and Applications*, Englewood Cliffs: Prentice-Hall

HORST, T.O. (1972a), "Firm and Industry Determinants of the Decision to Invest Abroad: An Empirical Study," *Review of Economics and Statistics*, August, pp. 258-266.

HORST, T.O. (1972b), "The Industrial Composition of U.S. Exports and Subsidiary Sales to the Canadian Market." *American Economic Review*, March, pp. 37-45.

Industries Assistance Commission (1973), *Annual Report, 1972-73*, Canberra: Australian Government Publishing Service

Industries Assistance Commission (1974), *Annual Report, 1973-74*, Canberra: Australian Government Publishing Service

Industries Assistance Commission (1976a), *Annual Report, 1975-76*, Canberra: Australian Government Publishing Service

Industries Assistance Commission (1976b), *Assistance to Manufacturing Industry in Australia*, Canberra: Australian Government Publishing Service

Industries Assistance Commission (1977), *Annual Report, 1976-77*, Canberra: Australian Government Publishing Service

Industries Assistance Commission (1978), *Annual Report*, 1977-78, Canberra: Australian Government Publishing Service

International Labour Organisation (1976 and other issues), *Year Book of Labour Statistics*, Geneva

JACKSON, R.J. *et al* (1975), *Policies for the Development of Manufacturing Industry (Report)*, Canberra: Australian Government Publishing Service

213

JANSSON, J.O. (1974), "Intra-Tariff Cross-Subsidization in Liner Shipping", *Journal of Transport Economics and Policy*, September, pp. 294-311.

JOHNS, B.L., HOGAN, W.P. (1967), "Some Applied Problems in Overseas Investment in Australia." paper presented to Section G of ANZAAS, January.

JOHNSTON, J. (1960), *Econometric Methods*, (2nd ed.) New York: McGraw-Hill

KENDALL, M.G. (1957), *A Course in Multivariate Analysis*, New York: Charles Griffin

KENDALL, M.G. (1976), *Multivariate Analysis*, New York: Charles Griffin

KENDALL, M.G. and STEWART, A. (1968), Advanced *Theory of Statistics*, Volume 3, New York: Charles Griffin

KRUGMAN, P.R. (1979), "Increasing Returns, Monopolistic Competition, and International Trade", *Journal of International Economics*, 9, pp. 469-479.

LACHENBRUCH, P.A., SNEERINGER, C. and REVO, L.T. (1973), "Robustness of the Linear Quadratic Discriminant Function to Certain Types of Non-Normality," *Communications in Statistics*, 1(1), pp. 39-56.

LAING, E.T. (1975), *Containers and Their Competitors : The Economics of Deep Sea General Cargo Shipping in the 1970s*, Liverpool: Maritime Transport Centre, University of Liverpool

LEAMER, E.E. and STERN, R.M. (1970), *Quantitative International Economics*, Boston: Allyn and Bacon, Inc.

LEIBENSTEIN, H. (1966), "Allocative Efficiency vs X-Efficiency." *American Economic Review*, June, pp.392-415.

LINNEMAN, H. et al. (1962), "An Analysis of World Trade Flows" in Tinbergen

LINNEMAN, H. (1966), *An Econometric Study of International Trade Flows*, Amsterdam: North Holland Press

LIPSEY, R.E. and WEISS, M.Y. (1974), "The Structure of Ocean Transport Changes." *Occasional Papers*, New York: National Bureau of Economic Research

LLOYD, P.J. (1973), *Non-Tariff Distortions of Australian Trade*, Canberra: Australian National University Press

MacCHARLES, D.C. (1978), *The Cost of Administrative Organisations in Canadian Secondary Manufacturing Industries*, Toronto: University of Toronto, Unpublished Phd. Dissertation

McDIAMID, O.J. (1946), *Commercial Policy in the Canadian Economy*, Cambridge: Harvard University Press

McDOUGALL, I.A. and SNAPE, R.H. (1970), *Studies in International Economics*, Amsterdam: North-Holland

MacINTOSH, W.A. (1940), *The Economic Background of Dominion - Provincial Relations*, Ottawa: Queens Printer

MELVIN, J.R. and WILKINSON, B.W. (1968), *Effective Protection in the Canadian Economy*, Ottawa: Economic Council of Canada, Special Study No. 9

MONETA, C. (1959), "The Estimation of Transport Costs in International Trade." *Journal of Political Economy*, February, pp.41-58.

NEILL, R. (1979), "Tweedle-Dum and Fiddle Dee Dee: Conservatives, Liberals and the National Policy." *Carlton University Economic Papers*, March

OFFICER, L.H. and HURTUBISE, J.A. (1969), "Price Effects of the Kennedy Round on Canadian Trade." *Review of Economics and Statistics*, August, pp. 320-330.

OKSANEN, E.H. and WILLIAMS, J.R. (1978), "International Cost Differences — A Comparison of Canadian and United States Manufacturing Industries." *Review of Economics and Statistics*, February, pp. 96-101.

ORR, D. (1975), "The Industrial Composition of U.S. Exports and Subsidiary Sales to the Canadian Market: Comment," *American Economic Review*, March, pp. 230-234.

PARRY, T.G. (1977), *The Structure and Performance of Australian Manufacturing Industries*, paper prepared for the Industries Assistance Commission.

PORRITT, E. (1908), *Sixty Years of Protection in Canada*, London: MacMillan

RATTIGAN, G.A., *et al.* (1973), *Report on Possible Ways of Increasing Imports*, unpublished.

RAYNES, J. (1977), "Transport Costs as a Barrier to Trade." *Economic Council of Canada, Discussion Paper, No.78*, January.

REITSMA, A.J. (1960), *Trade Protection in Australia*, Brisbane: University of Queensland Press

ROBINSON, E.A.G. ed. (1960), *Economic Consequences of the Size of Nations*, London: MacMillan

ROSENBLUTH, G. (1957), *Concentration in Canadian Manufacturing Industries*, Princeton: NBER, Princeton University Press

ROUND, D.K. (1974), "The Industrial Organisation Vaccum in Australia," *Economic Record*, June, pp. 169-198.

Royal Commission on Corporate Concentration (1977), *Studies in Canadian Industrial Organisation, Study No. 26*, Ottawa: Supply and Services Canada

SAMPSON, G.P. and YEATS, A.J. (1977), "Tariff and Transport Barriers Facing Australian Exports." *Journal of Transport Economics and Policy*, March, pp. 141-154.

SAMUELSON, P.A. (1954), "The Transfer Problem and Transport Costs, II: Analysis of Effects of Trade Impediments," *Economic Journal* June, pp. 264-289.

SCHERER, F.M. (1973), "The Determinants of Industrial Plant Sizes in Six Nations." *Review of Economics and Statistics*, May, pp. 135-145.

SCHERER, F.M. *et al.* (1975), *The Economics of Multi-Plant Operations: An International Comparison Analysis*, Cambridge: Harvard University Press

SHNEERSON, D., "The Rationality of Conference Pricing and Output Policies", *Maritime Studies and Management*, April 1976, pp. 245-248.

SHOWERS, V. (1979), *World Facts and Figures*, New York: John Wiley and Sons

SIEGEL, S. (1956), *Non Parametric Statistics for the Behavioral Sciences*, Tokyo: McGraw Hill

SPENCE, A.M. (1977), "Efficiency, Scale and Trade in Canadian and United States Manufacturing," In Royal Commission on Corporate Concentration

Statistics Canada (1971), *Census of Population*, Ottawa

Statistics Canada (1979b), *Concepts and Definitions of the Census of Manufactures*, Ottawa: Supply and Services Canada

STERN, R.M. (1973), "Tariffs and Other Measures of Trade Control: A Survey of Recent Developments." *Journal of Economic Literature*, September, pp. 857-888.

STURMEY, S.G. (1962), *British Shipping and World Competition*, London: Athlone Press

Study Group on Structural Adjustment (1979), *Report*, Canberra: Australian Government Publishing Service

Tariff Board (1967), *Annual Report, 1966-67*, Canberra: Commonwealth Government Printer

TINBERGEN, J. (1962), *Shaping the World Economy*, New York: The Twentieth Century Fund

U.S. Department of Commerce (1975), *U.S. General Imports*, May.

VERNON, J. *et al.* (1965), *Report of the Committee of Economic Enquiry*, Canberra: Commonwealth of Australia

VERNON, R. (ed.) (1970), *The Technology Factor in International Trade*, New York: Columbia U.P.

VINER, J. (1929), "The Australian Tariff." *Economic Record*, pp. 306-315

WATERS, W.G. II (1970), "Transport Costs, Tariffs and the Patterns of Industrial Protection." *American Economic Review*, December, pp. 1013-1020.

WEST, E.C. (1971), "Canada-United States Price and Productivity Differences in Manufacturing Industries, 1963," *Economic Council of Canada Staff Study 32*, Ottawa: Information Canada

WILKINSON, B.W. (1968), *Canada's International Trade: An Analysis of Recent Trends and Patterns*, Montreal: Canadian Trade Committee

WILKINSON, B.W. and NORRIE, K. (1975), *Effective Protection and the Return to Capital*, Ottawa: Economic Council of Canada

WILLIAMS, J.R. (1978), *The Canadian - United States Tariff and Canadian Industry: A Multisectoral Analysis*, Toronto: Toronto University Press

WONNACOTT, R.J. (1975), *Canada's Trade Options*, Ottawa: Economic Council of Canada

WONNACOTT, R.J. and WONNACOTT, P. (1967), *Free Trade Between the United States and Canada: The Potential Economic Effects*, Cambridge, Mass.: Harvard University Press

World Bank (1976), *World Tables*, Washington

YEATS, A.J. (1976), "The Incidence of Transport Costs on Indonesia's Exports to the United States," *Bulletin of Indonesian Economic Studies*, November, pp. 61-76.

YEATS, A.J. (1977), "Do International Transport Costs Increase with Fabrication? Some Empirical Evidence," *Oxford Economic Papers*, September, pp. 458-471.

YOUNG, J.H. (1957), *Canadian Commercial Policy*, Ottawa: Govt. Printer

ZERBY, J.A. and CONLON, R.M. (1977), *Major Determinants of Ocean Freight Rates for Australia's Exports to Selected Areas*, Sydney: The University of New South Wales

ZERBY, J.A. and CONLON, R.M. (1978a), "Capacity Utilisation in Liner Shipping." *Journal of Transport Economics and Policy*, January, pp. 29-46.

ZERBY, J.A. and CONLON, R.M. (1978b), "A Statistical Analysis of Some Influences Determining Ocean Tariff Rates." *Papers of the Australian Transport Research Forum*, May, pp. 297-325.

216